PASSAGE TO
EAST AFRICA

A COOKBOOK OF EAST AFRICAN ISMAILI AND INDIAN CUISINE

SHENAZ SHAMJI

JAMBO

Jambo wote!
Karibuni jikoni ya Sheni Shamji.
Tuta pika chakula pamoja
tamu tamu.

Translation
Hello everyone!
Welcome to the kitchen of Sheni Shamji.
We will all cook mouth-watering dishes together.

NOTE TO READERS

1 cup equals 250ml.

1 mug equals 350ml.

1 teaspoon (tsp) equals 5ml.

1 tablespoon (tbsp) equals 15ml.

1kg equals 2.2lb.

All references to **garam masala** in the ingredients section of the recipes are to the powdered version of garam masala (recipe included), unless specified otherwise.

Where reference is made to **ghee** in the recipes, you may substitute butter in its place. NB butter burns more easily than ghee, so extra care is needed when substituting butter for ghee.

Any **lentil** named includes its husk e.g. moong. However, if a lentil is mentioned as a 'daal' then it would be without its husk e.g. moong daal.

Coriander is cilantro. Coriander seeds or dhana seeds are seeds of coriander. Coriander powder or dhana powder is crushed coriander seeds.

Double cream is heavy cream and the nearest equivalent in North America is whipping cream.

Gram flour is chickpea flour. Other names are channa flour or besan.

Green, yellow, orange and red peppers are also called bell peppers.

Oil is any unflavoured vegetable oil e.g. Corn oil, sunflower oil, rapeseed oil etc. Avoid using olive oil as it has a distinct flavour. However unflavoured olive oil is available and ok to use.

Single cream is light cream and the nearest equivalent in North America is half and half.

Spring onions are scallions.

Tempering or wagar or tarka is a cooking process where spices or seeds are thrown into hot oil to impart the flavours. Leaving them in hot oil after the spices or seeds have popped will burn them. So be careful.

White flour is plain flour or all-purpose flour.

CONTENTS

Please note that for ease of reference, the common Indian or Swahili names of the dishes are in brackets alongside the recipe name. They are also included in the Index at the back of the book.

Please also note that the vegetarian recipes may include egg.

DEDICATIONS

This book is dedicated to my dad and mum Fatehali and Gulshan Babul (adoptive parents), to my biological parents Bahadur and Roshan Babul, to my mother-in-law Sherbanu Shamji (my mentor), to my wonderful companion, soulmate, and husband Amin Shamji and to my dear children Aalia and Naadim.

Dads Fatehali and Bahadur Babul

Sherbanu Shamji

My mum Gulshan and me

Mums Gulshan and Roshan Babul nee Boghani

My mum Roshan and me

My husband Amin, my children Aalia and Naadim and me

With my cooking partner in crime Amin Shamji

INTRODUCTION

A dhow

The dhow was the principal means of passage from India to East Africa up until the beginning of the twentieth century. The journeys were often long and arduous, and several sadly died en route. My ancestors are likely to have travelled by dhow to East Africa, eventually settling in Tanzania and surrounding countries.

This is where our culinary story now begins.

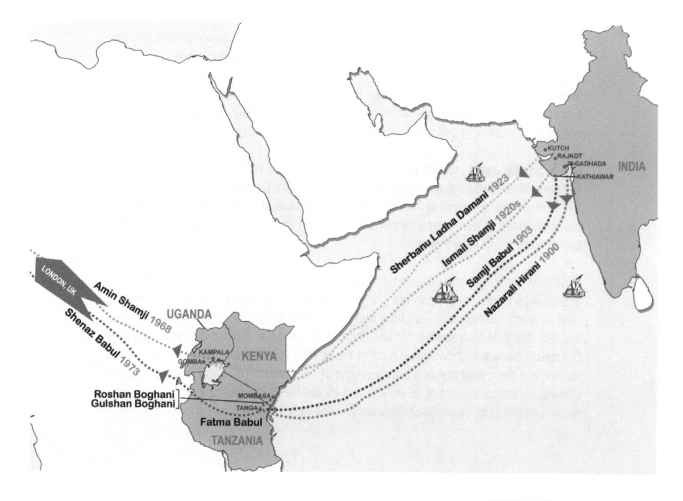

I was born in Tanga, Tanzania on 29th October 1956. Tanga was a beautiful port town with lots of sunshine and beaches and well-maintained streets.

I was born to Bahadur Babul and Roshan Babul née Boghani. Roshan's elder sister, Gulshan, was married to Bahadur's elder brother Fatehali and, once married, both couples lived together in the same house very happily. Since Fatehali and Gulshan sadly could not have their own children, Bahadur and Roshan gave me up for adoption to them with all their love when I was three days old.

I was raised calling Fatehali and Gulshan (my adoptive parents) "dad" and "mum" respectively whereas I called Bahadur and Roshan (my biological parents), "Bahadur Chacha" and "Munira aunty" respectively. Roshan allowed me to call her by the name Munira as I loved it as a young girl. I've called her by it ever since.

Roshan and Bahadur had three other daughters: Tasnim (also known as "Tashu"), Nina and Karima. I also had a brother. We all lived together happily in the same house being raised with four parents to all five children!

From my early childhood I loved food. Anything at home, at parties or different community gatherings and all sorts of street food in my hometown Tanga. I recall enjoying the crispy daal bhajias of Blue Room restaurant; the mouth-watering mishkaki (barbecued lamb cubes also known as nyama choma) from Central restaurant; the nariyal wara (coconut) channa bateta at Rudi masi's stall outside our mosque; the street food from Pakori's mobile tuck shop; the bher from the school tuck shop; the fried mogo from Mangi (a local seller) at school; and roasted peanuts in a conical newspaper at school too – all at recess time. We were given limited pocket money each day and we could never get enough of these goodies.

Due to political unrest I moved to London in 1973 with my dad Fatehali and mum Gulshan and my brother. My biological parents Bahadur and Roshan, together with my sisters Tasnim, Nina and Karima, all moved to Canada eventually. We were all heartbroken and devasted by this separation and were deeply saddened yet relieved and glad to be settling in a safe and economically stable environment.

Moving to London, I was delighted and overwhelmed by the plethora of different tastes and cuisines from this cosmopolitan city. Overnight I had access to cooking from different continents and countries such as China, Mexico, Thailand, Spain, Italy, America, and Vietnam and this alongside lip-smacking fish and chips by the seaside, filling and hearty roast (and Christmas) dinners and Caribbean food at the Notting Hill Carnival. They all aroused the senses, and these new wonders were a source of inspiration. One thing I realised was that I was quite unique in wanting to indulge and try out these diverse cuisines. To me these cuisines stood out as unchartered taste territory and were becoming very popular in Britain.

I did my A-levels in London followed by a pharmacy undergraduate degree at Brighton University. I qualified as a registered pharmacist shortly after in 1980 and am still currently working part-time.

Our registry wedding photo 27th Nov 1982

Our religious wedding 4th Dec 1982 with my family

I met my adorable husband and soulmate Amin Shamji, originally from Kampala, Uganda, in 1982. We got engaged two months later in August and were married in December the same year.

This is where my cooking experience was enhanced and enriched by watching and helping my mother-in-law Sherbanu Shamji cook her traditional Indian recipes. She lived with us for 28 years, was a tremendous cook, great mother-in-law, and fantastic grandmother. She loved cooking for my family, my in-laws, friends, at community gatherings, for the mosque and all the parties we used to have at home.

Indian cooking is more of an art than a science and each family uses their own measures of spices to conjure up different tastes and distinctive styles. No precise measures were used. Quantities were measured by the eye, or referenced as a splash or shake, so it was difficult to know exactly how much went into each recipe. Hence it took time and "aasre" (Gujarati for discretion or guesswork) to refine the measures to get the taste just so. The dilemma was always, more of this or less of that?

My mother-in-law also developed her cooking in this bespoke way. Over the years I scribbled down her recipes roughly but later I re-cooked them and wrote them down accurately and electronically. It was a laborious task which took a long time and many, many hours over many years to get to write a total of over 250 recipes, which also included my own recipes, my husband Amin's recipes and other recipes from family and friends. Amin is also a passionate cook and a real foodie. There are several recipes of his in this book and his signature dishes are spaghetti bolognese (which our daughter Aalia claims is even better than what the Italian's make!), dhokra (steamed savoury sponge) and lamb ni akni (rice cooked with lamb).

We have been blessed with two children: our elder daughter Aalia and younger son, Naadim. They are foodies like their parents and are great budding cooks too!

Aalia Shamji and grandmaa Sherbanu Shamji

Naadim Shamji and grandmaa Sherbanu Shamji

Aalia's most loved dishes made by us are chilli paneer salad Chinese-style, jugu wari daal (sweet daal with peanuts) and spaghetti bolognese (by her dad Amin).

Naadim's best loved dishes made by us are also chilli paneer salad Chinese style (like his sister), aubergine parcels, seero (by his grandma/dadimaa Sherbanu Shamji), baba ghanoush and lamb biriani. Naadim makes lovely (Ismaili) sherbet (recipe within) and has also made it for a mosque celebration which hosted 200 people and for his cousin's engagement party.

Juggling between cooking with my mother-in-law, working part time, raising a family, enjoying family life and doing community and voluntary work, choreographing and performing in 40 dance shows for community and charities, entertaining family and friends with home parties and barbeques and travelling, life has been pretty hectic!

My passion for food was clear though and I always dreamed of sharing this love with others. The Meghji family (of Chachi's Kitchen fame) really encouraged me to publish a cookbook as they were aware I was writing my recipes and taking photos of them. Thankfully they also enjoyed my cooking! It was quite a daunting and overwhelming task but with a lot of encouragement also from Amin, my children and other family members and friends who enjoy my food, I caved in and decided to go ahead.

I am a lover of both traditional and modern cooking, street food, simple foods, and international food. The art of food photography and food styling fascinates me. I love visiting food markets both in the UK and abroad. It is like leaving me loose in Aladdin's Cave. To me food brings together families, friends and is the tool to build new relations. Food excites the tastebuds, the eyes, the nose, the ears, and the touch. Food photos in recipe books and online delight me visually.

This recipe book contains food of mostly traditional Indian and East African Ismaili cuisine with some Chinese, Thai, Spanish, Greek and Mediterranean recipes, amongst others, which are family favourites. This is because I love the variety and inspiration of food from different cultures and cuisines, using local and distinctive ingredients in different ways for an array of different dishes to tempt the tastebuds. As you may notice my recipes are not in a standardised format and vary in the portions, measures etc. as I had originally only intended to write these recipes to pass on to my children and family but not for a published cookbook.

The book also contains delicious recipes of my dear family and friends whose cooking has also inspired me. I would like to thank them from the bottom of my heart. I treasure these greatly. I hope you enjoy making these recipes that I share with you from my family to yours. Just take your pick and cook whatever you fancy and your heart desires!

Bon appetit!

My sisters, my mum Roshan and me

Brief introduction into my family ancestry

My paternal grandfather (i.e., my dad's father) was Samji Babul Nathoo. He was born in Rajula, Kathiawar, India in March 1894. Samji's parents, and his sister Sombai, remained in India. Samji (aged nine) and his brothers Nanji and Premji travelled by boat or dhow to East Africa around 1903. Nanji died young of malaria.

Samji worked as a childminder for an Ismaili family by day and would sleep on the floor by night. He eventually married my grandmother Fatma Hirani, affectionately known as Fatu Kachhi, who was born on 18th Jan 1907 in Tanga, Tanzania. Fatu Kachhi's father was Nazarali Hirani and her mother was Motibai. They originally came from Gadhada, Gujarat. Fatu Kachhi had three elder brothers and their names were Janmohamed and Valimohamed, and we do not know the name of the third brother.

Fatu Kachhi was born under German colonial rule. During the Battle of Tanga (1914) Fatu Kachhi gave water to an injured Indian soldier fighting for the British. The Germans found out and her father was later arrested and imprisoned. The British won soon after and he was thankfully released. To honour Fatu Kachhi and her dad, the British awarded them for their bravery, the medal for which we have sadly lost.

Nazarali Hirani (from Gadhada, India) - Father of Fatma Babul

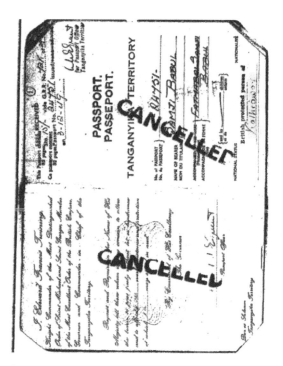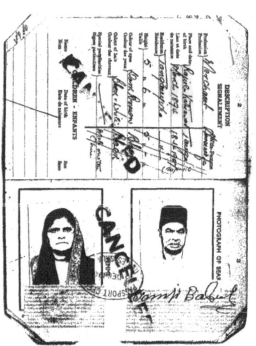

Samji Babul's 1949 Tanganyika Passport

Samji and Fatma Babul

Samji Babul family in the 1960s

My paternal grandparents ran a shop (duka) and they had 13 children – including my adoptive dad Fatehali and my biological dad Bahadur – and faced much hardship and poverty.

My sister Nina recalls some of the stories and recollections from our dad Bahadur Babul. In particular she remembers that Fatu Kacchi lost her mum when she was very young, and she had a physically challenged brother (the nameless brother mentioned earlier) who she carried on her back. He would supervise her cooking and other duties as she carried him on her back. She got married to my grandfather at a young age. Many proposals had come her way but as she had been promised to my grandfather the family honoured their word. She was a tough lady, was very principled, believed very much in equality and was very charitable.

Poverty was part of their married lives. Their 12 children were made to share three eggs between them, accompanied by hot ghee, crushed black pepper and white, unsliced bread. This was the cheapest form of food and was one of their regular home foods. My siblings and I, as kids, would share this experience of eating this food which we called ghee-mari by sitting on the floor with our dad Bahadur and mum Roshan, enjoying this simple but delicious dish. Dad would also talk to us of old Bollywood movies, and we would sing along with him on our drives in the car to Raskazone (the beach drive in Tanga). He was a lovely man and a favourite to many of our cousins!

Boghani family with friends. Back row (from left): Hassanali Boghani, Nurali Boghani, Jafferali Boghani, Abdulmohamed Boghani, unknown boy. Next row (from left): unknown standing girl, Sakar Boghani, unknown lady holding baby, unknown seated child, Mrs Jafferali Boghani, Kulsum Boghani, unknown standing girl. Next row (from left): Roshan Babul (kneeling), unknown child (standing), Gulshan Babul (kneeling). Seated on the floor (from left): first three children unknown, last two children are Noori Boghani and Sultana Essani.

As time went along, the 12 (Zarina, the youngest, died at a young age) siblings grew up and the sons, under the guidance of their brother Fatehali, my dad, led the family into prosperity.

As for my maternal ancestry my adoptive and biological mums, who were also sisters, were born to Abdulmohamed Boghani and Sakar Boghani née Gilani. Their mother Sakar died soon after giving birth to their sister Dolat, who sadly died too. Incapable of looking after his two young daughters their father agreed for them to be brought up by his mother Nanbai, who together with her son, Hassanali and his wife Sakar raised them together with their own children. My grandfather Abdulmohamed remarried to Khadija Giga and they had two sons Mehdi and Hassanali.

With my adoptive mum being the sister of my biological mum, and my adoptive dad being the brother of my biological dad, it was natural that they should want to all live in a shared household, which they did in Tanga. Each sister had a different role to play. Gulshan, my adoptive mum, looked after the children. She was energetic, playful, and fun and took us out on to the local swimming hotspot each day and on day trips to beaches. With five children between the two couples, entertainment was a fulltime job outside of school times! The other sister, Roshan, my biological mum, had a more administrative role and ran the household. This meant cleaning and cooking for the family.

Of the two brothers, who had married these two sisters, Fathehali (Gulshan's husband and my adoptive dad) steered the children's education. He was enamoured by the British colonial influence and requested Gulshan to only cook "English food" for him. Bahadur was the fun dad and took the children out on drives. He loved street food, Gujarati food and his paan (a crunchy sweet and savoury mix wrapped in leaves, eaten as a mouth freshener).

Lunchtime was a big meal, and every day the family (including our paternal uncles) all sat around the table to share a meal which was followed by a siesta. As per my adoptive dad's requirements soup was always the first course (which was not to be slurped) followed by Indian food. I was not allowed in the kitchen so never learnt to cook from Munira aunty, who having to cook to everyone's tastes, understandably needed her space.

Brief introduction to my husband Amin Shamji's family ancestry

Amin's paternal grandfather was Shamji Keshwani and his paternal grandmother was Manekbai Lalani, also known as Monghibai. They had four children: Jamal, Manibai, Hassam and Ismail. Ismail was Amin's father and was originally given the name "Anandji". It was customary for Khoja Ismailis of that time to have Hindu names. As times changed his name became Ismail, a more Muslim sounding name. He was born in Mota Devalia near Rajkot, Gujarat in 1910 and moved to Kiriri, in the Gomba district of Uganda in search of a better life.

Amin's father Ismaili Shamji married Rahemat Kurji Lalani initially and they had two daughters Sherbanu and Gulbanu. Rahemat died at a young age and Ismail Shamji remarried. His second wife was Sherbanu Ladha Ramji Damani, Amin's mother.

Sherbanu Ladha Ramji Damani was born in Nagalpur, Kutch, India on 1 January 1923. Like others of her generation the "1 January" birthday was given to her by the British government as she had no birth certificate. Her great grandparents came from Kera, in the princely state of Kutch in Gujarat, India. In the 1920s her parents Ladha and Labai took a dhow to East Africa. They lived in jungles that had to be cleared to set up a village which consisted of four to ten shops, with a small prayer hall doubling as a school. All the necessities of living had to be made by hand, including their homes, food, clothing, and furniture.

Sherbanu had four siblings: Sakina, Mohamed, Nurbanu and Amina. Amina had three daughters and two sons, all of whom my husband and I still regularly visit today. Amina, together with her daughter Dr Sajeda Meghji, would later become the authors of the hit recipe book and blog Chachi's Kitchen. Amina sadly passed away in early 2021. All sisters were excellent cooks and had very similar recipes incorporating Indian cuisine with local African cuisine and available ingredients.

Ismail Shamji and wife Sherbanu with daughters Sherbanu and Gulbanu in the 1940s

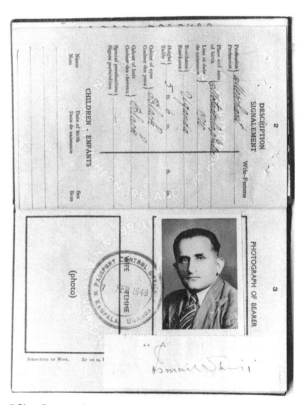

Ismail Shamji passport

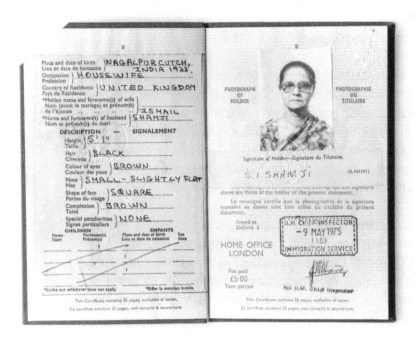

Sherbanu Shamji Passport

The Ismail Shamji family with Sherbanu Shamji, the sons Shiraz, Nasir and Amin; daughters-in-law Yasmin, Shamim and Shenaz; and grandchildren Adil, Faiza, Aalia, Naadim, Rozina and Nabeela

My mother-in-law was 16 years old when she married and became stepmother to two daughters who were only a few years younger than she was, as her husband (Ismail) was many years her senior. She took this in her stride and provided love and motherly care to her new children, and to the children she bore and lost. My mother-in-law had five children: Rozina, Shiraz, Sadru, Amin (my husband) and Nasir. Rozina and Sadru both sadly died at a young age.

As well as bringing up children, Sherbanu also supported her husband in the running of the shop (duka) and the household. My mother-in-law was not academically educated but was an excellent cook and seamstress. She would make lovely clothes for all her children and even later down the line for her daughters-in-law and grandchildren. So many of my Indian outfits (sari blouses, Punjabi suits etc. were made expertly by her) and her high standards and meticulous nature showed. In the realm of cooking, like other women of her generation, she memorised all her recipes. Unlike other women however she was openminded and learnt international dishes (from me) such as Chinese recipes, in exchange for teaching me her own. I really cherish all I learnt under her stewardship, and we regularly still make her food years after she passed away (2011). My mother-in-law Sherbanu was very inspirational to me towards learning to cook traditional Indian recipes.

Sherbanu Shamji with her children

STARTERS & SNACKS

Non Vegetarian

19/ Beef fried kebabs (Kaari kebab)
20/ Chicken kebabs
22/ Chicken satay
23/ Chinese crispy shredded beef
24/ Chinese Peking chicken thighs
25/ Chinese spring rolls
26/ Chinese sweet and sour chicken wings
27/ Fish cutlets (cakes) (Machhi ni cutlets)
28/ Jeera chicken
29/ Lamb chop cutlets
30/ Lamb cubes barbequed (Mishkaki or nyama choma)
31/ Lamb and chicken samosas
32/ Potato and mince champs (Bateta Champ)
33/ Sheekh mince kebab
34/ Spicy masala prawns
35/ Spicy masala prawns
36/ Tandoori chicken
38/ Tandoori lamb chops
40/ Thai chicken fritters and kebabs Version 1
41/ Thai chicken fritters and kebabs Version 2
42/ Thai chicken fritters and kebabs Version 3
43/ Thai chicken fritters and kebabs Version 4

Vegetarian

Beef fried kebabs (Kaari kebab)

Delicious straight from the fryer with coconut chutney!

SERVES 8 /
Makes 40 Kebabs

INGREDIENTS

1kg beef lean mince
4 medium onions very finely chopped
4 slices of white bread (crusts removed)
soaked in water then squeezed to let the
water out or 2 rounded dessertspoons
of millet/bajra flour
5 to 6 green chillies finely chopped
(optional)
20 stalks coriander leaves chopped
2 tbsp finely chopped or pasted ginger
20 cloves garlic peeled and pasted
1 tbsp dried mint or 2 tbsp fresh
chopped mint
2 tsp garam masala
salt to taste
oil for deep frying

METHOD

1. Mix all ingredients except oil. Knead the mixture till it is thoroughly mixed.

2. Shape into sausage type kebabs with wet hands and place on tray.

3. Deep fry in hot oil approximately 7 to 8 at a time. Do not turn until after a few minutes of cooking otherwise they break. Then reduce to medium heat till kebabs turn dark brown.

4. Drain and serve with raita (p303) or lemon wedges or coconut chutney (p289).

NB instead of frying the kebabs at step 3, you can instead combine the whole mixture with two beaten eggs, place in an oiled oven dish and bake at medium-high temperature, uncovered, until cooked as a type of meatloaf.

Should you use millet/bajra flour or bread? - it will come down to personal preference, but the bread adds crispiness to the kebabs whereas the millet/bajra flour simply adds body. Beef mince can be substituted with lamb mince too.

Chicken kebabs

Makes approx. 40 Kebabs

A very easy, fast and healthy starter dish

INGREDIENTS

1kg chicken mince
4 slices white bread (crusts removed) soaked in water and squeezed to remove water
2 tsp garam masala
1 tsp jeera powder
1 tsp dhana (coriander) powder
1 tbsp pasted ginger
4-6 cloves pasted garlic
20 stalks chopped coriander leaves
salt to taste
2 chopped green chillis (optional)

METHOD

1. Mix all ingredients and knead till thoroughly mixed.

2. Roll like sausages using slightly wet hands. Make 40 sausages.Add oil onto the outside of kebabs and grill them turning occasionally.

3. Serve hot with raita (p303) or tamarind sauce (ambli) (p306) or lemon wedges.

Chicken satay

SERVES 6-8 / *main dish*
Makes 30 skewers each containing approx. 4-5 pieces

This is a dish that always reminds me of my daughter Aalia as she loves it so much

INGREDIENTS

2.4kg chicken breast boneless or 18 small breasts cut to bite sizes
2 tsp salt
10 cloves garlic minced
2 tbsp grated ginger
5 tbsp soya sauce
4 tsp dhana or coriander powder
1 tsp red chilli powder or more
2 tbsp oil
juice of 3 limes or lemons
1 tsp black pepper
7 tsp of sugar

SATAY SAUCE:
makes about 1 litre
7 tbsp oil
4 tsp tomato paste
30 cloves garlic minced
8 tbsp of peanut butter coarse or smooth
or 10 tsp crushed roasted peanuts
400g coconut milk plus 400ml water
5 tbsp soya sauce
2-4 tsp chilli powder
6 tbsp sugar
few drops of orange food colour

METHOD

1. Mix all the above chicken ingredients and marinate in fridge for 6-8 hrs.

2. Place chicken in skewers and grill or barbeque or griddle or deep fry in hot oil.

3. For the sauce fry the tomato paste in oil for one minute, then add the garlic and fry for 30 seconds, then lastly add the rest of the sauce ingredients and cook for 4-5 minutes stirring.

4. Add sauce onto the cooked chicken.

5. Serve on its own.

SERVES 3 /

Chinese crispy shredded beef

INGREDIENTS

MARINADE:
500g rump steak very thinly sliced into long strips
6 cloves garlic pasted
4 tbsp dark soya sauce
2 tbsp toasted sesame seed oil
5 tbsp cornflour
1 tsp salt
1 tbsp five spice powder

DIPPING FOR FRYING:
3 egg whites whisked

SAUCE:
1 large spring onions/scallions finely chopped
5 tbsp sweet chilli sauce
1 tsp toasted sesame seed oil
3 tbsp toasted sesame seeds
1 tbsp chilli flakes
2 tbsp soya sauce
2 cloves garlic minced
2 tsp pasted ginger
2 tbsp oil

METHOD

1. Marinate the beef with the marinade for 1-2 hours.

2. Make the sauce by heating the oil and adding the garlic and ginger and fry for a minute.

3. Take it off the heat.

4. Dip the beef into egg white and fry in batches till beef is crispy outside.

5. Add the rest of the sauce ingredients to the garlic-ginger oil and then mix it with the fried beef.

6. Serve with rice or noodles or on its own.

SERVES 4 /

Chinese Peking chicken thighs

Usually duck is used for this dish but I have substituted it with chicken thighs as they are readily available. And the taste is still excellent!

INGREDIENTS

8-10 chicken thighs with bone and skin on

200ml hoisin sauce

1 small cucumber cut into long very thin slices about 5cm long

I bunch spring onion/scallions cut into very thin and long slices about 5cm long

12 mini Chinese pancakes steamed

MARINADE:

2 tbsp dark brown sugar

4 tsp Chinese 5 Spice powder

1 tbsp vinegar and 2 tbsp molasses mixed

salt to taste

METHOD

1. Mix the marinade ingredients. Take half of the marinade and mix with the chicken. Leave to marinate for a few hours - or for improved taste marinate overnight in a fridge.

2. Preheat the oven to 220C/420F and cook the thighs skin side up, open in the oven, in an oiled tray.

3. Towards the end of the cooking time maybe in 45 minutes or so add the rest of the marinade to the chicken and cook until the glaze is set.

4. Take the chicken out and take the meat off the bone.

5. Paste the hoisin sauce onto the steamed pancake, add the chicken meat on top, then add the cucumber and spring onion. Roll the pancake!

6. Have your pancake and eat it!

Chinese spring rolls

Makes 30 spring rolls

This is one of my daughter Aalia's and my favourite dishes. I wait for her to come home so she and her dad can do the laborious task of rolling the spring rolls

INGREDIENTS

30 spring rolls pastry sheets. If frozen use defrosting instructions
3 bunches (each bunch has about 4-6 spring onions) spring onions/scallions finely cut
750g boneless chicken breast, cut into thin slices and marinated with 5 cloves garlic minced, 3 tbsp minced ginger, 3 tbsp soya sauce, 3 tbsp sesame seed oil, 5 tsp cornflour and 2 tsp sugar
2 packets beansprouts 300g each

DIP INGREDIENTS:
Dip made of one part soya sauce, one part tabasco sauce (or any other hot sauce) and two parts sweet chilli sauce

METHOD

1. Stir-fry the chicken in batches in little oil. Let it cool. Add spring onions and bean sprouts uncooked.

2. Make a cereal bowl portion of paste using white/plain flour sieved and add little water at a time to make the paste.

3. Open the pastry one at a time and add some mixture in the centre of the sheet and roll and seal using paste making into a spring roll shape. The pastry can dry so keep it covered with damp cloth to stop it drying.

4. Deep fry or shallow fry in medium hot oil.

5. Have with the dip as shown above.

SERVES 4 /

Chinese sweet and sour chicken wings

These sticky wings are delicious straight from the oven and are a favourite of both adults and children. The glazing with sauce and the cooking can be done just before serving so they are fresh and hot from the oven!

INGREDIENTS

1kg chicken wings with skin on

MARINADE:
2 tbsp ginger paste
2 tbsp soya sauce
2 tbsp sesame seed oil
2 tsp sugar
1 tbsp cornflour

SAUCE:
1 cup white vinegar
1 cup brown sugar
3 tbsp cornflour
1 tbsp soya sauce
½ tsp red food colour (optional)

METHOD

1. Marinate the chicken wings in the marinade for few hours or overnight.

2. Make the sauce by mixing the ingredients in a saucepan and bringing to boil. Simmer for 2 minutes.

3. Heat the oven to 200C/400F.

4. Lay the wings on 1 or 2 lined baking trays and cook for a total of 45 minutes turning and basting the wings once.

5. Take the wings out of the oven and glaze both sides of the wings with the made sauce. Either place the wings back into the oven for 10-15 minutes turning them once or grill under hot grill and turn once till the glaze is browning and crispening.

6. Serve on its own with a bowl of water to clean the fingers!

Fish cutlets (cakes) (Machhi ni cutlets)

My dad Fatehali loved fish, and this was one of his favourites!

Makes 25 cutlets or cakes

INGREDIENTS

1kg cod fish skinned and boned. Steam the fish till cooked and flake it
1kg potatoes boiled and then mashed
3 green chillies finely chopped
8 garlic cloves pasted
salt to taste
juice of one large lemon
washed and chopped 15 sprigs of coriander
fine semolina or breadcrumbs or white/ plain flour to coat the cutlets
oil for deep frying
4 eggs beaten

METHOD

1. Mix all the above except the flour or semolina or breadcrumbs, eggs and oil.

2. Make 25 patties disc shaped. Coat each one in the semolina, or breadcrumbs or white flour. Then dip in egg just before frying. Fry each batch in medium heat oil (maybe 5 at a time) and let each side get medium brown.

3. Serve with lemon, or a mild tomato dip. Strong dips will mask the delicate flavour of the fish.

Jeera chicken

A fast and easy dish to make

INGREDIENTS

1kg boneless chicken breast cubes to bite size pieces
2 tsp salt
2 tbsp garlic paste
2 tbsp ginger paste
2 tsp haldi (turmeric)
3 green or red peppers cut into strips (bell peppers)
2 large red onion cut into fine rings
8 tbsp oil any veg oil e.g. corn, sunflower (not olive oil)
125g butter
2 tbsp jeera seeds
2 tbsp jeera powder
1 tsp chili powder
3 limes/lemon
½ bunch coriander
2 tsp garam masala

METHOD

1. Marinate the chicken in salt, garlic, ginger and haldi/turmeric for at least half an hour.

2. Heat the oil and add jeera seeds and let them pop, then the chicken and butter and stir fry Add jeera powder and chili powder. Cook till chicken is nearly ready.

3. Then add green/red pepper and coriander chopped. Cook for 3 minutes.

4. Add lemon/lime juice and garam masala. Adjust taste.

Garnish with onion rings.

SERVES 4 /

Lamb chop cutlets

INGREDIENTS

8 large lamb chops preferably chump chops with fat at ends
3 tsp garlic paste
4 tsp ginger paste
½ tsp salt
Oil for deep frying
White/plain flour to coat the chops
2 beaten eggs

METHOD

1. Marinate the chops in garlic and ginger paste and salt for few hours or overnight in the fridge.

2. Boil the chops in minimum water till cooked.

3. Remove chops and let them cool.

4. Coat in the flour and then dip in the beaten egg.

5. Deep fry till golden brown.

6. Serve with any tomato chutney.

SERVES 15 /

Lamb cubes barbequed (Mishkaki or nyama choma)

A signature barbequed street and restaurant food of East Africa. The aroma of the cooking fills one's heart with childhood memories of enjoying this feast back home

INGREDIENTS

4kg boneless cubed lamb mixed with 4 tsp salt and juice of 4 lemons and let to stand for half an hour

MARINADE:
2kg plain yogurt (not Greek yogurt)
1 tbsp hing/asafoetida
4 tbsp ginger paste
4 tbsp garlic paste
2 tbsp dhana powder
2 tbsp jeera powder
1 tbsp garam masala
4 tbsp mint sauce (Coleman's brand is fine or any brand-if you find that vinegary then use equivalent dried mint leaves)
1 tsp orange food colouring powder caution spillage can cause staining
4 tbsp mustard oil
2 tsp red chili powder
3 tbsp tandoori powder (see below)

Tandoori powder:
To make tandoori powder, see p339

METHOD

1. Mix the marinade and pour onto the lamb that is already standing with the salt and lemon juice. Mix thoroughly and leave to marinate for at least 12 hours in the fridge.

2. Barbecue lamb in skewers.

3. Serve with naan and salad and raita (p303).

Lamb and chicken samosas

Makes 20 samosas

You can make the samosas in advance and freeze them. To deep fry them while frozen, cook slowly.

A must dish to have at a party. The fresher they come out of the fryer the better! Lovely with a squeeze of lemon as you take each bite! Readymade pastries/pars are available but nothing can beat the home-made pastries

INGREDIENTS

LAMB SAMOSAS:
500g lamb mince good quality
juice of one lemon
salt to taste
10 cloves of garlic pasted
2 tbsp ginger paste
2 tsp garam masala
2 green chillies chopped
6 medium onions finely chopped
10-12 sprigs of coriander washed and chopped

PASTRY (PAR):
Full recipe on page 272

METHOD

1. Put the mince on a heated wok and add the lemon juice and salt to taste. Stir fry till all the juices have evaporated.

2. Add garlic, ginger, green chillies and stir well and cook for 10-15 minutes or till mince is cooked.

3. Take the wok off the heat and let the mixture cool down. Add onions and mix. Add coriander and garam masala and mix.

4. The mixture is ready to be stuffed into the pars and sealed using the flour and water mixture.

5. Deep fry in hot oil and serve with lemon.

INGREDIENTS

CHICKEN SAMOSAS:
500g chicken mince
16 spring onions or 2 bunches of spring onions/scallions finely chopped
1 tbsp salt or to taste
juice of 2 lemons
4 tbsp oil
8 tbsp garlic paste
5 tbsp ginger paste
½ tsp garam masala
½ bunch coriander washed and finely chopped
2 tsp coriander powder
4-5 green chillies finely chopped

PASTRY (PAR):
Full recipe on page 272

METHOD

1. Heat the oil on medium heat in a wok and add chicken, green chillies, coriander powder, salt, and lemon juice and stir fry. The chicken will get into clumps and un-clump using masher or stirrer. Cook till chicken is just cooked.

2. Add garlic and ginger and cook for 1 minute.

3. Let the mixture cool and add spring onions and coriander and garam masala.

4. Stuff the chicken mixture into the pars.

5. Deep fry in hot oil and serve with lemons.

Potato and mince champs (Bateta Champ)

Makes 20 bateta champs

Who does not love this dish? We can't get enough of it! My daughter Aalia loves this dish!

INGREDIENTS

THE MINCE MIX:
**500g lamb mince good quality
juice of one lemon
salt to taste
7 cloves of garlic pasted
2 tbsp ginger paste
1 tsp garam masala
2 green chillies chopped
4 medium onions finely chopped
15-20 sprigs of coriander washed and
chopped**

**2kg potatoes boiled and mashed and
salt added to taste
3 eggs beaten
½ mug white flour with ½ tsp salt added
oil to deep fry**

METHOD

1. Put the mince on a heated wok and add the lemon juice and salt to taste. Stir fry till all the juices have evaporated.

2. Add garlic, ginger, green chillies and stir well and cook for 10-15 minutes or till mince is cooked.

3. Take the wok off the heat and let the mixture cool down.

4. Add onions and mix. Add coriander and garam masala and mix.

5. Let the mixture cool.

6. Divide the mash into 40 portions.

7. Using wet hands and palm flatten the mash portions into flat discs about 7cm diameter. Place on a grease proof paper.

8. Place one disc on palm and add two tablespoons of meat mixture onto the disc. Add the second disc on top and fold over to make the bateta champ slightly oval shaped. This makes 20 champs.

9. Coat the champ with the salted flour all over and shake off excess flour and place the champ on grease proof paper.

10. Dip each of this champ into beaten egg.

11. Deep fry in medium hot oil till champ is golden brown.

12. Alternatively make a medium consistency paste of equal parts of channa/gram flour and white flour with little salt to taste and coat each of the champ with paste avoiding stage 9-10. then deep fry as above.

13. Serve with tomato ketchup or chilli and ketchup mixed sauce.

Sheekh mince kebab

Makes 20 large sheekh kebabs

Now which East African meat eater will say NO to a BBQed Sheekh kebab from the streets or the restaurants. The art is in making sure that the kebab does not collapse or slip onto the charcoal from the skewers!

INGREDIENTS

1kg fatty lamb mince (make sure it is not too finely ground. Do need some coarseness). The fat will drip away and cause smoke if barbequing- which is good

7 tbsp garlic paste

2 tbsp ginger paste

8 minced green chillies-this quantity makes it quite hot -use less if needed.

2 tbsp kasuri methi leaves (dried methi leaves available from Indian stores) this ingredient is quite important as it gives the kebabs a kick!! Try rehydrating the methi leaves in minimum water and squeeze out the water

4 tbsp dhana or coriander powder

1 tbsp jeera powder

6 very finely minced medium onions (700g in weight)

½ bunch coriander leaves washed and very finely chopped

4 tbsp plain flour (can add slightly more flour if the kebabs do not stick to the skewer)

4 tsp salt or to taste

METHOD

1. Mix all ingredients very thoroughly. Keep the mixture cool to make sure it sticks on the skewers.

2. One can use slightly wet hands to shape mince over the skewers. Best to use the 4-sided iron skewers so turning is easy.

3. Do not add any oil into the mixture as it causes the mixture to slip off the skewers. Only use oil when grilling or barbequing over the sheekh kebabs.

4. Try brushing or spraying the kebabs with water when nearly set to moisturise them.

SERVES 4 /

Spicy masala prawns
by Amin Shamji

A very quick and easy dish to impress the guests!

INGREDIENTS

40 king prawns raw and shelled
8 cloves garlic minced
2 tsp salt or to taste
juice of two limes
8 large spring onions/scallions sliced
4 tbsp butter
1-2 tsp chilli powder

TOMATO SAUCE:
3 tbsp tomato paste
4 cloves garlic pasted
2 tbsp oil
¼ tsp haldi or turmeric
½ tsp salt
¼ tsp red chilli powder

METHOD

SAUCE:
1. Heat oil and add garlic and fry for ½ minute. Then add all the ingredients and cook for 1 minute only.

PRAWNS:
2. Stir fry the prawns in melted butter and garlic till pink.

3. Add salt, the tomato sauce of above and chilli powder and cook till prawns are cooked. May take 3-4 minutes.

4. Switch off heat and add spring onions and lime juice and serve with parotha **(p275)**, naan or rice.

SERVES 4 /

Spicy masala prawns
by Roshan Babul

My dad Fatehali Babul used to love this dish made by his sister-in-law Roshan Babul. Living in Tanga on the coast of Tanzania, fresh prawns were easily available

INGREDIENTS

360g jumbo king prawns frozen (I get them from Iceland UK) or fresh
12 cloves garlic pasted
4 tbsp ginger paste
6 tbsp oil
2 tsp salt
4 tsp dhana/coriander powder
4 tsp jeera powder
2-3 tsp red chilli powder
4 tbsp tomato paste
4 tbsp lemon juice

METHOD

1. Defrost the prawns if frozen. Heat the oil on medium heat and fry the garlic and ginger for ½ minute.

2. Add the dhana and jeera powder and cook for ½ minute.

3. Add the tomato paste, salt and red chilli powder and cook for 1 minute mixing it all.

4. Add the prawns and cook till prawns are cooked. This takes about 3 to 5 minutes.

5. Add the lemon juice and serve with naan or parotha **(p275)**.

SERVES 15 /
Written for many people as I normally cook it when we have large crowds!

Tandoori chicken

This was a recipe created by me after researching many Indian cookbooks. The recipe has a Bengali twist to it by the addition of mustard oil. Another of our family signature dishes!

INGREDIENTS

20 chicken breasts boneless cubed mixed with 4 tsp salt and juice of 4 lemons and let to stand for half an hour

MARINADE:
2kg plain yogurt (not Greek yogurt)
1 tbsp hing/asafoetida
4 tbsp ginger paste
4 tbsp garlic paste
2 tbsp dhana/coriander powder
2 tbsp jeera powder
1 tbsp garam masala
4 tbsp mint sauce (Coleman's brand is fine or any brand-if you find that vinegary then use equivalent dried mint leaves throughout the recipe)
1 tsp orange food colouring powder
4 tbsp mustard oil
2 tsp red chili powder
3 tbsp tandoori powder (see below)
250g butter

Tandoori powder:
To make tandoori powder, see p339

METHOD

1. Mix the marinade except butter and pour onto the chicken that is already standing with the salt and lemon juice. Mix thoroughly and leave to marinate for at least 12 hours.

2. Preheat the oven to 200C/400F and put foil onto oven trays and altogether melt 250g butter and pour half onto the trays. Add the chicken.

3. Add the rest of butter on the top and open roast till cooked and the chicken browns on the top.

4. Siphon off the juices from the trays and use as a gravy.

5. Grill the chicken to brown.

6. Alternately barbeque chicken in skewers.

7. Serve with naan and rice and raita **(p303)**.

SERVES 15 /

Tandoori lamb chops

A favourite at our family barbeques

INGREDIENTS

30 lamb chops. Best to use Chump chops cut as it has a lot of meat and is tender. Beat the chops with a kitchen mallet (hammer) to flatten the chops. Add 4 tsp of salt and juice of 4 lemons, mix and let it rest for half an hour before adding marinade

MARINADE:
2kg plain yogurt (not Greek yogurt)
1 tbsp hing/asafoetida
4 tbsp ginger paste
4 tbsp garlic paste
2 tbsp dhana/coriander powder
2 tbsp jeera powder
1 tbsp garam masala
4 tbsp mint sauce (Coleman's brand is fine or any brand-if you find that vinegary then use equivalent dried mint leaves throughout the recipe)
1 tsp orange food colouring powder
4 tbsp mustard oil
2 tsp red chili powder
3 tbsp tandoori powder (see below)

Tandoori powder:
To make tandoori powder, see p339

METHOD

1. Mix the marinade and pour onto the lamb chops that are already standing with the salt and lemon juice. Mix thoroughly and leave to marinate for at least 12 hours.

2. Barbeque the lamb chops.

3. Serve with naan and salad and raita.

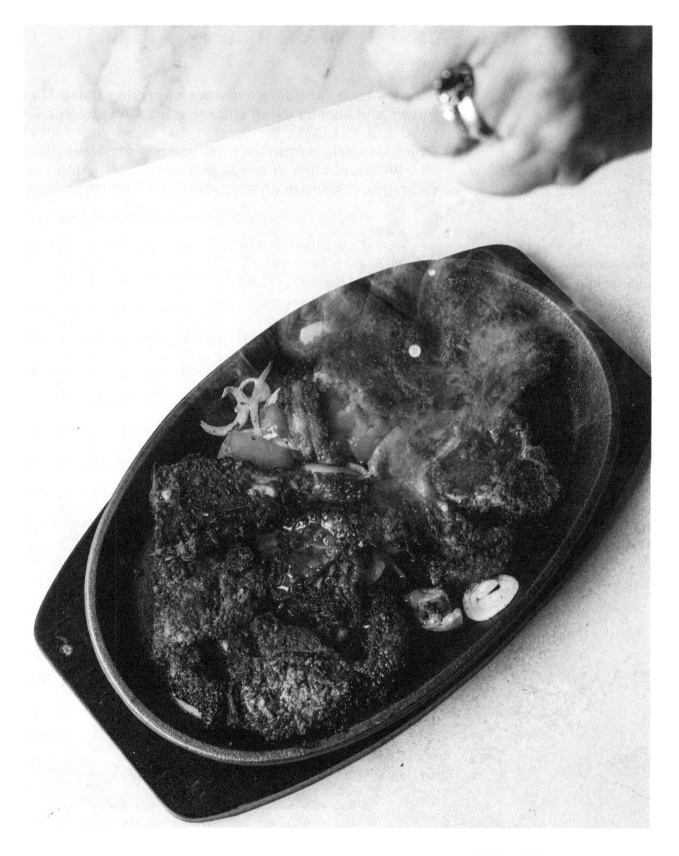

Thai chicken fritters and kebabs
Version 1 using cornflour

Makes 15 fritters

Here we have four different ways of making these Thai fritters and kebabs using chicken mince. All are equally good and just make the version that takes your fancy! Delicious straight from the fryer/bbq grill etc. Have them all with sweet chilli Thai sauce. Why not try using raw cod mince instead of chicken mince for a variation?

INGREDIENTS

20 kaffir lime leaves veins removed and finely chopped
350g minced raw chicken
3 tbsp green curry paste
2 tsp nam pla (Thai fish sauce)
1 tsp sugar
1 tbsp cornflour
1 tbsp chopped coriander
juice of half lime
1 tbsp ginger pasted
2 tsp salt or to taste
50g fine green beans finely chopped
2 stalks lemon grass-the soft part of bulb finely chopped for use
oil to shallow fry
white/plain flour with little salt for coating for frying

METHOD

1. Mix all ingredients (except the oil to shallow fry and white flour) and shape into flat discs or patties–not too thin. Use wetted hands to shape patties. Coat both sides of patties with the white flour.

2. Heat oil and fry the discs for 4-5 minutes or more till cooked.

3. Drain. Serve with sweet chilli sauce.

For an alternative version, add 1 small beaten egg into the mixture and drop golf-sized balls of that mixture into deep frying oil and cook for 4-5 minutes. Makes 20 balls.

Thai chicken fritters and kebabs
Version 2 using boiled potatoes

Makes 18 fritters

INGREDIENTS

500g raw chicken mince
500g boiled potatoes mashed
4 cloves garlic minced
3 inches of ginger grated
2 red chillies or more-chopped
¼ bunch chopped coriander leaves
3 lemon grass bulbs-the soft part of
bulb chopped for use
10 kaffir lime leaves (veins removed)
crushed
juice of ½ lime
1 small onion finely chopped
1 tbsp Thai fish sauce-nam pla
1 grated medium carrot or fine beans
equivalent chopped raw
salt to taste
oil to shallow fry
white/plain flour to coat the discs

METHOD

1. Mix all the above ingredients except oil and flour. Make into 18 flat discs.

2. Coat with white flour and shallow fry in hot oil for 4-5 minute or till cooked. Serve with sweet chilli sauce.

Thai chicken fritters and kebabs
Version 3 using bread slices

Makes 12 fritters

INGREDIENTS

500g raw chicken mince
1 tsp garlic paste
1 tsp ginger paste
2-3 green chillies chopped
salt to taste
2 white bread slices soaked in water.
Excess water should be squeezed out
6-7 stalks chopped coriander stalks
4 lemon grass bulbs - the soft part of
bulb chopped for use
4 kaffir lime leaves (veins removed)
crushed
juice of ¼ lime
1 shallot or medium onion finely chopped
(mix all of above very well and make
into 12 discs)
white/plain salted flour for coating the
discs
oil for shallow frying

METHOD

1. Coat each disc with white flour and
   shallow fry for five minutes or till cooked.
   Serve with sweet chilli sauce.

Thai chicken fritters and kebabs
Version 4 using egg

Makes 5 kebabs

INGREDIENTS

Chopped soft bulb from 4 lemon grass
400g raw chicken mince
1 small red chilli chopped
½ small egg white only
1 medium carrot finely grated
1-2 tsp nam pla or Thai fish sauce
6 cloves garlic minced
4 tsp ginger grated
3 tbsp fresh coriander leaves chopped
10 kaffir lime leaves (veins removed)
crushed
salt to taste
1 tsp black pepper
(can add 2 tsp corn flour to make the
mixture stickier)

METHOD

1. Mix all and the corn flour if necessary.

2. Roll onto skewers with wet hands (or on
   Lemon grass stalks) to make kebabs.

3. Rub a bit of oil onto the kebabs and grill
   or BBQ till cooked. Serve with sweet
   chilli sauce.

Aubergine parcels

This is one of our favourite barbeque sides. They can be prepared in advance to be finally barbequed or baked in the oven, to enjoy the melting cheese and vegetables infused with herbs and smoke flavour. Mm mm…

INGREDIENTS

2 very large aubergines cut into 24 discs total
100ml oil
1 tsp salt
6-8 large tomatoes cut into 36 discs discard the tops
24 square slices of cheddar cheese cut into 0.8cm thickness and to fit round the discs
12 strong foil squares of 25 x 25cm
Rock salt or normal salt to sprinkle on tomatoes
dried mixed herbs to sprinkle on tomatoes
oil to coat the foils

METHOD

1. Mix the aubergine discs with 100ml oil and 1 tsp salt .Leave for 5 minutes. Cook the aubergine discs on a barbecue to cook and smoke or alternatively place on an oiled oven dish and bake in a hot oven till aubergines are cooked.

2. Oil the foil and place in the centre an aubergine disc, followed by tomato disc and sprinkle a pinch of the rock or normal salt and a pinch of mixed herbs on the tomato. Place the cheese on top followed by another aubergine disc, the tomato with the salt and mixed herb sprinkle, then cheese again and tomato on top with the salt and mixed herb sprinkle.

3. Loosely bring the edges together and tightly roll all the edges on top to form a turnip like parcel.

4. Make the rest of the parcels and place on a hot barbeque grill for about 20 minute or until the cheese is melting. Alternatively cook in a hot oven for about 20 minutes or until the cheese is melting.

5. Remove and open the parcel gently and eat with fork and knife without removing the aubergine dish from the foil to enjoy all the juices captured!

SERVES 6 /

Aubergine puree curry (Bhurto or Indian Baba Ghanoush)

I call it the Indian Baba Ghanoush curry! Nice and smoked

INGREDIENTS

3 large aubergines
2 tsp oil
2 tsp garlic paste
1-2 green chillies finely chopped
8 stalks coriander with leaves chopped
salt to taste
1 medium onion finely chopped

METHOD

1. Remove stalks of aubergine and pierce aubergine all over with knife and oil the skin.

2. Using 2 skewers at each end rotate the aubergine over the gas flame for 4-5 minutes till aubergine is cooked inside and smoke is being emitted from the slits.

3. Wash the aubergines under cold water and peel the skin off. Mash the aubergine well and leave in a bowl.

4. Heat the oil and fry the onions, garlic and chillies for 1 minute.

5. Add the aubergine pulp, salt and chopped coriander and cook till all is heated up.

6. Serve with naan or rotlas (p267) and yogurt.

SERVES 4 /

Baked beans-home made

INGREDIENTS

½ medium onion diced finely
1 stick celery finely sliced
3 cloves garlic pasted
400g boiled haricot beans or mixed beans or white beans
200g pulped tomatoes
60ml water
1 tbsp tomato paste
1 tsp vinegar
2 tsp smoked paprika
2 tsp salt
1 tbs sugar
2 tbsp oil

METHOD

1. In a medium pan warm the oil, then add onion, garlic and celery and cook slowly for 15 minutes until softened.

2. Add pulped tomatoes and tomato paste with the water. Bring to boil and simmer for 10 minutes until sauce is reduced. Add salt, sugar, vinegar and smoked paprika.

3. Blend this mixture till nearly smooth and add the drained beans and simmer for 10 minutes.

Baked savoury cake (Hondwo)
by Malekbai Somani

SERVES 6 /

Makes one big oven tray

Ideal oven dish size is 25 x 33 cm with depth of 7cm

Did use roasting Aluminium trays size 29 x 22 cm and height of 6cm. It was still OK

Naaz Manji's (my husband's nephew, Aneez's wife) mum, Malekbai Somani from Toronto gave me this recipe verbally many years ago. I formalised this recipe in my kitchen and this tasty dish is the result. Delicious and very popular in parties

INGREDIENTS

3 mugs soji/coarse semolina (make sure it is not fine semolina!)

4 tbsp grated ginger

4 tbsp minced garlic

2 medium potatoes peeled and grated

500g cabbage sliced thinly

2 medium onions finely chopped (approximately 180g)

carrot grated 1 mug/350ml size

peas 1 mug/350ml size

2 tbsp sugar

2 teaspoons citric acid

500g sour yogurt (not Greek yogurt as it is too thick)

coriander leaves chopped 1 mug/350ml size

1 tbsp salt

3-4 green chillies chopped

1 teaspoon haldi (turmeric)

2 tbsp sesame seeds

1 tbsp Eno

mix all of the above well except the Eno

WAGAR (TEMPERING)

300ml oil

10 cloves (laving)

limbro or curry leaves a handful

rai or mustard seeds 4 tsp

jeera 4 tsp

sesame seeds 3 tbsp

hing/asafoetida 1 tbsp

METHOD

1. Heat the oil in a small saucepan till very hot and do wagar/tempering by throwing in the rest of the wagar ingredients and letting the seeds pop. Let the oil cool slightly.

2. Strain the oil using a metal sieve and add the strained oil into the mixture plus half of the strained wagar seeds etc.

3. Save the other half for later. Stir thoroughly.

4. Add the Eno to the mixture and stir thoroughly and pour the mixture onto the oiled oven dish and pour little oil onto the top layer.

5. Place in a preheated oven at 300F/170C.

6. Cook open for one hour and check by piercing a knife to see if inside is cooked. If still uncooked allow a bit more time.

7. Sprinkle the other half strained seeds onto the top of the hondwo and let it set.

8. Take out of the oven and let it rest and then tease it out of the dish onto a plate with tissue placed at the bottom.

Naaz Manji and me with her mum's hondwo recipe

SERVES 6 /

Battered droplets in yogurt (Boondi raita)

Battered droplets in a spicy yogurt mix

INGREDIENTS

½ mug white/plain flour

½ mug channa/gram flour

1 mug water

1 tsp salt

½ tsp haldi/turmeric

oil to fry

1kg natural yogurt (not Greek yogurt as it is too thick) mixed with 2 tsp salt, 2 tsp powdered roast jeera seeds, 20 sprigs of coriander chopped and 1 tsp red chilli powder

METHOD

1. Mix and sieve to make a smooth batter from the first five ingredients.

2. Heat the oil and pour the batter onto a strainer and shake the batter into the hot oil. Do not over crowd the oil with too many droplets otherwise it ends up as a big lump!

3. Fry the droplets till crispy and plunge them in a bowl of cold water. Squeeze the water out of the droplets and mix with the yogurt mix above.

4. Serve as an accompaniment to various curries or have with puris.

SERVES 3-4 /

Bean and dumpling snack (Saak dhokri)

A lovely snacky dish

INGREDIENTS

1 mug (350ml) vaal beans or gungo peas (bharazi) soaked overnight and boiled in adequate water for 1½ to 2 hours till soft (that makes 3 mugs of boiled vaal/bharazi). (Vaal is a better option, taste-wise.) Retain water
4 tbsp oil
½ tsp ajma/carom seeds/ajwain
2 tsp jeera seeds
1 tsp haldi or turmeric
1-2 tsp red chilli powder
add salt to taste in the boiled beans
juice of one lemon

DHOKRI (DUMPLINGS) INGREDIENTS:
2 mugs rotli flour preferably medium type
½ mug channa/gram flour
1 tsp salt
1 tsp haldi
2 green chillies chopped
5 tbsp of oil

METHOD

1. To make the dhokris, mix the flours, salt, haldi, green chillies and oil thoroughly, and then add enough water to make into pliable dough. Knead for 2-3 minute and divide the dough into two portions. Roll out the dough into 2 circular rotlis (chapattis) on a floured board and roll to about ¼ cm thickness each. Cut the rotlis into diamond shapes should make altogether about 70 diamonds. Leave aside.

2. Heat the oil in a large saucepan and add the ajma and jeera and let it pop for about 30 seconds. Add the haldi, boiled beans and three and half mugs of water using the water from the boiled beans to make up to this quantity. Add chilli powder and salt to taste.

3. Add the diamond cut dhokris slowly into the pot and bring it to boil. Cover the pot and simmer for 25 minutes or so till the dhokris are cooked.

4. You may need to occasionally separate the dhokris from clumping together. Switch off the cooker and add the lemon juice. Let the saucepan rest for 5 minutes and then serve.

SERVES 4 /

Bharazi or gungo peas or pigeon peas curry in coconut sauce (Bharazi in Swahili)

A typical East African Swahili dish to be consumed in the morning for breakfast!

INGREDIENTS

3 x 400g tins of boiled Gungo peas (good quality and well boiled)
1 x 400g tin coconut milk
4 tsp garlic paste
1 tsp turmeric/haldi
2 tbsp oil
juice of ½ to one lemon
salt to taste

METHOD

1. Drain the beans.

2. Fry the garlic in the hot oil for ½ minute and add the haldi and cook for another ½ minute.

3. Add the drained peas, salt and coconut milk.

4. Cook for about 4-5 minute on simmer.

5. Semi-mash the beans to give the sauce a thick consistency.

6. Add lemon juice and serve with mandazi (yeasted deep fried bread) or white crusty loaf slices.

SERVES 4 /

Bhel or bher

A proper street food dish that teases the taste buds with its hot, sweet, sour, and crunchy munch

INGREDIENTS

3 medium boiled potatoes cut into small cubes
2 small onions very finely chopped
2 tsp salt
1 tin 400g boiled chickpeas drained
1 tbsp fresh mint chopped
20 sprigs of coriander finely chopped
2 tsp coriander powder
3 tbsp green/lili chutney
Ambli/tamarind sauce (enough to coat the assembled ingredients at the end)
6 tbsp sev mamra or Bombay mix/ chevdo or fine/jinni sev
1 tsp chilli powder
4 tbsp fried or roasted peanuts

METHOD

1. Add salt, chilli powder and coriander powder to the potatoes and mix.

2. Assemble the bhel as follows: onto a plate lay the potatoes, then chickpeas on top, then sev mamra etc on top, then peanuts on top, then onions on top, then mint and chopped coriander on top, then green/lili chutney on top.

3. Pour enough tamarind sauce/ambli onto the assembled bhel to coat the ingredients. NB the ambli needs to be sweetened with additional sugar to ensure the flavour balance is correct.

4. Mix and enjoy.

Bombay mix (Chevdo)
by Sherbanu Shamji

Makes 13 mugs of chevdo

Nothing beats this version of home-made chevdo I used to make with my mother-in-law Sherbanu Shamji. It is definitely labour-intensive!

INGREDIENTS

Channa daal 350g equivalent to 1½ mugs, washed and soaked for a minimum of 18-24 hours in water with ½ tsp sodium bicarbonate. Then strained and rewashed and laid on a towel to dry for a couple of hours. This is equivalent to 400g ready fried channa daal from the shops. Cofresh brand is good

Large moong with husk 350 g equivalent to 1½ mugs, washed and soaked for a minimum of 18-24 hours in water with ½ tsp sodium bicarbonate. Then strained and rewashed and laid on a towel to dry for a couple of hours. This is equivalent to 300g ready fried moong daal from the shops

cashew nuts raw 160g

salted crisps 200g preferably Walkers brand

almonds raw 160g

peanuts raw 250g

flat rice pawa (rice flakes from Indian stores) 250g

3 tbsp salt

2 tbsp haldi or turmeric

2-3 tbsp red chilli powder

1 tbsp citric acid (limbu na phool)

3 tbsp sugar or less

oil for deep frying

if using ready-made fried daals from the shop reduce the salt, haldi and red chilli powder accordingly

WAGAR/TARKA/TEMPERING INGREDIENTS:

40ml vegetable oil

2 tbsp hing (asafoetida)

4 tsp cloves

4 tbsp rai (black mustard seeds)

2 fistful limbro/curry leaves

Lots of kitchen towel to soak up oil from frying

Each time anything is fried first place on kitchen towel to remove excess oil

This gives the chevdo its crispiness

METHOD

1. Heat oil high to 240 degrees centigrade (465F) or medium to high heat. Add 250ml of channa and let it come up and float stirring the channa in the oil. It takes around 2 minutes. Fry the rest of the batches. Place on kitchen towel. Frying channa is very tricky as under frying can make it soft and over frying makes it stone hard on cooling. So it's very confusing. Best to get ready fried channa daal from the shops.

2. Heat oil high to 240 degrees centigrade (465 F) or medium to high heat. Add 250ml moong and let it come up and float stirring the moong in the oil. The moong daal should be taken out when it just starts to turn golden brown. No later. Fry the rest of the batches. Place on kitchen towel. Frying moong is also very tricky as under frying can make it soft and over frying makes it hard on cooling. So it's very confusing. Best to get ready fried moong daal from the shops.

3. Add part salt, turmeric and chilli powder on each batch after soaking excess oil from frying leaving some for the pawa.

4. Mix the fried ingredients in a very large dish.

5. Fry pawa in 200C/400F oil, in batches. Pawa cooks very fast and remains white. As soon as it floats on top take it out and bloat the oil in kitchen towel. Add remaining salt, turmeric and chilli powder. Add to the mixture.

6. Fry the nuts as above temperature 200C/400F in batches. Cashews are ready when they just turn golden brown. Almonds need to be checked inside to golden brown. Same with peanuts.

7. Place the nuts on kitchen towel and then mix with the rest.

8. Add the slightly crushed crisps, sugar and citric acid.

9. Do wagar/tempering in hot oil. When the oil just starts to smoke throw in the mustard seed and cloves and let the mustard seeds pop. Then immediately add hing, curry leaves, and cook for 30-40 seconds. Pour this oil over the chevdo and mix thoroughly. Test for salt and adjust. Let the chevdo rest to cool. Store in an airtight container. Chevdo will keep well in a dark and cool place for a few weeks.

SERVES 6 /

Corn in coconut sauce (Makai paka)

This is a coastal version of corn on cob in coconut sauce. To be enjoyed and slurped away with lots of lemon juice

INGREDIENTS

6 full corn on cobs cut into 18 pieces total
2 large onions or 4 medium onions chopped finely
2 medium tomatoes chopped
3 tbsp oil
5 tsp ginger paste
8 cloves garlic pasted
1 tsp haldi/turmeric
¼ bunch coriander-washed and the stalks chopped separately and leaves chopped separately
2 tbsp gram flour/channa flour pasted with 2 tbsp of water
200ml water
4 tsp salt or to taste
1-2 green chillies chopped
600g coconut milk or 1 slab of pure creamed coconut (200g each) made with 400ml water total (slabs are better as they are thicker and tastier)
juice of 1-2 limes or lemons or to taste

METHOD

1. Boil the corn in 200ml of water till cooked and soft. Save the stock.

2. Fry the chilli and onion in oil till onions are translucent but not brown.

3. Add garlic and ginger and haldi and cook for 2 minutes.

4. Add tomatoes and coriander stalks and cook for 2 minutes.

5. Add stock from the cob (add 100ml and then add 50ml later if you feel the sauce is too thick in the end), the cooked cobs and salt and bring to boil.

6. Add coconut milk. Add pasted gram flour slowly and mix as you pour into the saucepan to avoid lumps. Cook on simmer for 10-15 minutes.

7. Add coriander leaves and lemon/lime juice. Take off the heat and let the makai paka rest for 10-15 minutes.

SERVES 6 /

Corn in peanut sauce African style (Makai or kasori in peanut sauce)

A very Ugandan dish using peanuts to make a sauce African style

INGREDIENTS

6 fresh corn on the cob cut into 4-5 pieces each or frozen 25 pieces corn on cob same size pieces

water to cover the cobs when put to boil

2-3 tbsp salt or to taste

1 flat tsp of haldi/turmeric

1½ mug of peanuts with skin grinded into a coarse powder

4 green chillies

½ inch ginger peeled and pasted

2 medium size onions sliced finely

2 medium tomatoes cut into small squares

lime juice from 3 limes

400g chopped tin tomatoes or fresh chopped tomatoes pulped

coriander leaves to garnish

METHOD

1. Place all the corn on the cob pieces, water enough to just cover the corn, salt to taste and turmeric into reasonable size saucepan and warm the contents to boil. Cover. The contents are to be left to simmer on a low heat for 1½ hours or the time to cook the corn.

2. Once the corn is cooked, add the ground peanuts, finely sliced green chillies and ginger and continue heating for 45 minutes.

3. Add sliced onions, chopped fresh tomatoes, pulped tomatoes and continue heating for next 30 minutes. Add lime juice.

4. Serve garnished with coriander leaves.

SERVES 3 /

Curried chapattis (Batakia)

A perfect way to cook up a nice snack using left over or dried chapattis/rotli

INGREDIENTS

2-3 tbsp vegetable oil
1 large onion
3-4 cloves of garlic pasted
1 tbsp ginger paste
1 green chilli
1 tsp jeera powder
1 tsp coriander/dhana powder
½ tsp turmeric
400g tin tomato pulped
2 cups of water
⅔ cup yogurt
6-7 chapattis cut in small squares of 5 x 5cm size
juice of ½ lemon
2 tsp salt or to taste

METHOD

1 Put oil in pan and heat.

2 Add chopped onion and fry until the onions go clear and heat further just before onions turn red.

3 Add garlic and ginger paste followed by green chilli, coriander and jeera powder and turmeric powder. Stir on low heat for 1-2 minutes.

4 Add tin tomatoes and continue on low heating for 20-25 minutes.

5 Add at this point water and yogurt and slowly warm to gentle boil and then add chapatti pieces and cook for 10-15 minutes.

6 Add lemon juice and stir.

SERVES 8 /

Curried chickpeas (Channa vagaria)

Lovely accompaniment to Akni or vegetable pilau

INGREDIENTS

6 mugs boiled brown chickpeas or Kabuli channa (1 mug dried chickpeas that has been pre-soaked overnight and boiled till soft yields 2½ mugs boiled chickpeas)
4 tsp jeera powder
4 tsp coriander powder
salt to taste
2 tbsp garlic paste
2 tbsp ginger paste
100ml broth from the boiled chickpea or water
2 tsp turmeric
6 tbsp tomato paste
200g tin tomatoes pulped
8 tbsp oil
juice of half lemon
1-2 tsp red chilli powder

METHOD

1. Heat the oil and sauté tomato paste for 1 minute. Add garlic and ginger and sauté for ½ minute. Add all the dry spices and sauté for a minute.

2. Add the chickpeas, water/broth, salt, tomato pulped and bring to boil then simmer covered for 20 minutes or so adding very little water if needed. The mixture should be dryish.

3. Add lemon juice and serve with akni or biriani as a side.

SERVES 12 /

Curried stir-fried vegetables (Sambharo)

A very satisfying crunchy accompaniment to any vegetarian curry dish or in a thali/platter of different vegetarian items!

INGREDIENTS

½ white cabbage equivalent to 500g finely shredded (discard the hard bits)
4 large carrots peeled and cut to thin slices or like matchsticks equivalent to 500g
3 medium raw mangoes from Indian shop equivalent to 375g. Discard the stone, leave the skin on and remove any fibrous tissues around the core. Cut to thin slices
50 limbro/curry leaves
5 tsp channa/gram flour pasted medium consistency with water
1½ tsp sugar
1 tbsp hing/asafoetida
4 tsp rai/mustard seeds
8 tbsp oil
Juice of half a lemon or one lime
4 tsp haldi/turmeric
1-2 longitudinally cut green chillies
1 tbsp salt
200ml water

METHOD

1. Heat the oil on high and when it starts smoking add the rai and let it pop for 30 second or until all the rai is almost popped.

2. Immediately add the limbro, green chillies, hing and haldi. Cook for half a minute or so.

3. Add all the vegetables and salt and mix well for 3-4 minutes.

4. Add the water and let it cook till vegetables are all soft and cooked.

5. Add sugar and gram flour paste and mix well and keep stirring on medium heat for 3-4 minutes. Add very little water if necessary.

6. Add lemon juice and mix well.

7. Have it with rotlis or puris or parothas or any vegetarian meal as a side dish.

SERVES 4 /

Curried sweetcorn (Makai or Kasori curried) in peanut sauce

This is the currified version of corn on cob with peanut sauce

INGREDIENTS

4 corn on the cob cut into 4-5 pieces each

3 medium size onions finely chopped

1x400g tin of tomatoes (pulped) + 3-4 fresh tomatoes (chopped)

5 tsp ginger paste

5 tsp garlic paste

1 tbsp dhana powder (coriander powder)

1 tbsp jeera powder

½ tsp haldi powder (turmeric powder)

2 green chillies chopped

1 cup of blended raw red or pink peanuts (do not use jumbo or large peanuts as these do not cook easily)

1 tbsp salt or to taste

10-15 sprigs of chopped stalks and leaves of coriander

1 litre broth from the boiled corn

juice of two large lemons

METHOD

1. Place the corn pieces into the pan and cover with water (1litre) and add the salt. Boil the corn until soft. Will need to top up from time to time with water.

2. In another pan fry the onions until just golden brown. At this point, add sliced green chillies and fry for 1-2 minutes.

3. Add the fresh tomatoes and cook until soft for about 5 minutes.

4. Add to (3) paste of garlic and ginger followed by dhana and jeera powders and haldi powder. Cook the mixture for 10-15 minutes.

5. Add the pulped tomatoes followed by chopped coriander stalks.

6. Simmer the mixture for 30minutes covered until all the ingredients are all well-cooked.

7. Add the boiled corn from (1) and mix, followed gradually by the corn broth from (1). Bring it to boil and simmer for 10 minutes and add to it the blended peanuts.

8. Leave it to boil until oil from the peanuts begins to float. This takes 30-40 minutes or maybe slightly longer. Add the lemon juice and coriander leaves.

Daal bhajias or fritters in yogurt sauce (Dahi wada)

Makes 40 dahi wadas

INGREDIENTS

1 mug moong split (chilka)
1 mug urad daal
(Soak both daals overnight, strain and blend next day without any water)
10 cloves minced garlic
7 tbsp ginger paste
3 green chillies chopped
salt to taste
into 1500ml yogurt add 2 tsp roasted ground jeera or more, ½ tsp red chilli powder (optional) and ¼ bunch chopped coriander
½ tsp Eno
bowl of cold water to soak the wadas

METHOD

1. Add the garlic, ginger, salt and green chillies to the blended mixed daals.

2. The mixture will need to be fried in a number of batches. Therefore you will need to divide the amount of Eno by the number of batches. Eno is added to each batch just before frying. From each batch you will need to make flattened discs of approximately 5cm diameter. Deep fry the wadas/discs in medium hot oil. When done, drop the wadas/discs into a bowl of cold water.

3. After 2-3 minutes squeeze the wadas gently to remove the water and add to the yogurt mixture.

4. Keep doing with each batch.

5. Garnish with roasted jeera powder, red chilli powder and coriander leaves.

Makes 50 medium bhajias

Daal bhajias or fritters using mixed daals
Version 1

INGREDIENTS

1 mug urad daal
1 mug black eye beans/chora
1 mug moong daal
Soak all daals overnight. The next day strain and blend the daals into a thickish paste (you should blend the daals separately as they have different consistencies). Do not add any water when blending. Then mix all the blended daals. Leave out for 6-7 hours or more to ferment once mixed.

THEN ADD:
15 cloves minced garlic
12 tbsp ginger paste
6 green chillies blended
4 tsp salt
½ bunch chopped coriander leaves
1 tsp citric acid
3 tsp kasuri methi presoaked and water squeezed out (optional)
1 large very finely chopped onion
mix thoroughly

METHOD

Pat each bhajia in your hand or make golf size balls and deep fry on medium heat. Serve with coconut chutney **(p289)**.

Daal bhajias or fritters using split moong or chilka
Version 2

Makes 80 small bhajias

INGREDIENTS

3 mugs split moong (chilka) (soaked for 1½ days. Sieved and blended to thickish sticky paste)
12 cloves minced garlic
10 tbsp ginger paste
3 medium onions chopped very fine
½ bunch coriander chopped
6 green chillies chopped
salt to taste
1 tsp Eno

METHOD

1. Add all the ingredients except Eno to the pasted daal.

2. Add Eno just before frying.

3. Make into flattish discs or golf size balls and deep fry into medium hot oil till cooked.

Bhajias are quite crispy.

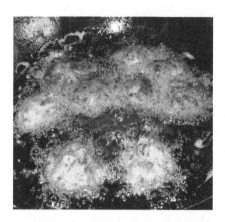

Daal bhajias or fritters - Crispy
Version 3

Makes 18 walnut size bhajias or 15 disc shaped bhajias

In my hometown of Tanga, Tanzania there is a famous restaurant call Blue room. There, everyone flocked in to enjoy their sizzling hot crispy daal bhajias. Of course, their recipe is a top secret but this is the nearest I could guess! Lovely with coconut chutney

INGREDIENTS

¾ mug moong daal without husk pre-soaked for a minimum of 6 hours

¼ mug basmati rice pre-soaked for a minimum of 6 hours

1 medium finely chopped onion

3 green chillies finely chopped

¼ bunch fresh coriander chopped

1 tsp kasuri methi

4 cloves garlic pasted

4 tbsp ginger pasted

1½ tsp salt

¼ tsp Eno

METHOD

1. Strain the daal and rice and blend separately with no water till the paste is quite fine. Mix the pastes.

2. Add the rest of the ingredients except Eno and let it stand for three to four hours though you can use immediately if needed.

3. Add Eno and mix vigorously and make into balls or discs and deep fry in hot oil.

4. Serve with coconut chutney **(p289)**.

SERVES 4 /

Green bananas (Matoke) in peanut sauce

This is *the* fusion of Ugandan and Indian ingredients giving this green banana recipe its uniqueness!

INGREDIENTS

10 matokes (green cooking bananas) skin removed with knife and each cut into 6 pieces and plunged into cold water to stop it going dark
3 medium size onions finely chopped
400g tin of tomatoes (pulped) + 3-4 fresh tomatoes (chopped)
5 tsp ginger paste
5 tsp garlic paste
1 tbsp dhana powder (coriander powder)
1 tbsp jeera powder
½ tsp haldi powder (turmeric powder)
2 green chillies chopped
1 cup of blended raw red or pink peanuts (do not use large or jumbo nuts as they do not cook easily)
1 tbsp salt or to taste
10-15 sprigs of chopped stalks and leaves of coriander
800ml water including water from boiled matoke stock
juice of 1-2 large lemons
3 tbsp oil

METHOD

1. Place the strained matoke pieces into the pan and add enough water to cover. Boil the matoke until soft (around 10 minutes), strain, and save the water for use later.

2. In another pan fry the onions in oil until just golden brown. At this point, add sliced green chillies and fry for 1-2 minutes.

3. Add the fresh tomatoes and cook until soft for about 5 minutes.

4. Add paste of garlic and ginger followed by dhana and jeera powders and haldi powder. Cook the mixture for 10-15 minutes.

5. Add the pulped tomatoes and salt followed by chopped coriander stalks. Add blended peanuts and the water from the boiled matoke (up to 800ml, and if short, top up with more water).

6. Simmer the mixture for 30 minutes covered until all the ingredients are all well-cooked.

7. Add the boiled matoke from and mix. Bring it to boil and simmer for 5 minutes.

8. Add the lemon juice and coriander leaves.

Indian onion pancakes (Reshmi Bhajia)

This is basically tikha chilla (savoury pancakes) but with onions added to it

Makes 8 flat bhajias/pancakes

INGREDIENTS

3 large cloves garlic minced

5cm long ginger minced

3 green chillies minced

8 stalks of coriander all chopped or 4 tbsp methi leaves

1 mug channa/gram flour

1 mug white/ plain flour (the white flour gives silkiness texture to the bhajias)

2 tsp salt

1 medium onion minced

¼ tsp citric acid or juice of half large lemon

½ tsp turmeric powder/haldi

1½ mugs of water

oil to fry

METHOD

1. Mix the salt, haldi, flours and water and mix.Sieve through a strainer to get a smooth texture. Add the rest of the ingredients except oil, and mix.

2. In a 20cm diameter shallow very non-stick frying pan add 1 tbsp oil and add ⅓ mug of batter and swirl quickly to cover the base. Cook till brown (about 2-3 minutes) and flip over and cook for about 2-3 minutes or so till cooked.

Serve with any tomato chutney (p311) or kokum chutney (p296).

Indian pancakes savoury (Tikha chilla)

My husband's niece Salima Yunus nee Manji's favourite snack

Makes 8 chillas/savoury pancakes

INGREDIENTS

3 large cloves garlic minced
2 inches of peeled ginger minced
3 green chillies minced
8 stalks of coriander all chopped
1 mug channa/gram flour
1 mug white/plain flour (the white flour gives silkiness texture to the chillas)
2 tsp salt
½ tsp citric acid or juice of one large lemon
½ tsp turmeric powder or haldi
2 mugs of water
oil to fry

METHOD

1. Mix the salt, haldi, flours and water and mix.Sieve through a strainer to get a smooth texture. Add the rest of the ingredients except oil and mix.

2. In a 20cm diameter, shallow, non-stick frying pan add 2 tsp oil and add ⅓ mug of batter and swirl quickly to cover the base. Cook till brown (about a minute or two) and flip over and cook for about 2 minutes or so till cooked.

3. Serve with kokum chutney (p296) or any tomato chutney (p311).

Indian pancakes sweet (Mitha chilla)

Makes 8 pancakes

INGREDIENTS

1 mug white/plain flour
approximately ½ mug sugar alter
according to taste
add milk to pouring consistency
oil

METHOD

1. Mix all ingredients thoroughly.

2. Heat 1 tsp oil in a 20cm diameter frying pan. Pour ⅓ mug batter into the pan. Tilt the pan to cover the base. Cook till brown underneath.

3. Flip the pancake and cook on the other side till cooked. Can pour maple syrup over it to eat.

Khichdi fritters (Khichdi na bhajia)

A good way to use left over lisi khichdi

Makes 20 bhajia walnut size

INGREDIENTS

1 mug lisi khichdi (p270)
4 cloves garlic pasted
2 tbsp ginger paste
2 green chillies finely chopped
1 tsp haldi
1 tsp salt
3 tbsp kasuri methi (dried methi leaves)
or 3 tbsp chopped fresh coriander
5 tbsp gram flour/besan/channa flour
1 tbsp yogurt
1 medium very finely chopped onion
oil for deep frying

METHOD

1. Mix all the ingredients and mix thoroughly and knead for a couple of minutes.

2. Leave for ½ hour.

3. Make into 20 balls and deep fry in medium hot oil till the bhajias are crispy outside and cooked inside.

4. Serve with coconut chutney or tamarind/ambli sauce or any tomato chutneys in this recipe book.

If the balls stick to the palms on forming, use wet hands.

SERVES 4 /

Kidney bean curry in coconut sauce (Marage in Swahili)

An East African breakfast dish to be savoured in the morning with mandazi!

INGREDIENTS

3 x 400g tins of boiled kidney beans (good quality and well boiled)
1 x 400g tin coconut milk
4 tsp garlic paste
1 tsp turmeric/haldi
2 tbsp oil
juice of ½ to one lemon
salt to taste

METHOD

1. Drain the beans.

2. Fry the garlic in the hot oil for ½ minute and add the haldi and cook for another ½ minute.

3. Add the drained beans, salt and coconut milk.

4. Cook for about 4-5 minute on simmer.

5. Semi-mash the beans to give the sauce a thick consistency.

6. Add lemon juice and serve with mandazi (yeasted deep-fried bread) or white crusty loaf slices.

SERVES 4 /

Mashed potato

INGREDIENTS

4 mugs starchy and sticky potato mash
6 tbsp chopped parley
½ mug butter
1½ mugs milk
salt to taste
4 tsp horseradish (optional)
little dollop of butter

METHOD

1. Heat the butter and milk in a large pan, and add the mash. Add salt to taste. Mix till the mass becomes one large lump.

2. Add parsley and a little dollop of butter and horseradish (optional).

3. Serve.

Mixed flour fritters (Dhebra)

Makes 30 dhebras

INGREDIENTS

2 mugs bajra flour
1 mug fine cornmeal
1 mug rotli flour (medium atta)
3 tbsp ginger paste
15 cloves minced garlic
10 green chillies chopped finely
1 tsp citric acid
7 tbsp oil
2 tbsp salt
2 tbsp sugar
1 mug yogurt preferably sour
2 bunches washed methi leaves chopped finely
12 tbsp sesame seeds
7 tsp dhana powder
7 tsp jeera powder
2 tsp haldi
1 tbsp red chilli powder
2 tsp (flat level) bicarbonate of soda

METHOD

1. Make the dough by mixing all the ingredients (except bicarbonate of soda) with enough water to make a pliable dough like rotlo dough as guidance. Knead for 3-4 minutes. Leave for 2-3 hours at least covered.

2. Dissolve the bicarbonate of soda in a little oil (for even distribution) and mix into the dough and knead for a minute or two.

3. With wet hands make golf ball sizes portions and then flatten them to 5 cm diameter discs and deep fry in hot oil. Reduce heat to medium and fry till dhebras become dark brown.

4. Serve with yogurt.

SERVES 2 /

Mogo spicy (Masala)
Version 1

Another spicy version to the finger licking fried mogo

INGREDIENTS

**10-12 pieces of sticks of fried mogo
(can use fresh or frozen mogo boiled
in salted water and drained and cooled
and then fried) Each stick is 10cm
length by 2.5cm thick**
1 large onion thinly sliced
½ tsp jeera seeds
2 large ripe tomatoes
1 tbsp tomato paste
3 cloves of garlic pasted
2 inches ginger grated
6-8 sprigs of chopped coriander
1 green chilli sliced
¾ tsp dhana/coriander powder
¾ tsp jeera powder
salt to taste
2 tbsp oil
½ tsp ground black pepper
juice of one lime

METHOD

1 Place oil in sauce pan and heat. Add and stir in whole jeera for half a minute followed by sliced onions and sprinkle a little salt. Stir and fry onions until light brown.

2 At this point, add garlic and ginger paste and stir for 1 minute followed by sliced green chilli. Stir for 1-2 minutes.

3 Add dhana and jeera powder stir and mix for half a minute followed by chopped tomatoes, tomato paste and chopped coriander and simmer the mixture for 15-20 minutes on low heat. At half stage add coarse ground black pepper. The mixture looks a bit thick with red rich sauce. Also add salt to taste.

4 Switch off the heat and add pieces of fried mogo and serve with lime and sprinkled coriander and have the masala mogo with a fizzy drink!

SERVES 4 /

Mogo spicy (Masala)
Version 2

This is a spicy version to the standard fried mogo. Lovely for parties. The sauce can be used for masala fish too

INGREDIENTS

20 mogo chips-use frozen or fresh. Each stick is 10cm long and 2.5cm thick-boil the mogo in salted water till nearly cooked and then rinsed and left to cool
8 cloves garlic pasted
8 inches of pasted ginger
4 tsp tomato paste
2 tsp dhana powder (coriander powder)
2 tsp jeera powder (cumin powder)
1 tsp haldi/turmeric
½ bunch washed and chopped coriander stalks and leaves
juice of 2 lemons
200g tin tomatoes pulped
½ tsp or more of chilli powder
10 tbsp oil
salt to taste
oil to deep fry

METHOD

1. Deep fry the boiled mogo till crispy outside. Leave aside.

2. Heat the oil and fry garlic, ginger, haldi, dhana and jeera powder, tomato paste and coriander stalks for one minute.

3. Add tomatoes and salt and cook for 7-8 minutes.

4. Add fried mogo and lemon juice to the sauce and mix and cook for 2-3 minutes.

5. Stir in coriander leaves and serve with tamarind sauce (ambli) **(p306)** or coconut chutney **(p289)**.

SERVES 2 /

Mogo stir-fried with peppers

We had this version of stir-fried mogo in a restaurant in Leicester, UK in the 1990's and it was quite a unique experience!

INGREDIENTS

10 sticks mogo (size 10 x 2.5cm) boiled in salted water
2 red or green peppers/bell peppers diced
3 green chillies
4 cloves minced garlic
10cm long minced peeled ginger
¼ bunch coriander chopped
1 tsp haldi or turmeric
juice of 1 lemon
oil for deep frying

METHOD

1. Deep fry the boiled mogo till crispy. Leave aside.

2. In 4-5 tbsp oil fry green chillies, garlic, ginger, then green peppers, turmeric and salt.

3. Add mogo and stir and cook till mogo is heated.

4. Add coriander and lemon juice.

5. Serve with coconut chutney (**p289**).

Mogo with sweetcorn

Delicious for the vegetarians and all alike!

SERVES 4 /

INGREDIENTS

16 sticks of mogo (size 10 x 2.5cm) from frozen packet. Covered with enough water to cover and boiled with 2 tsp salt till soft

300g pulped tomatoes

6 cloves garlic pasted

4 tsp ginger paste

2 green/bell peppers chopped

½ tsp turmeric/haldi

1-2 green chillies chopped

400g cooked sweetcorn

4 tbsp oil

300ml coconut milk

20 sprigs fresh coriander stalks and leaves chopped separately

juice of 2 lemons

100ml stock from the boiled mogo

METHOD

1. Heat the oil on medium heat and fry the green chillies, garlic and ginger for ½ minute.

2. Add turmeric and green peppers and fry for a minute.

3. Add tomatoes and coriander stalks and cook for 2 minutes.

4. Add the boiled mogo, sweetcorn, stock from the boiled mogo and cook for 5-6 minutes adding more stock if required. This recipe should be of thick consistency.

5. Adjust salt if required. Add lemon juice and coriander leaves and Serve with coconut chutney **(p289)** or tamarind sauce (ambli) **(p306)**.

SERVES 4 /

Moong curry-dry (Suki moong nu shaak)

A dry daal accompaniment to any dish

INGREDIENTS

1 mug moong daal
1 medium onion finely chopped
1 tsp salt
1 large tomato finely chopped
3 cloves garlic finely chopped
1 tsp asafoetida/hing
3 tbsp oil
1 tsp coriander powder
1 tsp jeera powder
1 tsp turmeric
1 green and 1 red pepper (bell pepper)
- chopped
1 tsp sugar
2 mugs water
juice of ½ lemon
½ tsp garam masala
few sprigs of coriander chopped

METHOD

1. Pre-soak the washed daal in 2 mugs of warm water for an hour and then boil until it's nearly cooked.

2. Strain the daal and retain the water.

3. Heat the oil in the pan and add the green chillies and onions and fry till the onions are transparent.

4. Add the jeera powder, garlic, asafoetida, coriander powder, turmeric and fry for 30 seconds. Add the tomatoes, sugar and salt and cook for 2 minutes.

5. Add the nearly cooked moong. Then leave to cook till daal is cooked and nearly dry.

6. Add lemon juice, coriander leaves and garam masala and serve with puris or eat on its own as a side dish.

Onion bhaji or bhajias fritters

A must in all British Indian restaurants since the 1970s. Delicious straight from the fryer!

SERVES 4 /
Makes around 50 bhajias

INGREDIENTS

1 mug channa flour (gram/besan flour)
1 mug white flour
2 tsp salt
1 tsp turmeric or haldi
4 tsp dhana/coriander powder
6 minced cloves of garlic
4 tsp minced ginger
3 large onions finely chopped
16 sprigs coriander
juice of 1 lemon
2 green chilies chopped
2 tbsp hot oil
oil for deep frying

METHOD

1. Sieve the flours and mix well with the salt and turmeric. Add dhana powder.

2. Add water little by little and make into a medium thickish paste. Add the onions and the rest of the ingredients and mix. Add 2 tbsp hot oil into batter to make bhajias soft.

3. Form spherical balls of around 7.5cm (3 inches) diameter from the batter. Deep fry the bhajias in medium-hot oil until cooked. NB do not flip the bhajias prematurely while frying as they may otherwise break.

4. Serve with coconut chutney **(p289)** or tamarind sauce (ambli) **(p306)**.

Paneer Chilli Indian style

This is the red and spicy Indian version of chilli paneer Delicious

INGREDIENTS

300g paneer cut into pieces of 2.5cm x 1cm each
2 tbsp oil
3 tbsp garlic chopped
1 tbsp ginger paste
4 green chillies cut into small slices or less
juice of half a lime
1 tbsp coriander/dhana powder
1 medium onion finely chopped
3 tbsp cornflour
1 tbsp white/plain flour
salt to taste
2 tbsp coriander leaves for garnish
10 curry leaves/limbro
1 green and 1 red pepper (bell pepper) - chopped
4 tsp soya sauce
1 tbsp vinegar
2 tbsp tomato paste

METHOD

1. Combine the cornflour and white flour in 4 tbsp water to make a loose paste.

2. Marinate the paneer with this paste and green chillies. Shallow fry the paneer and chillies till paneer becomes light brown in colour. Remove from oil.

3. Heat 2 tbsp oil in a pan and add chopped garlic and cook for a few seconds. Add ginger and cook for a few seconds. Add onions and curry leaves and fry for 3-4 minutes till onions become translucent.

4. Add coriander powder and fry for 1 minute adding 1-2 tsp water. Add green and red peppers and cook for 3-4 minutes. Add soya sauce, vinegar, tomato paste, paneer and salt and cook for 3-4 minutes.

5. Add the remaining paste in the marinade to the pan —may need to add a little water. Let the mixture thicken. Add lime juice and take off the heat. Garnish with coriander leaves.

6. Serve on its own or as an accompaniment.

Paneer Chilli Salad (Chinese-Indian style)

My family and I visited a restaurant in North London in the 1990s and had this version of chilli paneer. It had a Chinese twist to it. We were so impressed that when we came home my daughter Aalia and I tried to guess the ingredients! After a few trials we cracked it. Somehow this version is not readily available in restaurants

INGREDIENTS

MARINADE:
2 tbsp garlic paste
6 tbsp soya sauce
3 tbsp sesame seed oil

SALAD:
1 small lettuce washed and chopped
1 cucumber cut into quarter and then chopped to fine pieces
12 stalks spring onions/scallions finely chopped

SAUCE:
4 tbsp garlic paste
12 tbsp soya sauce
6 tbsp sesame seed oil

OTHER:
12 tbsp sesame seeds, dry roasted in a wok till well toasted
8 mildish long chillies or 4 green chillies fried in 2 tbsp oil
750g paneer cut into small pieces of 2.5cm x 1cm each
4 green or red peppers/bell peppers cut into small pieces, then stir fried with 3 tbsp oil
oil to fry

METHOD

1. Marinate the paneer in the marinade overnight or for 2-3 hours.

2. Cut the salad and mix and spread on a large dish.

3. Mix the sauce ingredients and leave aside.

4. Deep-fry the paneer in hot oil in batches till paneer starts to brown on the sides.

5. Mix the fried paneer, green or red peppers, toasted sesame seeds and sauce ingredients and spread over the salad.

6. Serve with fried chillies on top as required.

The paneer mixture can be served without salad but with boiled or stir-fried noodles.

Peanuts roasted

INGREDIENTS

3 cups jumbo peanuts (525g) or any other peanuts
2 tbsp salt
500ml boiling water
Oven set at 170C/340F

METHOD

1. Add 500ml of boiling water into a pan with the salt and peanuts.

2. Leave it soaking for 7 minutes. Then sieve.

3. Transfer the strained peanuts onto an oven tray and place into a preheated oven at 170C/340F.

4. After 15 minutes remove the tray and toss the peanuts. Return the tray to the oven for a further 15 minutes.

5. Again toss the peanuts and cook for a further 5 minutes.

6. Take the tray out and let the peanuts cool.

Potato and chickpea snack in coconut sauce (Channa bateta nariyal wara)

A special type of Channa bateta with coconut milk found in the streets and homes of people from the coastal strip of East Africa. This dish is eaten with crisps and coconut chutney

SERVES 10 /
Makes 20 servings –Therefore serves 10 if each one has 2 bowls!

INGREDIENTS

**12 medium potatoes peeled and cubed
4 mugs boiled channa/chickpeas kabuli
or brown channa/chickpeas (1 mug dry
channa yields 2½ mugs boiled channa)
600ml coconut milk
3 tbsp or less channa/gram/besan flour
pasted finely in little water
salt to taste
2 tsp haldi or turmeric
2 tsp red chilli powder
2 tbsp oil
2.5 litres water including water from
channa if boiled at home
lemon juice of 3-4 lemons or more**

METHOD

1. Heat the oil and add the potatoes and turmeric. Fry for a few minutes.

2. Add the boiled channa and water, salt, chilli powder and cook till potatoes are nearly done.

3. Add coconut milk and the pasted channa flour and stir well so the channa flour mixes well.

4. Cook for 4-5 minutes.

5. Add lemon juice and serve with crisps and coconut chutney **(p289).**

SERVES 8 /

Each person has 2 helpings

Rudi Masi's picture reproduced with kind permission of her grandson Shafin Kamalu Jamal.

Potato and chickpea snack with tomatoes (Channa bateta)

Now who of my generation does not remember enjoying endless bowls of channa bateta mixed with chevdo/Bombay mix, ambli and coconut chutney? This street food was our staple diet to be bought from stalls at school recess times, outside Jamatkhanas after prayers were over and at restaurants! Channa bateta always reminds me of Rudi Masi in Tanga selling them outside Jamat Khana or Mrs Nanji selling them at our primary Agakhan School. Rudi Masi used to scold me if I went for refills as she told me off for wasting my father's money for buying too many of these delicious snacks! I still would take the scolding and buy more till her late arrival customers would be deprived of this snack as I had consumed her stock. Ha ha..good old memories

INGREDIENTS

(1 mug is 350ml)
1.5kg potatoes peeled and cubed small
3 tbsp rai (mustard seeds)
3 tbsp oil
30-40 limbro leaves (curry leaves)
4 x 400g tins equivalent or 4 mugs of boiled chickpeas/channa dark brown or light brown (1mug dry channa/chickpeas yields 2½ mugs boiled channa)
2 tbsp channa/gram flour pasted with little water
1 tbsp turmeric/haldi
8 small raw mangoes skinned, de-stoned and cubed. If not using raw mangoes then add 2 tsp citric acid or 5 tsp amchoor powder (dry mango powder) pasted with a little water. If additional sharpness is required add more lemon juice
800g pulped tomatoes
5 mugs water which includes water from boiled channa/chickpeas if using

Red chili powder to taste
Salt to taste

METHOD

1. Heat the oil and do the wagar (tempering) of rai/mustard seeds in oil by throwing it in till the rai pops.

2. Then add the curry leaves and haldi/turmeric and cook for 30 seconds.

3. Then add potatoes and cook for 4-5 minutes.

4. Add channa/chickpeas, tomatoes, water, salt and raw mangoes if using and cook for 5 minutes.

5. When potatoes are nearly cooked add pasted channa flour little at a time and stir.

6. Add citric acid or pasted amchoor powder if not using raw mangoes and red chili powder to taste and stir. Cook for 5 minutes and add more water if required. Serve tamarind sauce (ambli) **(p306)** and chevdo (Bombay Mix) **(p54)**.

SERVES 4 /

Potato and flat rice curried (Bateta pawa)

by my besty Jayshree Patel's mum Kusumben Patel

This is something I loved having at my best friend Jayshree Patel's house. Her mum Kusum aunty would make this dish that I had never tasted before and absolutely loved it. I was in my 20's and that taste still lingers in my mouth. The hotter it was the better! After being married I rang her to get a rough recipe and have now written it accurately for us all to enjoy. Thank you so much Kusum aunty

INGREDIENTS

1kg potatoes peeled and chopped into small cubes

1½ mugs medium rice pawa (flat rice) washed in warm water a few times and strained (flat rice is available from Indian stores)

10 cloves (laving)

2 tsp jeera seeds

3 sticks medium length cinnamon

2 tsp hing/asafoetida

2 tsp haldi/turmeric

2 tsp sugar

1 green chillies finely chopped

30 curry leaves

4 tsp mustard seeds

Juice of 1 lemon

4 tsp salt

3 tbsp oil

15 sprigs fresh coriander-stalks and leaves chopped separately

METHOD

1. Heat the oil and when the oil is just smoking throw in the mustard seeds and jeera seeds and let them pop.

2. Immediately add the curry leaves ,hing, cinnamon, cloves, green chillies and haldi and cook for 30 seconds.

3. Add the potatoes, coriander stalks and salt.

4. Stir and cook for 2 minutes and then cook covered on gentle heat for 10 minutes or so till potatoes are almost cooked.

5. Add the washed pawa and sugar and mix.

6. Cook till potatoes and pawa are cooked.

7. Add lemon juice and chopped coriander leaves.

8. Serve on it's own.

SERVES 6 /

Potato and sweetcorn snack in peanut sauce or channa flour (Corn bateta)

An alternative to channa bateta. This is a tasty snack especially for those who cannot digest channa

INGREDIENTS

500g potatoes peeled and cubed to bite size

400g tin tomatoes pulped

1 tsp rai (mustard seeds)

1 tsp jeera seeds

½ tsp haldi (turmeric)

½ tsp hing (asafetida) (optional)

2 green chilies

10-15 limbro leaves (curry leaves)

lemon juice to taste

salt to taste

½ tsp dhana powder (coriander powder)

½ tsp jeera powder

700g of sweetcorn from tin or cooked from frozen

2 tbsp oil

1-2 tsp red chili powder

(if using peanut butter for recipe) 2 tbsp crunchy peanut butter

(if using channa flour for recipe) 1-3 tsp channa (gram/besan) flour pasted in little water

METHOD

1. Temper (wagar) the following ingredients in hot oil: rai, limbro, hing, jeera seeds and green chilies. Cook the ingredients till the seeds pop.

2. Add potatoes salt, turmeric, dhana powder, jeera powder and red chili powder. Stir. Cook for 3 minutes.

3. Add enough water to cover the potatoes and boil. Cook for a while (10 minutes or so).

4. Add tomatoes and corn. Add more water to cover if required.

5. When potatoes are nearly cooked add the peanut butter or enough channa flour (pasted with little water) to required thickness. Peanut butter already has salt so be careful. Cook for 5 minutes and adjust taste with salt and lemon etc. Serve with chevdo (Bombay Mix) **(p54)** and tamarind sauce (ambli) **(p306)**.

SERVES 4 /
Makes chutney for four

Potato fritters-Nylon (crispy) bhajias and Maru's style chutney

Maru's Bhajia was a very famous dish served at Maru's Restaurant in East Africa in the 1960s. The dish was also called "Nylon" Bhajia because it's silky appearance resembled the then new fabric called "nylon" – an alternative to cotton that needed no ironing. Our generation took pride in wearing nylon dresses, saris and frocks. London Indian restaurants sell these bhajias as crispy fried bhajias

INGREDIENTS

7 medium potatoes peeled and thinly sliced but not too thin
15 cloves garlic
4 tsp ginger pasted
4 green chillies minced
4 tsp haldi/turmeric
4 tsp salt
10 sprigs coriander finely slices
¼ tsp citric acid
10 tbsp sieved gram/channa flour

METHOD

1. Add the salt to the potatoes and leave for 10 minutes to let the water come out of the potatoes.

2. Add all the other ingredients to the potatoes and mix thoroughly. No water is needed as the water from the potatoes will be enough.

3. Leave for 20 minutes (max 50 minutes including time between frying batches).

4. Heat oil to high temperature and deep fry in batches till the batter looks golden brown and the potatoes are cooked.

5. Serve with Maru's style chutney **(p300)**.

INGREDIENTS & METHOD

MARU'S STYLE CHUTNEY
1 green pepper (bell pepper)
1 red pepper (bell pepper)
½ cucumber
1 large carrot
juice of two lemons
salt to taste
1 tbsp tomato ketchup (be careful as more ketchup will make it too sweet)
coarsely chop all the vegetables and blend without ketchup
add ketchup and mix well

Punjabi fritters (Pakodas)

Makes about 40 walnut size pakodas

The gist of this recipe was given to me verbally by Dilshad Hemani. I had to quantify it and create this recipe. Thank you so much Dilshad. Love these pakoras, especially throwing them into the Punjabi kadhi to make Punjabi pakora kadhi!

INGREDIENTS

¼ cauliflower finely chopped
4-5 medium potatoes finely cubed
2 medium onions finely chopped
4 tsp yogurt
2 tsp oil
4 tbsp grated ginger
2 tbsp garlic paste
5 chopped green chillies
2 tsp ajma/carom seeds/ajwain
5-6 sprigs of chopped coriander
1 tsp haldi/turmeric
2 tsp dhana/coriander powder
2 tsp jeera powder
salt to taste
1 tsp garam masala
8-10 large or 20 small spinach leaves chopped
gram/channa flour-quantity to see in method-need approximately 25 tablespoons or less
oil for frying

METHOD

1. Mix all except channa flour and oil for frying. Then add channa flour little by little to coat all the mixture. Leave for few minutes for water to be drawn so a thickish batter is formed in the mixture. If need be can add trace amount of water.

2. Fry the walnut size pakoda initially in hot oil to get them to set and then reduce heat so they cook inside. Turn them as they cook.

3. Cook in batches and serve with coconut chutney **(p289)** or tamarind sauce (ambli) **(p306)**.

SERVES 3 /

Red pepper bake with goat's cheese
by Aalia Shamji

This is my daughter Aalia's very favourite dish

INGREDIENTS

3 red peppers (bell pepper) cut into half
as cups and seeds and pulp removed
20 baby cherry tomatoes cut into halves
and 1 tsp sugar plus 2 tsp balsamic
vinegar mixed into it
4 tbsp olive oil
6 cloves garlic finely sliced
salt
20 basil leaves
2 tbsp toasted pine nuts
250g of soft goat's cheese cut into 6
discs
6 tbsp of garlic croutons

METHOD

1. Preheat the oven to 200C/400F.

2. Into each of the pepper cups add the
tomatoes, garlic and 1 tsp olive oil.

3. Bake for 35 minutes.

4. Remove from oven and tuck in the
basil leaves and pine nuts into the cups
followed by goat's cheese on the top and
then the garlic croutons. Pour another
teaspoon of olive oil onto the croutons.

5. Bake again for 5 minutes.

Vegetable samosas

A must-have dish at a party. The fresher they come out of the fryer the better! Lovely with a squeeze of lemon as you take each bite! Readymade pastries/pars are available but nothing can beat the home-made pastries

Makes 25 Vegetable samosas

You can make the samosas in advance and freeze them. To deep fry them while frozen, cook slowly.

INGREDIENTS

500g potatoes peeled and cut into small cubes
1¼ mugs frozen peas (petit pois is best) one mug is 350ml
1¼ mug frozen or tin sweetcorn
2 medium carrots scraped and cut into small cubes
1-2 green chillies finely chopped
2 tbsp ginger paste
2 tbsp garlic paste
½ tsp mustard/rai seeds
½ tsp fenugreek/methi seeds
1 tsp hing (asafoetida)
2 tbsp oil
15 curry leaves (limbro)
1½ tsp salt or to taste
½ tsp citric acid or juice of ½ to 1 lemon
1 tbsp sugar
½ tsp haldi or turmeric
⅛ bunch coriander washed and chopped fine
2 tsp garam masala

PASTRY (PAR):
Full recipe on page 272

METHOD

1. Boil potatoes, carrots, frozen peas and frozen sweetcorn in minimum salted water till nearly cooked. Strain. If using tin sweetcorn do not boil the sweetcorn (add to strained vegetables).

2. Heat oil in wok and when just smoking add the mustard and fenugreek seeds and let them pop for a minute or so.

3. Add limbro, hing, garlic and ginger paste, turmeric and green chillies and cook for half a minute.

4. Add the strained cooked vegetables and salt and stir fry for 10 minutes or so till vegetables are almost cooked.

5. Add sugar, citric acid or lemon juice and cook covered on slow heat for 5 minutes or less.

6. Let the mixture cool and add the coriander and garam masala.

7. Stuff the mixture into the pars. (See p273 for method to fold and seal the samosas.)

8. Deep fry in hot oil and serve with lemon.

SERVES 2 /

Semolina curried porridge with vegetables (Upma)

A South Indian morish savoury semolina pudding! I first tasted it at my good and dear friend Jayshree Patel's house. Her dad had just returned from India and he had made this snack for us. I couldn't get enough of it! I recently contacted my friend Jayshree and went through the recipe with her

INGREDIENTS

1 cup coarse semolina flour

2 tbsp ghee

½ tsp hing/asafoetida

1 tsp urad daal

1 tsp mustard seeds/rai

1 small onion very finely chopped

½ to 1 green chilli finely chopped

10 curry leaves

1 tbsp finely sliced ginger

¼ cup boiled and diced carrots

¼ cup boiled and cut fine beans

2 tbsp roasted cashew nuts semi-crushed

½ tsp chilli powder (optional)

salt to taste

2 ¼ cups water

juice of half to one lemon

METHOD

1. Place the semolina in a large pan and dry roast over medium heat until it looks toasty.

2. Transfer the semolina to a dish.

3. In the same pan heat the ghee and when hot add the mustard seeds and urad daal to splutter for about 30 seconds.

4. Add onion and fry for about a minute till onions are very light brown.

5. Add green chillies, curry leaves, ginger, hing and cook for a minute.

6. Add the carrots and fine beans, chilli powder and mix all. Cook for a minute.

7. Add the toasted semolina and mix and cook for a minute.

8. Add salt and water. The mixture will bubble. Be careful. Reduce heat and add cashews.

9. Cook for two minutes and add lemon juice.

10. Switch off cooker when mixture is still slightly runny.

11. Let the mixture rest for 3 minutes.

SERVES 4 /

Spicy masala chips

INGREDIENTS

1kg any potatoes peeled and cut into chips. Sprinkle with 1 tbsp salt
4 tsp jeera seeds
2 tsp haldi/turmeric
2 tsp jeera/cumin powder
2 tbsp ginger paste
2 tbsp garlic paste
2 green chillies finely chopped
4 tbsp tomato paste
1 tsp salt
4 tsp sugar
140ml water
6 tbsp oil
1 tsp garam masala
15 sprigs coriander chopped
1 tsp red chilli powder
oil for frying

METHOD

1. Fry the potato chips till cooked. Leave aside.

2. In the heated 6 tbsp oil, fry the jeera seeds till they pop. It takes about 30 to 40 seconds.

3. Add the turmeric, ginger paste, garlic paste, jeera powder, green chillies, tomato paste, salt and sugar and cook for a minute.

4. Add the water and chilli powder and cook for 3-4 minutes.

5. Add the chopped coriander and garam masala and mix.

6. Add the freshly fried potatoes and mix.

7. Serve.

Spicy potato balls (Bateta wada)

Makes 15 giant bateta wadas - the size of a cricket ball!

My memories go back to Tanga, Tanzania my birthplace and where I grew up. My mum Gulshan Babul frequently took us to Central restaurant in Tanga to eat the lovely street foods like mishkaki, coconut channa bateta and those GIANT potato balls called bateta wada. One was enough to fill our little tummies. We would water it down with Tanga's famous drink Healtho! This is my version of this delicious recipe

INGREDIENTS

POTATO STUFFING:
15 medium boiled potatoes semi-mashed
20 large garlic cloves
10 green chillies-adjust to taste
½ bunch coriander stalks and leaves chopped
½ tsp haldi/turmeric
salt to taste
juice of 2 limes or one large lemon or more

BATTER:
1 cup gram/channa flour
1 cup plain white flour
½ tsp salt
water to make a batter of medium consistency

METHOD

1. Mix the potato stuffing and make into 15 balls. If the stuffing sticks to the hands, wet the hands while shaping.

2. Sieve the flours and salt and mix with water to make a batter of medium consistency.

3. Dip each ball into the batter and deep fry in medium hot oil till batter is cooked.

Serve with ambli or coconut chutney **(p289)** or tomato chutney **(p311)**.

Spicy potatoes (Masala bateta)
by Tasnim Jaffer aka Tashu

SERVES 4 /

My dear older sister Tasnim Babul Jaffer also known as Tashu (RIP) would make this dish for us. It always reminded me of the Patwa restaurant in Tanga where we would go to have masala bateta with coconut chutney

INGREDIENTS

10 medium potatoes boiled and cubed to bite size pieces
2 tsp garlic pasted
10 tbsp oil
salt to taste
2 tsp red chilli powder
6 tbsp tomato paste
3 tbsp water
2 tsp turmeric

METHOD

1. Heat the oil in a saucepan and add garlic to fry for ½ minute.

2. Add turmeric and fry for ½ minute.

3. Add tomato paste and salt and fry for 2-3 minutes.

4. Add potatoes, chilli powder and water and cook for 4-5 minutes on simmer.

Adjust salt if needed and serve with coconut chutney **(p289)**.

Makes 6 large ladwas/balls or 10 small ladwas/balls

Spring garlic and millet balls (Lasan na ladwa)

These are savoury balls that are delicious with yogurt

INGREDIENTS

2 mugs washed, cleaned and finely chopped spring garlic
250g or more of butter or ghee
salt to taste
2 crumbled rotlas (p267)

METHOD

1. Heat the ghee in a saucepan and add the spring garlic and fry for a minute or less.

2. Add the crumbled rotlas and mix and cook till all the mixture is heated.

3. Taste and adjust salt. Try forming one ladwa and if the mixture does not bind add more ghee and reheat.

4. Take off the heat and make the ladwas when the mixture is still hot but does not burn the hands!

5. Serve with salted yogurt.

Note: Can be frozen. Make sure when you eat them, they need to be warmed.

SERVES 4 /

Makes 12 dumplings

Steamed rice dumplings (Khichi)
by Gulbanu Manji

Lovely and steamy rice dumplings to comfort the soul

INGREDIENTS

1 mug medium coarse rice flour
2½ mugs water
1 tsp sodium bicarbonate
1½ tsp salt
½ tsp black pepper powdered
2 tsp slightly crushed jeera seeds
1 tbsp sesame seeds
2 tsp slightly crushed ajma (ajwain/ carom seeds)
1 green chilli or more chopped
2 tbsp oil
oil to pat on dumplings

METHOD

1. Heat the water in a large pan and add salt, jeera seeds, black pepper, sesame seeds, ajma, green chillies, oil and sodium bicarbonate.

2. Bring to boil and slowly add the rice flour stirring vigorously to remove any lumps that may form. Keep doing it continuously for about 7-8 minutes till the product is smooth.

3. Let the mixture rest for 3-4 minutes and then pour onto a large stainless steel tray to cool it slightly.

4. With oiled hands make donut shaped dumplings with a hole in the middle and pat them again with oil.

5. In a wok, place a trivet and on top of it place a holed pizza type oven pan so as to let the steam penetrate into the dumplings. Place the dumplings onto the pan and add water to the wok to reach just under the pan.

6. Place a muslin cloth over the dumplings so that the steam from the wok cover does not fall onto the dumplings. Cover the wok.

7. Let the water boil and cook for 5 minutes.

8. Take the pan off the wok and let the dumplings cool as they will be sticky to remove.

9. Once slightly cooled and peelable remove the dumplings and serve with chilli oil or chilly garlicky oil.

Steamed savoury cake (Dhokra)

Makes 1 dhokra

This version was introduced to my husband Amin by my dear relative Azmina Kassam, and we all love it!

INGREDIENTS

250ml coarse semolina and add 1 tbsp (level) of chana nu lot/besan/gram flour
300ml yogurt (Onken Yogurt is Good)
300ml cold water
3 tbsp oil
1 tsp coarse jeera seeds pounded in pestle and mortar slightly
Lemon juice, maybe 1-2 tbsp, if the yogurt is not sour
½ tsp sugar
1½ tsp salt
2 tsp garlic pasted
2 tsp ginger pasted
¼ tsp turmeric
1-2 green chillies pasted
5 sprigs fresh coriander chopped
1 tsp Eno
2 tbsp methi (fenugreek) leaves or
1 tbsp dried kasuri methi

METHOD

1. Mix all ingredients thoroughly adding Eno at the end. Stir this for a full minute.

2. Mix well and pour in a greased thali (steel dish), 23-25cm in diameter and about 2.5cm high. Can sprinkle chilli powder for garnish.

3. Place the thali on a tripod (steam ring) which is placed in a wide saucepan or wok which has boiling water covered till the tripod. Cover the pan and let the water boil firmly for steam cooking for 20-25 minutes. Take the thali out.

4. Let it cool. Carefully tease the dhokra out. Have with garlicky tomato chutney **(p311)**/chilli sauce.

SERVES 6 /

Stir fried colocasia leaves (Patra or Arvi na bhajia vagharela)

A very easy, tasty and fast snack to make

INGREDIENTS

2 x 400g tins ready made patra leaves or arvi na bhajia (take out of the tin and cut into thin slices)
60 curry leaves or limbro
2 tbsp sesame seeds
2 tbsp dessicated coconut
50ml water
3 tbsp oil
10 sprigs of coriander stalks with leaves chopped

METHOD

1. Heat the oil in a wok. Then for wagar (tempering) add the curry leaves and let it sizzle for about a minute. Then add sesame seeds and coconut and cook for a few seconds to let the sesames seeds and coconut turn just a bit brown.

2. Add patra leaves and mix gently. Then add the water and cover and let it cook gently for 4-5 minutes till the patra is thoroughly warmed.

3. Switch off cooker.Let it rest for 4-5 minutes covered.

4. Add coriander leaves and serve with tamarind sauce (ambli) **(p306)**.

SERVES 4 /

Stuffed peppers (Lot wara mircha)

A nice accompaniment to vegetarian Gujarati cuisine

INGREDIENTS

12 padron peppers (or other mild peppers) cut open longitudinally and seeds removed
1 mug channa/gram flour
1 tbsp salt
1 tbsp sugar or grated gaur/jaggery
1 tsp haldi/turmeric
4 green chillies minced (if the peppers above are not hot)
juice of 1 lemon
mix all of above except the peppers and make into a medium runny paste with water. Fill the paste into the peppers and secure with thread if necessary

WAGAR OR TEMPERING:
1½ tsp rai or mustard seeds
1½ tsp methi/fenugreek seeds
50 limbro leaves (curry leaves)
1 tbsp hing/asafoetida
5 tbsp oil

METHOD

1. In the hot oil do wagar/tempering by adding rai and methi seeds and let them pop for around 30 seconds. Add hing and curry leaves and immediately add the stuffed peppers carefully so that the paste does not spill out.

2. Add a little water. Cover to steam for around 7 minutes on low heat or till peppers and paste are nearly cooked. Turn peppers around to cook on the other side for about 3 minutes. Keep adding more water if necessary and cover. Cook till the peppers and paste appear cooked.

Stuffed potato balls (Pack bateta)

Pack batetas remind me of Mombasa, Kenya where we used to go to collect these delicious potato balls made on the street near the Ismaili town Jamatkhana. The spicier they are the better

Makes 40 pack bateta

INGREDIENTS & METHOD

2.5kg potatoes boiled (and cut to roast potato size. Add 2 tsp salt over the potatoes and leave for 20-30 minutes)
1 tbsp oil
½ mug water
4 tsp salt
2 tsp haldi or turmeric
4 tsp red chilli powder
1 tsp limbu na phool or citric acid or juice of 2 large lemons
2 tsp paprika powder for colour and thickening the paste
25 cloves garlic minced (this quantity is correct!)

1. Make a paste of all ingredients except potatoes. The paste should be relatively thick. If it is thin, add more paprika.

2. Cut a cross into the potatoes till ¾ length down. Carefully put paste into the cross and press the potatoes back to its original shape. Leave for 1-2 hours to marinate.

BATTER:
1 mugs channa/gram flour
1 mugs plain white flour
1 tbsp salt
2 tsp haldi or turmeric
2 mugs water or slightly less

1. Mix the batter ingredients and then pass through a sieve to get a smooth paste.

2. Roll each marinated potato into the batter and deep fry in hot oil till batter is cooked.

3. Serve with coconut chutney (p289).

MAINS

Non Vegetarian

107/ Akni - chicken pilau Version 1

108/ Akni - chicken or lamb pilau and kachumber (Indian salsa) Version 2

110/ Akni - chicken pilau with channa daal Version 3

112/ Akni - lamb pilau Version 4

114/ Biriani (East African style) with chicken or lamb

116/ Biriani - Rajasthan style-chicken

118/ Chicken in coconut sauce curry (Kuku Paka)

120/ Chicken or lamb curry (Kukra or Ghosh nu shaak)

122/ Chicken or lamb kalio curry (Kukra or Ghosh no kalio)

124/ Chicken or lamb (ghosh) or lamb mince (kheemo) in spinach (Bhaji) curry

126/ Chicken stir fried in three styles (Original, Jalfrezi and Methi)

127/ Chicken - creamy in green peppercorn sauce

128/ Chilli Con Carne

129/ Chinese chicken and green, red pepper in black bean sauce

130/ Cinnamon and orange beef or lamb

132/ Daal using mixed daals and with chicken or lamb

134/ Fish curry (Machhi nu shaak)

136/ Fish pilau (Machhi Bhat) with the option of smoking

138/ Goulash

139/ Green banana (Matoke) and chicken or lamb stew (Kaacha kera)

140/ Gumbo Caribbean style - prawn or chicken

141/ Irish stew

142/ Karhai (wok) chicken

143/ Karhai (wok) lamb (ghosh) / lamb chops

144/ Khurdi lamb soup-Bohora speciality

146/ Kofta or Kebab curry (shaak) with lamb or chicken mince

148/ Lamb or chicken, lentil and daal thick stew (Khichdo)

150/ Millet dumplings stew (Muthia) with lamb or chicken

152/ Mince and pea curry (Kheema ane matar nu shaak)

154/ Minced meat curry baked with eggs (Mkate Mayai)

156/ Mogo (cassava) with chicken

157/ Moroccan chicken tagine

158/ Moroccan lamb tagine

159/ Moussaka

160/ Nihari with lamb shanks

161/ Paella - Spanish rice dish with fish and prawns

162/ Prawns - Thai coconut style

164/ Spaghetti Bolognese

166/ Spicy (masala) fish with aubergines and potatoes

168/ Spicy (masala) leg of lamb

169/ Steak-sweet balsamic

170/ Tandoori chicken in creamy sauce

172/ Tuna curry

Vegetarian

173/ Aubergine and chickpea vegetarian tagine

174/ Bitter gourd curry with jaggery (Gaur wara karela nu shaak)

176/ Biriani (East African style) with moong or masoor or vegetables with dhungar (smoke)

178/ Cabbage and potato curry (Gobi ane bateta nu shaak)

179/ Cauliflower and potato curry (Phool gobi ane bateta nu shaak)

180/ Channa daal curry (Akhi channa daal nu shaak)

181/ Chickpea curry (Channa nu shaak)

182/ Chinese chilli aubergine Schezuan

183/ Daal Masoor Version 1

184/ Daal Masoor Version 2

185/ Daal Moong

186/ Daal sweet with peanuts (Jugu wari mithi daal)

187/ Daal using mixed daals or with potatoes or aubergines or saragvo

188/ Daal-Urad Punjabi style (Daal Makhani)

189/ Drumstick vegetable curry (Saragvo Sing nu shaak)

190/ Dumpling and vegetable dry curry Gujarati style (Oondhiyo)

191/ Egg Indian scambled curry (Mayai dungri nu shaak)

192/ Egg omelette Indian style rotli roll

193/ Flat bean or cluster bean curry (Guvar nu shaak)

194/ Green moong curry (Moong nu shaak)

195/ Green pepper curry (mircha nu shaak)

196/ Ivy gourd curry (Tindora nu shaak)

197/ Kidney bean and aubergine curry

198/ Kidney bean curry

199/ Okra (Lady finger) curry (Bhinda nu shaak)

200/ Masala dossas including dossa, stuffing and South Indian Daal sambhal

202/ Paneer and pea curry (Matar paneer)

203/ Paneer and spinach curry (Saag paneer)

204/ Paneer and sweetcorn curry

205/ Potato, aubergine and pea curry (Ringna, bateta ane matar nu shaak)

206/ Potato and aubergine stuffed dry curry (Ringna bateta bharela nu shaak)

207/ Potato curry (Bateta nu shaak) Version 1

208/ Potato curry (Bateta nu shaak) Version 2

209/ Potato curry (Bateta nu shaak) Version 3

210/ Potato curry (Paida bateta nu shaak) Version 4

211/ Radish leaves curry (Mooli Bhaji nu shaak)

212/ Red cowpea curry in coconut sauce (Nariyal waru lal chori nu shaak)

213/ Ridged gourd curry (Ghisoda or turia or turai nu shaak)

214/ Spanish omelette

215/ Thai vegetable curry

216/ Vaal or lima bean curry (Vaal nu shaak)

217/ Valor (Indian runner bean) curry (Valor nu shaak)

218/ Yogurt runny curry Gujarat style (Kadhi)

219/ Yogurt runny curry Punjabi style with pakoras (Kadhi-Punjabi style with pakoras)

Akni - chicken pilau
Version 1

SERVES 6 /

Another specialty by husband Amin. Love it as its flavoursome

INGREDIENTS

1.5kg skinned chicken, washed and cut into pieces
2 tbsp for marinade + 2 tbsp garlic paste
2 tbsp for marinade + 2 tbsp ginger paste
4 x 5cm long cinnamon bark
2 black cardamom (elcho) pods (optional)
6 cardamom pods
2 tsp cumin seeds/jeera seeds
7 cloves
1 tsp black peppercorns
6 bay leaves
4 medium size onions chopped lengthwise
7 medium size tomatoes chopped
1 green chilli, finely minced
5 tbsp yogurt
3 tbsp of vegetable oil
2½ cups basmati rice washed and left to soak in water for 45 minutes
6 small to medium potatoes halved into 12 pieced total
salt 2 tsp for marinade and 1 tbsp for rice
4.5 cups water total
pinch of yellow food colour powder + 7-8 strands of saffron

METHOD

1. Marinate chicken in yogurt, 2 tbsp garlic paste, 2 tbsp ginger paste, chillies and 2 tsp salt for 2 to 3 hours.

2. Heat oil in large size saucepan and add black cardamoms, cinnamon, black peppercorns, cumin seeds, cloves and cardamom pods and fry for 1 minute.

3. Add to the above, chopped onions and fry the ingredients until the onions are golden brown not dark brown.

4. Add rest of garlic and ginger paste to the above. Stir continuously for ½ minute on medium heat. Then add chopped tomatoes and bay leaves. Add little water slowly (approximately half cup) to keep the sauce fluid. Stir these ingredients for 15-20-mins on low to medium heat.

5. Add to (4) the marinated chicken from step (1). Stir and add 1 cup of hot water and continue heating for 15 minutes.

6. Add potatoes and more hot water (3 cups) and continue heating at high heat for 10 minutes.

7. Add the washed and strained rice to the above (6). Heat for 10 minutes on low heat. At this stage, with the help of a wide spoon gently move the rice from the bottom of the pan to the top and then transfer the pan into a preheated hot oven set at 100C/210F for 10 to 15 minutes or till rice is cooked and then switch off the oven for Akni to rest. At the end of cooking time add saffron and yellow food colour powder mixed with a minimum of water.

8. Meal ready for consumption with kachumber/yogurt or raita and a Coke.

SERVES 3-4 /

Akni - chicken or lamb pilau and kachumber (Indian salsa)
Version 2

This dish is a lighter version of other akni recipes

INGREDIENTS

1 mug basmati rice washed a couple of times and pre-soaked in water for 1-2 hours

2 large boneless chicken breasts weighing 500g total cubed to bite size pieces, or chicken skinned but with bones weighing 750g cut up to bite size pieces. If using lamb then 750g of cubed leg of lamb with bones or 500g of cubed boneless leg of lamb

1 tbsp ginger pasted

3 large cloves of garlic pasted

5 cardamom pods

1 stick of cinnamon 5 inches long

1 tsp whole black peppercorns

2 tsp jeera seeds

10 cloves

¼ mug of yogurt

salt to taste

1 large onion finely chopped

2 medium tomatoes chopped

2 medium potatoes cut into 6 cubes

5 tbsp oil

METHOD

1. Marinate the chicken or lamb in ½ tsp salt, ¼ mug yogurt, garlic and ginger for 2-3 hours or overnight.

2. If using lamb boil in 1 mug water in a saucepan and simmer covered for 1½ hour or till lamb is soft.

3. Heat the oil in a saucepan and when oil is hot throw in the tempering spices i.e cardamom, jeera seeds, cinnamon, black peppercorns, cloves and cook for 30 seconds or till the jeera seeds start to crackle. Immediately add the onion and fry till onions get translucent. This may take 7-10 minutes.

4. Add the chopped tomatoes and potatoes and sauté for 3-4 minutes.

5. Add chicken with marinade or the cooked lamb strained and 2 tsp salt and cook for 3-4 minutes.

6. Add 1 mug water if using chicken or stock from lamb if using lamb and bring to boil and cook for 5 minutes. Potatoes should be nearly cooked.

7. Strain the rice and add to the mixture and mix well. Bring to boil and cook covered on very low heat for 10 minutes. Stir the whole mixture and cook again on low heat covered till rice is cooked. Check to see if rice needs little extra water. Add carefully and if necessary as it can make the rice soggy. Switch off cooker and the let the rice rest in its steam for the final cooking of rice.

8. Serve with kachumber **(p240)**.

SERVES 4 /

Akni - chicken pilau with channa daal
Version 3

This is a lighter version of akni with the bite of channa daal

INGREDIENTS

2 cups basmati rice washed a couple of times and pre-soaked in water for 1-2 hours

2 large boneless chicken breasts weighing 500g total cubed to bite size pieces, or chicken skinned but with bones weighing 750g cut up to bite size pieces

2 tbsp ginger pasted

2 tbsp garlic pasted

8 cardamom pods

2 stick of cinnamon 10cm long

1 tsp whole black peppercorns

1 tbsp jeera seeds

12 cloves

¼ cup of yogurt

salt

1 large onion finely chopped

2 medium tomatoes chopped

3 medium potatoes cut into 9 cubes

6 tbsp oil

1½ cups boiled channa daal (pre-soak channa daal in water overnight. Then change water and boil in water till soft. Add salt to taste. 1 cup dried channa daal yields 2½ cups boiled channa daal)

1-2 green chillies chopped

METHOD

1. Marinate the chicken in 1 tsp salt, ¼ cup yogurt, garlic and ginger for 2-3 hours or overnight.

2. Heat the oil in a saucepan and when oil is hot throw in the tempering spices i.e cardamom, jeera seeds, cinnamon, black peppercorns, and cloves and cook for 30 seconds or till the jeera seeds start to crackle. Immediately add the onion and green chillies and fry till onions get translucent. This may take 7-10 minutes.

3. Add the chopped tomatoes and potatoes and sauté for 3-4 minutes.

4. Add chicken with marinade and 1 tbsp salt and cook for 3-4 minutes.

5. Add 1¼ cup water and bring to boil and cook for 5 minutes. Potatoes should be nearly cooked.

6. Strain the rice and add to the mixture together with the channa daal and mix well. Add 1 cup water. Bring to boil and cook covered on very low heat for 10 minutes covered tight. Stir the whole mixture and cook again on low heat covered till rice is cooked. Check to see if rice needs little extra water. Add carefully and if necessary as it can make the rice soggy. Switch off cooker and the let the rice rest in its steam for the final cooking of rice.

7. Serve with kachumber **(p240)**.

SERVES 8 /

Akni - lamb pilau
Version 4

This akni is my husband Amin's specialty and is a flavorsome version. I just love the aroma in the house when its cooking and wait in anticipation as I prepare the kachumber and wash the dishes!

INGREDIENTS

2kg leg of lamb, cubed
4 tbsp + 4 tbsp garlic paste
4 tbsp + 4 tbsp ginger paste
10 x 5cm cinnamon bark
4 black cardamom (elcho) pods (optional)
12 cardamom pods
5 tsp cumin/jeera seeds
15 cloves
2 tsp black peppercorns
6 medium size onions chopped lengthwise
10 medium size tomatoes chopped
3 green chilies, finely sliced
120ml or 8 tbsp yogurt
6 tbsp of vegetable oil
3 cups of basmati rice soaked in water for ¾ hour
4 large potatoes quartered into 16 pieced total
1 tbsp salt for marinade and 4 tsp salt for rice
5½ cups of broth plus water total

METHOD

1. Clean, remove any fat on the lamb cubes and marinate in yogurt, 4 tbsp garlic paste, 4 tbsp ginger paste and 1 tbsp salt for 1.5 hours or overnight.

2. Boil the lamb with 4 cups water until soft. This takes about 1¼ hours or so.

3. Heat oil in large size saucepan and add elcho, cardamom, black peppercorns, cumin, cloves and cinnamon and fry for 2 minutes on medium heat.

4. Add to the above, chopped onions and fry the ingredients until the onions are golden brown not dark brown.

5. Add the rest of garlic paste and ginger paste to the above. Stir continuously for ½ minute followed by chopped tomatoes. Add very little water to keep the sauce fluid if needed. Stir these ingredients for 15-20 minutes on low heat.

6. Add strained boiled lamb. Add potatoes. Add 4 tsp salt.

7. Stir this on high heat for 5 minutes and add the broth from (2) and water if needed to make up to 5½ cups and stir for further 15-20 minutes on medium heat.

8. Add the strained rice to the above. Bring to boil and cook on medium to low heat covered for 15-20 minutes and then place in the oven at 120C/250F till cooked. This takes about 15 minutes.

9. Meal ready for consumption with kachumber **(p240)** and yogurt/raita **(p303)**.

Biriani (East African style) with chicken or lamb

SERVES 16 /
Quantity is large as it's done for festivals and parties

East African Biriani is heavier than the rest of the other birianis. A perfect and most appropriate dish to cook for any festivities and large parties. The aroma of saffron and fried onions at cooking and at serving puts anyone into the festive mood. The smoking/dhunghar of the biriani is optional but it definitely throws a twist into this rich dish!

INGREDIENTS

32 pieces of potatoes the size of roast potatoes cooked by deep frying in onion oil but nearly cooked otherwise they can fall apart later in the biriani if fully cooked

6kg skinned and cut up chicken assorted pieces if doing chicken biriani

6kg lamb pieces (half with bones and half boneless) if doing lamb biriani

2 cups i.e 500ml fried onions (1kg or about 16 medium onions deep-fried in oil yields 500ml fried onions).Leave the onion oil aside. Leave a few strands of fried onions for garnish

30 cloves/laving

8 large cinnamon sticks

24 black peppercorns

30 cardamom pods slightly crushed to open the pods

1kg plain yogurt

3 x 400ml pulped tin tomatoes

8 green chillies chopped or to taste

1 tbsp red chilli powder or to taste

5 tbsp garlic paste

5 tbsp ginger paste

juice of one lemon

salt to taste

2 tbsp tomato paste

1 cup butter (250ml)

1 cup oil from the fried onions (250ml)

4 heaped tsp saffron

4 mugs basmati rice (1 mug is 350ml) washed and soaked in 8 mugs water and salt to taste

5 charcoal pieces preferably the ones that light up instantly plus 5 tsp oil – not the onion oil

5 little cups to fit the charcoal made with foil

½ tsp yellow food colour and 2 tsp saffron mixed in little water for rice

3 tbsp garam masala

1 bunch coriander washed and chopped- stalks and leaves left separately

METHOD

CHICKEN OR LAMB BIRIANI:

1. Marinate the chicken or lamb in the mixture of tomatoes, tomato paste, 4 tsp saffron, chilli powder, garlic, ginger, coriander stalks, yogurt, green chillies, and salt to taste overnight or a few hours in a large saucepan. Cook till the meat is nearly tender. Lamb can take up to 1½ hours and chicken around ½ to ¾ hour.

2. In another small saucepan do wagar (tempering) using the 1 cup onion oil and 1 cup butter heated and adding the cloves, cinnamon, black peppercorn, cardamom for one minute or so.

3. Pour this tempered oil into the cooked mixture and mix it.

4. Add the 1½ cups fried onions to this mixture.

5. Cook this mixture for 10 minutes.

6. Add garam masala and lemon juice.

7. Cook the rice in another saucepan with 4 tbsp onion oil. When nearly cooked

add 2 tsp saffron and the food colour mixture and roughly fold into the rice to give it an uneven colour.

8. Light the charcoals meanwhile till all are red and burning.

9. In the saucepan of the cooked mixture add ½ cup fried onions and the coriander leaves on top and then add the cooked rice on the top.

10. Let this biriani cook very gently for 5-7 minutes to let the flavours permeate.

11. Make 5 holes in the rice and place the foil cups into them. Switch off cooker.

12. Add the burning charcoal in each cup and add 1 tsp oil in each cup. There will be a lot of smoke coming out. Quickly close the lid and place a heavy object on top to minimise loss of smoke.

13. Leave for 5-10 minutes, then remove the foil cups.

14. Can serve by folding in the mixture gently into the rice or by placing rice onto a dish topped up with mixture. Garnish with coriander leaves and fried onions. Serve with raita **(p303)** and kachumber **(p240)**.

Biriani - Rajasthan style-chicken
by Amin Shamji

This biriani is much lighter than the East African version. It is more fragrant and elemental where you can smell the individual ingredients like saffron, rose water etc

INGREDIENTS

2 cups rice (one cup is 250ml)

6 cups water

1kg cleaned and cut pieces of whole chicken

150g of yogurt

4 tbsp of garlic paste

4 tbsp of ginger paste

½ tsp turmeric powder

2 green chillies minced

½ tsp red chilli powder optional

2 tbsp of ground coriander powder

1 tbsp of cumin seeds (jeera seeds)

15 cardamoms

12 cloves

15 black peppercorns

2 large cinnamon stick

4 bay leaves

500g onions thinly sliced

500g tomatoes chopped

3 tbsp ghee

salt to taste

4 tsp saffron infused in 6 tbsp water plus 2 tsp saffron for marinade

6 tbsp rose water. (to make rose water from rose essence add 1 tsp rose essence to 2 tsp of water)

oil to fry the onions

toasted cashews, coriander leaves and pistachios for garnish

METHOD

ONIONS:
Heat oil to deep fry the onions. Add 1 tsp salt to onions and fry the onions to golden brown colour in the oil and store for later use.

MARINATE:
Mix chicken cut in pieces in garlic paste, ginger paste, green chillies, yogurt, 1 tsp salt and the 2 tsp saffron and leave to marinate at least for a minimum of 30 minutes. This can be marinated for longer period by leaving in the fridge overnight.

WAGAR/TEMPERING/TARKA:
In the hot oil (4 tbsp) from the fried onions, place 10 cardamoms, 1 large cinnamon stick broken into 5-6 pieces, cloves, peppercorns and stir and then add jeera seeds and bay leaves. Once the jeera seeds start to pop add turmeric, red chilli powder, ground coriander and salt (2 tsp). Mix well for 30 seconds.

Immediately to above mixture, add the chicken marinade and stir for 5 minutes with constant stirring to mix all the ingredients followed by chopped tomatoes. Cook open and if necessary, add small amount of water. Continue cooking and stirring to near dryness on medium heat in open. This will take 30-40 minutes. Leave the mixture aside.

RICE:
Half cook rice in the 6 cups water with 5 cardamoms, 1½ tsp salt, 1 large cinnamon sticks broken into 4 pieces and then put in the strainer. The condition of the rice should be soft on the outside and hard in the centre.

ASSEMBLING FOR BIRIANI:
a In a fresh pan, place 2 tbsp of ghee and heat. This is to prevent rice sticking on the pan. Add a splash of water (1 tbsp) to generate steam and then add one third of rice which is spread evenly in the pan. To the layer of rice, sprinkle 2 tbsp of saffron infused in water followed by 2 tbsp of rose water. Place on top of the rice now half portion of chicken followed by fried onion (⅓ portion).

b Repeat (a), layer of rice (one third) followed by 2 tbsp saffron infused in water, 2 tbsp rose water, fried onions (⅓ portion) and finally the chicken.

c At the end of (b), place the last layer of rice followed by 2 tbsp saffron infused in water, 2 tbsp rose water and fried onions (⅓ portion) and to stop the rice sticking on the side of pan add 1 tbsp of ghee on the side of pan. Cover the pan and continue cooking for 30 minutes on gentle heat or until all the rice is cooked.

SERVING:

When serving, garnish the biriani with coriander leaves and toasted pistachios and cashew nut.

Serve with raita **(p303)**.

SERVES 6 /

Chicken in coconut sauce curry (Kuku Paka)

A very authentic East African dish common to the Khojas, Bohoras and Mehmans of East Africa. A coconut gravy dish of chicken, boiled eggs and potatoes served with naan/white bread and rice

INGREDIENTS

1.5 kg chicken pieces (skinned) - make sure there are some pieces with bones as this gives the broth a better taste
10 boiled eggs
10 boiled potatoes (cut to the size of roast potatoes) - make sure the potatoes are not the ones that mash very easily
2 large onions or 4 medium onions chopped finely
2 medium tomatoes chopped
3 tbsp oil
2 tbsp ginger paste
8 cloves garlic pasted
1 tsp haldi/turmeric
¼ bunch coriander-washed and the stalks chopped separately and leaves chopped separately
1 tbsp gram flour/channa flour pasted with little water
150ml water
5 tsp salt or to taste
2 green chillies
600g tin coconut milk or 1 slab of pure creamed coconut (200g) made with 400ml water total (slabs are better as they are thicker and tastier)
juice of 1-2 limes or lemons or to taste

METHOD

1. Fry the chilli and onion in oil till onions are translucent but not brown.

2. Add garlic and ginger and haldi and cook for 2 minutes.

3. Add tomatoes and coriander stalks and cook for 2 minutes.

4. Add the chicken and stir fry this mixture for 5 minutes.

5. Add water (add 100ml and then add 50ml later if you feel the sauce is too thick in the end) and salt and bring to boil. Cover and simmer till chicken is nearly cooked.

6. Add boiled potatoes, boiled eggs and coconut milk or coconut slab as diluted with water and bring to boil then simmer for 8 minutes. Add pasted gram flour slowly and mix as you pour into the saucepan to avoid lumps. Cook for 3 minutes.

7. Add coriander leaves and lemon juice. Take off the heat and let the kuku paka rest for 10-15 minutes.

SERVES 4 /

Chicken or lamb curry (Kukra or Ghosh nu shaak)

My mother-in-law Sherbanu Shamji regularly made this dish and we all have fond memories of eating this lovely curry

INGREDIENTS

1kg chicken pieces skinned and preferably with bones for better flavour
500g onions finely chopped
400g pulped tomatoes
500g potatoes peeled and cut into pieces about the size for roast potatoes
2 tbsp fresh minced ginger
2 tbsp fresh garlic paste
2 tbsp tomato paste
2 tsp coriander powder
2 tsp cumin or jeera powder
2 tsp garam masala
½ tsp turmeric or haldi powder
1 tsp chilli powder (optional)
8 tbsp oil
1 tbsp chopped coriander leaves – optional
salt to taste
lemon juice to taste
2 cups water

WHOLE GARAM MASALA:
4 pods cardamom
2 sticks cinnamon 10cm each
6 cloves

METHOD

1. Wash the chicken pieces and add garlic, ginger and salt and marinate for one hour.

2. Heat oil in a saucepan. Fry the whole garam masala for about a minute.

3. Add the onions and fry until onions are golden brown.

4. Add the marinated chicken, pulped tomatoes and all the powdered spices (except garam masala) and fry. Add salt.

5. When well blended and thick add the tomato paste and cook on low heat.

6. Add two cups water and bring to boil, and cover and cook over low heat. Add potatoes 30 minutes before chicken is totally cooked. Add more water if you need.

7. Add chopped coriander leaves, lemon juice and garam masala.

8. Serve with naan, or bread and rice.

To make lamb curry substitute chicken with 1 kg lamb cubes with bone preferably and adjust cooking time for the meat or you can half cook the marinated lamb in minimum water to save time beforehand.

When eating the curry avoid chewing the whole garam masala. Discard as you eat.

SERVES 4 /

Chicken or lamb kalio curry (Kukra or Ghosh no kalio)

The difference between lamb/chicken curry and kalio is that kalio is thicker and richer than curry as it has added yogurt and saffron. Biriani masala in contrast is thicker, has more saffron and fried onions, and less water

INGREDIENTS

1kg chicken pieces skinned and preferably with bones for better flavour
500g onions finely chopped
400g pulped tomatoes
500g potatoes peeled and cut into pieces about the size for roast potatoes
2 tbsp fresh minced ginger
2 tbsp fresh garlic paste
2 tbsp tomato paste
2 tsp coriander powder
2 tsp cumin or jeera powder
2 tsp garam masala
½ tsp turmeric or haldi powder
2 tsp chilli powder (optional)
8 tbsp oil
1 tbsp chopped coriander leaves – optional
salt to taste
lemon juice to taste
8 tbsp natural yogurt
1 tsp saffron
1 cup water

WHOLE GARAM MASALA:
4 pods cardamom
2 sticks cinnamon
6 cloves

METHOD

1. Wash the chicken pieces and add saffron, yogurt, garlic, ginger and salt and marinate for one hour.

2. Heat oil in a saucepan. Fry the whole garam masala for about a minute.

3. Add the onions and fry until onions turn golden brown.

4. Add the marinated chicken, tomatoes and all the powdered spices (except garam masala) and fry. Add salt.

5. When well blended and thick add the tomato paste and cook on low heat.

6. Add one cup water and bring to boil, and cover and cook over low heat. Add potatoes 30 minutes before chicken is totally cooked. Add more water if you need.

7. Add chopped coriander leaves, lemon juice and garam masala.

8. Serve with naan, or bread and rice. To make lamb kalio substitute chicken with 1kg lamb cubes with bone preferably and adjust cooking time for the meat or you can half cook the marinated lamb in minimum water to save time beforehand.

When eating the curry avoid chewing the whole garam masala. Discard as you eat.

SERVES 8 /

Chicken or lamb (ghosh) or lamb mince (kheemo) in spinach (Bhaji) curry

A nutritious and delicious meal. The iron in the spinach will transform you into Popeye the Sailor Man!!

INGREDIENTS

1½kg chicken pieces skinned or leg of lamb (ghosh) cubed or lamb mince
Spinach (bhaji) frozen 1½kg
5 medium onions finely chopped
10 cloves garlic minced
3 tbsp ginger minced
8 tbsp oil
3 tbsp tomato paste
3 x 400g tins tomatoes pulped
4 tsp dhana/coriander powder
4 tsp jeera powder
2 tsp garam masala
2 tsp haldi (turmeric)
4 sliced green chillies
Leaves from one bunch fresh methi chopped
salt to taste

TARKA OR WAGAR OR TEMPERING:
4 tbsp butter or ghee
3 inch ginger peeled and cut into thin strips

METHOD

If using leg of lamb, preboil the meat in minimum water and salt for about 45 minutes or so and add the stock in minimum quantity to the dish at stage 3. Chicken has to be added raw at stage 2 and add the mince at stage 2 too. Mince may need a total of one hour cooking.

1. Fry the onions in oil till nearly brown and then add the green chillies.

2. Add methi leaves and fry for 1-2 minutes. Add haldi/turmeric, dhana/coriander and jeera powder, garlic and ginger and fry for one minute. Add chicken or mince and salt and cook for 3-4 minutes on medium heat adding a little water if needed to stop spices burning.

3. Add tomato paste and tomatoes. Cook for 3-4 minutes. Add spinach and add lamb at this stage if using and cook for 45 minutes or so until everything tastes cooked. Add garam masala.

4. The next stage is the tempering (wagar) process. Heat the butter or ghee in a small saucepan, add the strips of ginger and cook for a minute. Add the contents of the small saucepan into the main dish and cook for a further two minutes.
Add this to the dish and cook for 2-3 minutes.' at end of method.

5. Serve with lisi khichdi **(p270)** or parotha **(p275)** or rotlis (chapattis) **(p263)** or naan.

SERVES 4 /

Chicken stir fried in three styles (Original, Jalfrezi and Methi)

Three different versions of stir-fried chicken Indian style

INGREDIENTS

1kg boneless chicken cubed
4 medium onions pulped
10 tbsp oil
3 tbsp garlic paste
3 tbsp ginger paste
1 tbsp haldi (turmeric)
5 green chilies (optional)
3 tbsp dhana/coriander powder
3 tbsp jeera powder
2 tsp red chili powder
2 tbsp tomato paste
400g pulped tomatoes
175ml water
2 tsp garam masala
salt to taste

CHICKEN JALFREZI ONLY:
5 chopped green/bell peppers to bite size
2 tsp sugar

ORIGINAL ONLY:
¼ bunch coriander stalks and leaves chopped

METHI CHICKEN ONLY:
leaves from l bunch fresh methi

METHOD

1. **For Original recipe**. Fry onion and green chilies in oil till nearly brown. Add garlic, ginger, turmeric, dhana powder/coriander, jeera powder and chili powder and salt and then chicken. Fry for 5 minutes. Add tomato paste. Fry for 3 minutes. Add tomatoes. Stir and cook for 10 minutes or so till chicken is cooked. Add garam masala plus ¼ bunch coriander leaves.

2. **For Chicken Jalfrezi.** Follow step 1. but 5 minutes before the cooking is complete, add 5 chopped green peppers plus 2 tsp sugar. Also, do not add coriander leaves.

3. **For Methi Chicken.** Follow step 1. but add 1 bunch chopped methi leaves when onions are nearly fried. Do not add coriander leaves.

SERVES 5 /

Chicken - creamy in green peppercorn sauce

An excellent, quick and attractive dish to make for guests

INGREDIENTS

8 medium sized chicken breasts sliced horizontally to make into thin flat 16 slices-making thin cuts on each slice allows flavours to penetrate
15 garlic cloves pasted
100g butter
200ml fresh double cream
1 x 115g bottle of green peppercorn in vinegar – the vinegar to be strained away

METHOD

1. Marinate the chicken in all the garlic for at least 2 hours or overnight.

2. Melt butter in the pan and cook chicken breasts in batches and remove from pan.

3. Add the drained peppercorns to the butter in the pan and fry for 2-3 minutes.

4. Add chicken and double cream.

5. Only add salt if needed as there will be salt from the butter and peppercorn.

6. Cook for 4-5 minutes or more for the dish to be heated thoroughly.

7. Serve with mash and green beans and cooked spinach.

SERVES 4 /

Chilli Con Carne

One of my husband Amin's signature dish!

INGREDIENTS

4 tbsp olive oil

6 medium sized onions thinly sliced

10-12 garlic cloves or 1 bulb pasted

1 tbsp ginger pasted

1kg mince beef

4 tbsp tomato paste

800g tomatoes pulped

4 medium tomatoes chopped

3-5 green chillies

2 tsp coriander powder

2 tsp jeera powder

A generous splash of Worcester sauce

Seasoning with black pepper to taste

3-4 sticks of cinnamon 10cm each

2 x 400g tins of red kidney beans

3 cubes of chicken stock preferably Knorr brand

juice of one lemon

salt to taste

red chilli powder to taste

5 sprigs of coriander leaves (chopped)

METHOD

1. Place onions into hot olive oil. Fry until clear and beginning to show first signs of browning. At this point add garlic, ginger and green chillies and stir-fry for a few minutes until mixture is light brown.

2. Add the mince beef, constantly stirring and breaking lumps of beef until all the beef is brown. Stir at low-medium heat for the next 10 minutes. Add at this point salt, seasoning with black pepper, coriander and jeera powder, cinnamon sticks, and splash of Worcester sauce. Stir this mixture for 10 minutes.

3. Add chopped tomatoes, chilli powder, tomato paste and cubes of crumbled chicken stock. Cover and simmer the mixture for an hour on low heat.

4. Add 2 tins of red kidney beans and coriander leaves and simmer for 30 minutes. Add lemon juice and serve with long grain rice with tomato and onion salad on the side.

Chinese chicken and green, red pepper in black bean sauce

SERVES 6 /

INGREDIENTS

5-6 chicken breasts
4 tbsp vegetable oil
2 tbsp toasted sesame seed oil
8 cloves of garlic pasted
4 tbsp grated ginger
2 large onions cut in 2 x 2cm square pieces
4 green peppers cut 2 x 2cm square pieces
2 red peppers cut 2 x 2cm pieces
2 carrots cut in thin 6cm long slices
4 tbsp Chinese fermented black beans
4 tsp cornflour
1 tbsp soya sauce
400ml chicken stock made with water and a cube of chicken Knorr stock

MARINADE:
2 tbsp rice vinegar
½ tsp salt

METHOD

1 Cut the chicken into small cubes and mix with the marinade and leave for ½ to 1 hour.

2. Mix the cornflour with a little of the water or stock.

3. At the same time, soak the salted Chinese fermented black beans in enough water to cover.

4. Divide the garlic and ginger paste into 4 portions:

a. Heat the oil (1 tbsp) in a wok, add one portion of ginger and garlic with quick stir fry.

b. To the mixture at a. above immediately add onions and stir fry until the onions begin to soften slightly. Then leave aside.

c. Repeat steps a. and b. above, replacing onions with green pepper and carrot slices respectively. In the case of the carrots, stir fry until soft; this will require a longer heating period. Place all stir fried vegetables on one side.

5. Heat the remaining oil (1 tbsp) in the same wok and add last portion of garlic and ginger with a quick stir followed by the marinated pieces of chicken. Add 1 tbsp of soya sauce once the chicken is sealed. High heat until all the chicken is cooked.

6. Add all the stir fried vegetables from (4) into (5) and cook for a further minute.

7. Now add the black beans (and any liquid it comes in) and the cornflour paste; stir frequently whilst bringing the mixture up to the boil.

8. Reduce to a simmer and cover for 5 minutes.

9. Add the toasted sesame seed oil and serve with egg fried rice.

SERVES 6 /

Cinnamon and orange beef or lamb

A different kind of beef or lamb dish cooked on the cooker and then in the oven

INGREDIENTS

1.5kg beef silverside joint or 2kg leg of lamb with bone
2 medium onions coarsely chopped
1 medium leek washed thoroughly and chopped
4 large carrots-scrubbed and chopped
2 sticks celery washed and sliced
2 bay leaves
12-15 cloves

GLAZING:
5 tbsp demerara sugar
1 tbsp ground cinnamon
½ tsp dry mustard powder
juice of half orange

SAUCE:
500ml stock from the beef or lamb
salt to taste
1 tbsp cinnamon powder
2 tbsp demerara sugar
juice of one orange
1 tsp dry mustard powder
3 tbsp cornflour

METHOD

1. Place the joint in a saucepan with the vegetables and bay leaves and cover with enough water. Bring to boil, remove scum, cover and simmer gently for 2 ½ hours for beef and 1¾ hours for the lamb.

2. Allow to cool slightly in the stock, then drain and place the meat in a roasting pan. Stud the joint all over with cloves. Mix the glazing ingredients and spread half of it over the top half of the meat and cook in a moderate oven (180C/ 350F) for 15 minutes and repeat over the other side for another 15 minutes basting occasionally. Remove and keep warm and slice a little later.

3. Stir all sauce ingredients in the pan drippings and place in the oven and let it boil till all is mixed. Pour all this sauce into a saucepan and heat and pour over the sliced meat.

SERVES 4 /

Daal using mixed daals and with chicken or lamb

INGREDIENTS

1 mug of mixed daal (equal portions - by volume not weight - of urad daal, moong daal, channa daal, masoor daal and tuver daal) (Daals are the legumes without the husk)
4 tbsp oil
1 large onion finely chopped
400g tomato pulped
5 cloves garlic pasted
1 tbsp ginger pasted
1 tsp jeera seeds
1 tsp turmeric
½ tsp black peppercorns
6 cloves
6 cardamoms
2 x 10cm cinnamon stick
⅓ bunch coriander washed and stalks and leaves chopped separately
1-2 green chillies chopped
Juice of 1-2 lemons
3 tsp salt or to taste

EXTRA IF MAKING THE BELOW:
· **For chicken daal use 1kg chicken skinned pieces with bone boiled in minimum water with 1 tsp salt and 1 tbsp ginger pasted till nearly cooked**

· **For lamb daal use 2kg lamb with bones boiled till nearly cooked in minimum water with 2 tsp salt and 2 tbsp ginger pasted**

METHOD

1. Wash the daals with water and soak in 4 mugs of water for 2-3 hours.

2. Boil the daals and simmer covered till cooked. May take up to an hour. Add more water if needed.

3. Pulp the daal and add 2 tsp salt.

4. Then in hot oil in a large saucepan do the tempering (throwing of the spices in the hot oil till they pop or give aroma) of jeera seeds, peppercorns, cloves, cardamom and cinnamon. This takes about half a minute.

5. Add onions and green chillies and cook till onions are transparent.

6. Add garlic and ginger and turmeric and fry for ½ minute.

7. Add tomatoes and coriander stalks and cook for 4-5 minutes. Then add the pulped daal.

8. If making daal **without** chicken or lamb, add ½ to 1 mug of water as required and continue from step 10.

9. If making daal **with** chicken or lamb, add the relevant meat/poultry (as detailed below the core ingredients) to the daal with ½ to 1 mug of its stock and follow below.

10. Bring to boil. Simmer open till the ingredients are all cooked.

11. Add lemon juice and coriander leaves and serve with rotlis (chapattis) **(p263)** or parotha **(p275)** and rice.

SERVES 2 /

Fish curry (Machhi nu shaak)

INGREDIENTS

500g of any fish like cod, salmon, tilapia, red snapper, basa etc filleted or steaks. Steaks taste better as it has bones. If filleted cut into total of 15 pieces. If using steaks leave them as they are

2 tbsp garlic paste

1 tbsp ginger paste

1 tbsp coriander powder

1 tbsp jeera powder

½ tsp turmeric

½ tsp salt plus 1 tsp salt extra

1 tsp garam masala

1 tbsp tomato paste

¾ tsp red chilli powder

2 tbsp oil

200ml water

juice of two lemons

75ml coconut milk (optional)

METHOD

1. Add 1 tsp salt plus juice of one lemon onto the fish and leave to marinate for 1-2 hours.

2. Make a paste of garlic paste, ginger paste, coriander powder, jeera powder, tomato paste, turmeric, ½ tsp salt, chilli powder and 1 tbsp water.

3. Heat the oil on medium and fry the above paste for a minute.

4. Add 200ml water and bring to boil. Slowly add the fish making sure it does not mash.

5. Stir gently and cook simmered for about 5 minutes or so.

6. Add coconut milk if required and cook for a further 2 minutes.

7. Adjust salt and add juice of one lemon and the garam masala.

8. Serve with ugali (p265) or boiled rice.

SERVES 4 /

Fish pilau (Machhi Bhat) with the option of smoking

My dad Bahadur loved this dish when I first made it many years ago. It really reminded him of his childhood. He had not had it for many years and this experience brought his childhood back. I was really touched

INGREDIENTS

1kg good quality fish fillets or steaks e.g. cod, tilapia, red snapper

3 medium onions finely sliced

1 tbsp turmeric

4 green chillies sliced

400ml coconut milk

250ml water

1½ mugs basmati rice

3 tbsp ghee or 1 tbsp ghee and 2 tbsp oil

2 tbsp oil

1½ bunch coriander - chopped

4 tsp garam masala

juice of two limes or 1 large lemon

salt 1 tbsp plus 2 tsp

METHOD

1. Soak rice for 15-20 minutes and wash and dry the fish.

2. Heat the ghee or oil and ghee mixture, add turmeric , garam masala , chillies and coriander and 2 tsp salt and cook for 1 minute.

3. Add lemon juice and then the fish. When mixture is dryish turn the fish to the other side. Total cooking time is approximately 7 minutes.

4. Remove fish from pan leaving the herb mixture in the saucepan and add juice to lime/ lemon to the fish. Remove the herb mixture and set aside.

5. In the same saucepan add the 2 tbsp oil and fry the onions till brown at edges.

6. Add the herb mixture, 1 tbsp salt and the drained rice and stir for 3 minutes.

7. Add coconut milk and 250ml water, bring to boil and simmer covered till rice is nearly cooked. May need to add a little more water.

8. Add the fish on top, cover and cook till rice is cooked.

9. Mix the fish very carefully into the rice and switch off cooker.

To smoke the rice or do Dhungar heat 2 charcoal pieces and place the ready heated coal in a foil packed like a little basket. Make 2 deep holes in the rice mixture and place the foil with the burning coal into these holes. Quickly add 1-2 tsp oil onto each of the charcoals and cover the lid quickly and tightly for 10-15 minutes. Remove the foil and serve.

SERVES 4 /

Goulash

Goulash always reminds me of having it in Prague in the very cold winter and really enjoying it

INGREDIENTS

1kg stewing beef or diced beef
750g or 5 large finely chopped onions
6 medium ripe tomatoes finely chopped
15 cloves garlic pasted
1 tsp whole black peppercorns lightly crushed
2 tbsp paprika powder
½ tsp red chilli powder (optional)
1 tsp marjoram
2 bay leaves
2 beef OXO cubes
1 tsp salt or to taste
10 tbsp cooking oil
1 large red pepper (bell pepper) finely diced

METHOD

1. Add 1½ mugs of water to the beef in the saucepan and the salt. Bring to boil, remove the froth and cover simmered for 1½ to 2 hours till beef is very soft.

2. Heat the oil in another saucepan and fry the onions till medium brown. Can take 15-20 minutes. Add the garlic and bay leaves and cook for 30 seconds.

3. Add all the spices and red pepper and cook for 1 minute. Then add the tomatoes and cook for 2 minutes. Then add the crumbled beef OXO cubes and 150ml of the broth from the cooked beef.

4. Add the strained meat into the saucepan and let the mixture cook on simmer covered for 45 minutes or so. The beef chunks should be very soft. You can add more stock if required little by little. Taste the salt and adjust.

5. If you wish to thicken the sauce do so by adding a paste of 1 tsp butter in 1 tsp white flour and add it slowly to the goulash. Cook for 3-4 minutes.

6. May serve with bread dumplings or mash or American rice.

Green banana (Matoke) and chicken or lamb stew (Kaacha kera)

Makes 2-3 large servings

A green banana and meat/chicken fusion of Indian and East African cuisine containing coconut milk. I loved this dish as a child and could not get enough of it. My mum Gulshan would spoil me by treating me to this dish. Very fond memories. For the vegetarians one can substitute the meat with maybe sweetcorn

INGREDIENTS

6 kacha kera/matok/kachi ndizi/green cooking bananas-peeled cut into round thick pieces and left in water to stop it going dark
1 medium onion chopped
135ml coconut milk
juice of one lime/lemon
salt to taste
½ tsp haldi (turmeric)
1 chicken breast (raw) with bones cut into small pieces or 250g boiled cubed lamb with bones
2 tsp garlic paste
2 tsp ginger paste
2 green chillies chopped
¼ bunch coriander leaves washed and chopped
3 tbsp oil

METHOD

1. Boil the matoke in very little salted water till soft. Strain and mash the matoke. Leave aside.

2. Fry the onions in hot oil with chillies till onions are soft but not brown. Add garlic and ginger and turmeric and cook for ½ a minute.

3. Add chicken pieces (raw) and ¼ mug or less of water and boil chicken with salt to taste for 6-8 minutes. (If using boiled lamb, just add the meat with ¼ mug of its broth and cook for 2-3 minutes.)

4. Then add the mashed matoke, lime, coriander, coconut milk and more water if required. The dish should be dryish. Cook for 4-5 minutes making sure the chicken is cooked.

SERVES 6 /

Gumbo Caribbean style - prawn or chicken

Gumbo derives from "Kigombo" a type of African okra

INGREDIENTS

300g okra (bhinda) washed, dried, topped, tailed and cut into small pieces
400g pulped tomatoes
30g butter
1 medium onion, 1 green pepper (bell pepper) and 1 stalk celery – all to be chopped
2 cloves garlic chopped
2 tsp tomato paste
2 tsp Cajun spice
2 bay leaves
2 tsp chilli flakes
1 tbsp Worcester sauce
salt and pepper to taste
400ml water plus 1-2 stock cubes preferably Knorr brand to make stock
2 tbsp plain flour pasted with 2 tbsp butter. Mix well
600g prawns-raw and peeled or 600g chicken breast diced

METHOD

1. Combine okra and pulped tomatoes in a pan. Bring to boil, reduce heat, cover and simmer gently for 15 minutes.

2. Cook the vegetables in butter for 2-3 minutes, add garlic and cook for 20 minutes.

3. Add okra and tomato mixture to the vegetables with tomato paste, Cajun spice, chilli flakes, bay leaves, Worcester sauce and pepper. Stir for 2 minutes, then add stock and salt. Add some of the warmed stock to the butter and flour paste until a creamy texture is formed. Add that to the pan and cook a further 15 minutes.

4. Add prawns/chicken and simmer gently until cooked, season to taste. Serve with American rice.

SERVES 3 /

Irish stew

A food to warm up the cockles of the heart on a cold winter's night

INGREDIENTS

2 tbsp oil
500g frying steak or braising or stewing steak cut into one inch cubes or bigger sizes
2 med onions peeled and diced
1 large carrot peeled and diced
3 sticks celery chopped
3 tbsp pearl barley
2 tbsp Worcestershire sauce
¾ pint stock or water
3 bay leaves
salt and fresh ground pepper to taste

METHOD

1. Heat the oil in frying pan or wok and brown the meat, if necessary, in batches. Leave aside.

2. In the residual oil in wok add the vegetables and cook for 3 minutes.

3. Return the meat and the remaining ingredients into the wok, mix and transfer to a casserole dish.

4. Cover and cook in a preheated oven at 180C/350F for 1½ to 1¾ hours.

5. Taste and adjust seasoning, remove bay leaves and serve with mash or boiled potatoes.

Karhai (wok) chicken

SERVES 4 /

A thick and rich wok/karahi cooked chicken which is a must when dining out in an Indian restaurant

INGREDIENTS

1kg boneless chicken breast or skinned chicken with bones both cut to bite size pieces
5 tbsp ginger paste
5 tbsp garlic paste
5 tsp coriander/dhana powder
5 tsp jeera powder
1 tsp turmeric
2-4 green chillies sliced
⅓ cup oil
⅓ cup ghee
1 tsp ground black pepper
1-2 tsp Kashmiri chilli powder (Kashmiri chilli powder is mild and has intense red colour)
30 sprigs coriander (leaves and stalks chopped separately)
2 tsp salt plus 2 tsp salt
4 tsp kasuri methi (dried methi leaves)
2 tsp kalonji/nigella seeds/kala jeera/onion seeds
800g pulped tomatoes

METHOD

1. Marinate the chicken in half of the garlic and ginger and 2 tsp salt for an hour or overnight in the fridge.

2. In a wok/karahi heat the oil and ghee and fry the kalonji seeds and green chillies for ½ minute.

3. Add remaining garlic and ginger and fry for ½ minute.

4. Add turmeric, coriander and jeera powder and fry for ½ minute.

5. Add the chicken and cook till outside is cooked.

6. Add tomatoes, 2 tsp salt, chilli powder, black pepper and coriander stalks and cook open stirring occasionally on medium heat.

7. Add kasuri methi and cook open for another 15 minutes or until chicken is thoroughly cooked. The oil should be floating on the top.

8. Add coriander leaves and serve with naan or tandoori roti.

Karhai (wok) lamb (ghosh)/lamb chops

This is a delightful wok/karahi sister dish of karahi chicken. A must for lamb lovers!

SERVES 4 /

INGREDIENTS

1kg lamb cut to bite size pieces preferably with some pieces with bones to give flavour or 1kg lamb chops (preferably chump chops. I get mine from Iceland supermarket, UK frozen. Chump chops have a lot of meat) with some fat removed

5 tbsp ginger paste

5 tbsp garlic paste

5 tsp coriander/dhana powder

5 tsp jeera powder

1 tsp turmeric

2-4 green chillies sliced

⅓ cup oil

⅓ cup ghee

1 tsp ground black pepper

1-2 tsp Kashmiri chilli powder (Kashmiri chilli powder is mild and has intense red colour)

30 sprigs coriander (leaves and stalks chopped separately)

2 tsp salt plus 2 tsp salt

4 tsp kasuri methi (dried methi leaves)

1 tsp kalonji/nigella seeds/kala jeera/ onion seeds

600g pulped tomatoes

2 tsp garam masala

METHOD

1. Marinate the lamb or lamb chops in half of the garlic and ginger and 2 tsp salt for an hour or overnight in the fridge.

2. Pre boil the lamb or lamb chops in one cup water covered in a pan for 30 minutes.

3. In a wok/karahi heat the oil and ghee and fry the kalonji seeds and green chillies for ½ minute.

4. Add remaining garlic and ginger and fry for ½ minute.

5. Add turmeric, coriander and jeera powder and fry for ½ minute.

6. Add tomatoes, 2 tsp salt, Kashmiri chilli powder, black pepper and coriander stalks and bring to boil.

7. Add the strained meat with 250ml of its stock (may need to add a little water to bring to 250ml) and cook open for 25 minutes stirring occasionally.

8. Add kasuri methi and cook open for another 20 minutes or until meat is thoroughly cooked. The oil should be floating on the top.

9. Add coriander leaves and garam masala and serve with naan or tandoori rotli (chapatti) **(p263)**.

SERVES 4 /

Khurdi lamb soup-Bohora speciality

My mum and dad Gulshan and Fatehali had a lot of Bohora friends with whom they hosted many parties. Their Bohora friends would bring their authentic dish Khurdi to these parties. I used to love having it on these occasions. Sadly, after my parents passed away, I missed having Khurdi. So, I asked my mum's dear Bohora friend Akila Jivanjee for the recipe on the phone. Now I make it and reminisce on the good old days

INGREDIENTS

1kg lamb neck with bones or leg of lamb with bones cubed boiled in 700ml water, 3-4 tsp salt, 4 tsp ginger till lamb is soft
2 cups milk (or 1¾ cup milk and ¼ cup double cream/whipping cream)
1 tsp jeera seeds (cumin)
5 large cloves garlic pasted
½ tsp black pepper ground
20-30 mint leaves slightly crushed
2 tsp white flour
1 large or 2 medium onions finely chopped
500ml stock from above boiled meat
2 tbsp oil
1 green chilli finely chopped
juice of 1 lime

METHOD

1. Separate cooked meat from stock.

2. Heat oil in pan and add jeera seeds and let them pop, then add onions and fry them till soft.

3. Add strained meat, and 2 tsp white flour and sauté for 2-3 minutes.

4. Add garlic and sauté for 1 minute.

5. Add 500ml stock from boiled meat and the milk (or milk and double cream mixture) trying to remove some of the floating fat away from the stock, black pepper, green chillies, and mint and bring to boil. Simmer gently for 10-15 minutes.

6. Add juice of the lime to taste.

7. Serve with boiled moong or moong rice or plain rice.

Kofta or Kebab curry (shaak) with lamb or chicken mince

For 10 people (approx. 60 koftas or kebabs)

INGREDIENTS

KEBAB MIXTURE:

1½kg lamb or chicken mince
3 thick slices of white bread (crusts removed) very slighly soaked with water (excess water squeezed out) and then mash this bread into a paste
2 tsp coriander powder
2 tsp jeera powder
1½tsp garam masala
4 tsp garlic paste
4 tsp ginger paste
chopped 10 sprigs of fresh coriander (leaves and stalk)
1 medium onion finely chopped
1 green chilli finely chopped
salt to taste

OTHER:

250ml oil
3 large onions finely chopped
8 tsp garlic paste
8 tsp ginger paste
800g pulped tomatoes
15 medium new potatoes
4 tsp coriander powder
4 tsp jeera powder
1 tbsp garam masala or more to taste
1½ tsp turmeric powder or haldi
salt to taste
2 chopped green chillies or more to taste
1-2 tsp red chilli powder optional
10 sprigs of chopped coriander stalks and leaves
8 cardamom pods
8 cloves (laving)
2 long cinnamon sticks

Lemon juice if required
750ml boiling water

METHOD

1. Mix very thoroughly all the ingredients of the kabab mixture and knead for a few minutes. Leave for 1-2 hours or more. Then shape the meat portions into balls the size of golf balls.

2. Heat the oil and fry in the cardamom, cinnamon, cloves, green chillies and the onions till the onions turn dark brown. Add the dry spices except red chilli powder. Add garlic and ginger and fry for 2 minutes.

3. Then add tomatoes, salt, red chilli powder and the coriander chopped stalks and fry for 5 minutes. Add the 750ml of boiling water and cook on high heat till boiling for 5 minutes.

4. Add the mince balls (kofta) and after it has boiled cover and leave to simmer for at least 45 minutes. Then add the potatoes and boil and simmer covered for the next 30 minutes or so if lamb and less if chicken. Times may vary as both the meats should be quite soft. Lamb may require more than an hour and potatoes half an hour or so. Make sure the potates do not mash as this will spoil the recipe. If you feel the potatoes are cooked and the meat is not ready, remove the potatoes from the pan and add them at the end again.

5. When the dish is ready add the garam masala, lemon juice if required and add chopped fresh coriander leaves.

6. Serve with rice and white bread (thickly sliced) or parothas (p275).

Note on burgers – the kebab mixture also makes very nice lamb and chicken burgers (Indian style). Flatten portions of the mixture into burger sized patties and grill on both sides till just cooked. 500g of mince makes approximately 6 burgers.

SERVES 10-12 /
1 cup is 250ml volume
(Daals are the ones without the husk)

Lamb or chicken, lentil and daal thick stew (Khichdo)

Khichdo is a very typical Khoja Ismaili dish cooked for festivities and parties. It is quite the labour of love but utterly worth it! The Pakistanis make 'halim' which is very similar to khichdo

INGREDIENTS

2.5kg leg of lamb cut into curry size pieces or 2.5kg of skinned and cut chicken with bones-it is important to have the bones as this gives it more flavour (boneless chicken breasts do not give enough flavour)
1 cup pearl barley important as this gives it the stickiness!
½ cup basmati rice
¾ cup porridge oats (normally used for cereals) gives stickiness
¾ cup moong daal
⅓ cup gram daal or channa daal
⅓ cup urad daal
⅓ cup masoor daal
⅓ cup toover daal
8 medium onions finely chopped
800g pulped tomatoes
1¼ cup oil and 50ml of ghee
7 tbsp garlic paste
7 tbsp ginger paste
3 tbsp coriander powder
3 tbsp jeera powder
5 tsp haldi/turmeric
2 tsp red chilli powder
5 tsp garam masala
4 green chillies chopped
juice of 3-4 lemons depending upon your liking
¾ bunch coriander-washed and chopped-separate the chopped stalks from the chopped leaves

salt to taste
10 cloves
10 cardamoms
4 large sticks cinnamon

TEMPERING/WAGAR:
12cm ginger cut into thin matchstick like sizes
25ml ghee/butter

METHOD

1. Wash the pearl barley with water, strain and add 3 cups of water and soak for 2-3 hours. Then strain the water and add 3 cups of water again and 1 tsp salt and boil-then simmer gently covered till soft - approx. time is 1 hour. The pearl barley does not mash. Blend it using a blender.

2. Mix all the daals and rice and wash and strain. Add 4 cups of water and soak for 2-3 hours - after that time wash the daals and rice and strain and add 4 cups of water again and 1 tsp salt. Bring pan to boil removing the froth as it forms. Then cover and simmer gently for at least an hour till daals and rice is soft. Make sure the daals do not stick at the bottom. Puree the mixture but leave it slightly coarse.

3. Add 1½ cups water and ½ tsp salt to porridge oats and boil till cooked-takes about 10 minutes.

4. Add 5 tsp garlic paste, 5 tsp ginger paste, 2 chopped green chillies and 1 tsp salt to lamb/chicken and cover with just enough water and cook covered till tender. Lamb needs at least 1¼ hours cooking time. Chicken needs less time. Do not overcook the chicken otherwise it shreds.

5. Heat the oil and the 50ml of ghee in a large saucepan and fry the onions, cinnamon, green chillies, cardamom and cloves till the onions are nearly brown.

6. Add the coriander powder, jeera powder and haldi, and cook for 1 minute. Add the remaining garlic and ginger and cook for another minute.

7. Add tomatoes, chilli powder, coriander stalks only and cook on low heat for 10-15 minutes till sauce is well blended.

8. Add the meat with 2 cups of its stock and cook for 5 minutes.

9. Add all the daal mixture, porridge oats and pearl barley and salt to taste to the

saucepan and mix thoroughly and cook for ½ hour on low heat.

10. Add lemon juice and garam masala and mix. Keep khichdo on very low simmer and make sure it does not stick at the bottom.

11. Do the wagar/tempering by heating the ghee/butter in a small pan and add ginger and cook for 1 minute. Add the whole mixture to the khichdo.

12. Add coriander leaves into the khichdo and mix everything thoroughly. Switch off the cooker and let the khichdo rest for 10 minutes covered for the flavours to impart.

13. Serve with lemon juice - yum yum.

For 6 people if this is the only dish
1 cup is 250ml

Millet dumplings stew (Muthia) with lamb or chicken

This is *the* signature East African Khoja Ismaili dish, cooked on special occasions. This challenging recipe is the ultimate test for any budding chef!

INGREDIENTS

1kg chicken already skinned and cut into pieces (the bones in the chicken give taste) or 1kg lamb with bones cut into cubes
8 baby aubergines or 8 long aubergines or a very large aubergine cut into 8 cubes
frozen spinach 500g
bharazi (pigeon peas or gungo peas) ½ cup soaked overnight, water cleaned and boiled the next day till soft. This will yield 1 cup of boiled bharazi. Keep the stock for use later
chora or black eye beans ½ cup soaked overnight, water cleaned and boiled the next day till soft. This will yield 1 cup of boiled chora. Keep the stock for use later
4 green chillies slit
1½ bunch of methi/fenugreek–washed and the leaves plucked, chopped discard the stems. Or ½ mug of dried methi leaves pre-soaked and the water squeezed out
2 tbsp ginger paste
2 tbsp garlic paste
1½ tins coconut milk-total is 600ml
250g guvar/flat beans washed and top and tailed and boiled in minimum water till half cooked
400g tin of tomato pulped
¾ cup oil
1 cup peas

8 new potatoes medium size cut into half with skin on or 3 large potatoes cut onto 16 pieces
2 cups chopped onion
3 large sticks cinnamon
1 tbsp jeera powder
1 tbsp coriander powder
1 tsp turmeric/haldi
½ bunch washed coriander. Chop and keep stalks and leaves separately
salt to taste
juice of 2 lemons
2 tsp garam masala

MUTHIA INGREDIENTS:
(makes 24 muthias)
2½ cups millet flour or bajra flour
½ cup dessicated coconut-pre-soaked in water for 10 minutes and the water squeezed out. Retain the water
2 tsp garlic paste
1 tsp garam masala
1 tsp salt
¾ tsp jeera powder
¾ tsp haldi or turmeric
2 green chilli chopped
110ml coconut milk
8 tsp coriander leaves chopped
8 tsp fresh methi leaves chopped or pre-soak 1 tbsp dried methi leaves and squeeze water out

To make muthias mix all and add 150ml water using the water from the dessicated

coconut also. Make into a stiffish dough making it too soft makes the muthias dissolve upon cooking! Make 24 small balls out of the dough, and shape each one so that it looks like a sausage

METHOD

1. Cook chicken or lamb in 1½ cups water, 2 tsp salt and 2 tbsp ginger paste and bring to boil, cover, simmer till cooked. Chicken may take 45 minutes or so and lamb maybe 1¼ hours. Cook until soft- not too soft.

2. Heat oil, add cinnamon sticks and green chillies. Cook for 1 minute.

3. Add onions and cook till onions start turning brown.

4. Add methi leaves and cook for 2 minutes.

5. Add tomatoes, garlic, jeera powder, coriander powder, coriander stalks, salt, haldi/turmeric and cook for 3 minutes.

6. Cut the baby aubergines into criss cross and retain the stalks or slit the long aubergines and add to the pan with spinach, peas, chicken or lamb without its stock. Cook for 5-7 minutes

7. Add guvar, chora, bharazi, potatoes and cook for 10 minutes or so till aubergines are nearly cooked.

8. Mix the meat stock, bean stock and guvar stock and make up to 4¼ cups-add water if necessary-add this to the pan.

9. Add coconut milk and salt to taste and bring to boil. Make sure all ingredients are now cooked -if not, cook for a while till cooked.

10. Bring mixture to a boil then with a large stirring spoon move a portion of solids in the pan to the side and drop muthias vertically carefully into the pan. Do the same all-round the pan till all muthias are placed in the pan.DO NOT stir at this time as this will break the muthias. Let the mixture boil for 3-4 minutes shaking the pan to make sure solids do not stick at the bottom. The muthias should be set by now.

11. Add lemon juice, salt if necessary, coriander leaves and garam masala and stir very carefully.

12. Leave to rest for 3-4 minute and serve with coconut chutney (p289).

SERVES 4 /

Mince and pea curry (Kheema ane matar nu shaak)

INGREDIENTS

Whole garam masala: 4 x 7cm cinnamon sticks, 15 peppercorns, 10 cloves, 10 cardamoms and 4 tsp jeera seeds
4 tbsp vegetable oil
3 large onions finely chopped
1kg lamb mince
20 cloves garlic made into paste
4 tbsp grated ginger
2 green chillies sliced
½ tsp red chilli powder
1 tsp turmeric powder (haldi)
4 tsp of coriander powder
4 tsp jeera powder
600g of pulped tomatoes for drier curry or 800g of pulped tomatoes for thick sauce curry
2 tbsp yogurt
2 cups of peas
3-4 tsp garam masala or more to taste
1 tbsp salt or to taste
⅓ bunch coriander chopped into stalks separately and leaves separately
1 lemon

METHOD

1. Heat the oil, add all the whole garam masala.

2. At the moment the masala starts to crackle and splutter, add the onions and fry until golden brown.

3. At this point, add to (2) the mince, garlic paste, grated ginger, fresh coriander stalks and green chillies until the meat is brown and keep breaking the lumps in the process.

4. Add to (3) turmeric, red chilli powder, coriander and jeera powder. Stir, then add pulped tomatoes.

5. Bring to boil and add yogurt. Mix. Then cook for 20 minutes, stirring occasionally. Then add the peas.

6. Add salt to taste.

7. Simmer for 50 minutes or so covered until the mince is soft.

8. Add juice of one lemon. Add garam masala and fresh coriander leaves.

9. Serve with rice or rotli (chapatti) **(p263)**.

SERVES 4 /

Minced meat curry baked with eggs (Mkate Mayai)

This minced meat curry recipe was shared with us by Sajeda Meghji, my husband's cousin. I have adapted this recipe to make my own version with baked eggs

INGREDIENTS

Whole garam masala: 4 x 4cm cinnamon sticks, 15 peppercorns, 10 cloves, 10 cardamoms and 4 tsp jeera seeds
4 tbsp vegetable oil
3 large onions finely chopped
1kg lamb mince
20 cloves garlic made into paste
4 tbsp grated ginger
2 green chillies sliced
½ tsp red chilli powder
1 tsp turmeric powder (haldi)
4 tsp of coriander/dhana powder
4 tsp jeera powder
2 x 400g tins of chopped tomatoes (pulped)
2 tbsp yogurt
2 cups of peas
3-4 tsp garam masala or more to taste
1 tbsp salt or to taste.
⅓ bunch coriander chopped into stalks separately and leaves separately
6 eggs
oven dish roughly 35 x 35cm and 6cm deep
juice of one lemon

METHOD

1. Heat the oil, add all the whole garam masala ingredients.

2. The moment the masala starts to crackle and splutter, add the onions and fry until golden brown.

3. At this point, add to (2) the mince, garlic paste, grated ginger, fresh coriander stalks and green chillies until the meat is brown and keep breaking the lumps in the process.

4. Add to (3) turmeric, red chilli powder, coriander and jeera powder. Stir, then add the pulped tomatoes.

5. Bring to boil and add yogurt. Mix. Then cook for 20 minutes, stirring occasionally. Then add the peas.

6. Add salt to taste.

7. Simmer for 50 minutes or so covered until the mince is soft.

8. Add juice of one lemon.

9. Add garam masala and fresh coriander leaves.

10 Remove as much of the cinnamon sticks out of the mince as possible

11. Transfer the mince into the ovenproof dish.

12. Heat the oven to 180C/350F.

13. Into the surface of the mince make six little 'wells' and drop an egg into each of the wells.

14. Bake the dish now in the oven till eggs are nearly set.

15. Remove from oven.

16. Serve with rotlis (chapattis) **(p263)** or white crusty bread.

SERVES 6 /

Mogo (cassava) with chicken

This creamy coconut version of mogo/cassava with chicken is incredibly unique to the East African cuisine. It can be eaten on its own or with a spicy chilli or coconut chutney

INGREDIENTS

4 chicken breasts (preferably on the bone) cut to bite-size pieces
2kg frozen mogo (in cut pieces)
3-4 cloves garlic pasted
4 inches ginger pasted
1 medium onion finely chopped
200g pulped tomatoes
300ml coconut milk
2-3 green chilllies
coriander ½ bunch chopped
juice of 2-3 limes or lemon or to taste
salt to taste
4 tbsp oil
½ tsp haldi/turmeric

METHOD

1. Boil the chicken with salt in minimum water till cooked.

2. Boil the mogo in salt and minimum water till soft. Strain. Save the water in case you need it. Semi mash the mogo.

3. In the hot oil cook the chillies and onion till transparent.

4. Add garlic and ginger and haldi. Fry for 1 minute and add the tomatoes. Cook for 4 minutes.

5. Add the mogo and chicken (plus liquid) to the tomato mixture. Add salt to taste.

6. Add coconut milk. Mix. Cook for 10 minutes.If more liquid is required to be added use the strained mogo liquid. Add lemon/lime juice and coriander.

Moroccan chicken tagine

SERVES 4 /

This tagine is fragrant, limey and light. It reminds me of being in Marrakesh where we had this dish sitting outdoors in a lovely restaurant listening to Senegalese singers singing Sufic songs whilst swinging their heads to swirl the tassels on their hats!

INGREDIENTS

1.2kg chicken skinned
1 tsp each of dried ginger powder, jeera or cumin powder and coriander powder
½ tsp turmeric/haldi
1 medium onion finely chopped
2 tbsp olive oil
6 cloves garlic minced
2 pinches saffron soaked in little water
salt to taste
250ml water
750g butternut squash peeled and cut into bite size large cubes
100g drained queen green olives pitted
2 preserved limes chopped; seeds removed. (these can be found in middle eastern shops)
juice of one lemon
6 tbsp chopped Greek parsley leaves

METHOD

1. Combine the dried ginger powder, cumin powder, turmeric, 1 tsp salt and the coriander powder and rub half of it onto the chicken and leave to marinate for at least an hour.

2. Preheat the oven to 200C/400F. Heat 2 tbsp of olive oil in a wok and cook the whole chicken on all sides to brown it and seal it.

3. Remove chicken and place onto the tagine. In the remaining oil in the wok add the onions and cook till soft. Add the garlic and cook for a minute. Then add the rest of the combined dry spices, saffron and salt to taste, and cook for one minute. Add water and bring to boil.

4. Pour this mixture onto the chicken in the tagine and cover and cook in oven for 15 minutes.

5. Remove the tagine and add the butternut squash and mix gently. Cover and cook for 45 minutes again or till chicken is cooked.

6. Remove tagine from oven and stir in gently the preserved limes, lemon juice, olives and the Greek parsley.

7. Serve with couscous or American rice.

SERVES 4 /

Moroccan lamb tagine

The aroma of this beautiful dish reminds me of our holidays in Marrakesh as we strolled through the main square at Jemaa El Fna, weaving our way through the souks and losing our way in the food courts

INGREDIENTS

1kg leg of lamb cubed or shoulder of lamb cubed
¼ tsp chilli powder
1½ tsp ground black pepper
4 tsp ground dry ginger powder
1 tbsp turmeric/haldi
2 tsp cinnamon powder
4 tsp paprika powder
3 medium onions finely chopped
800g pulped tomatoes
2 tbsp argan oil (can substitute with olive oil)
2 tbsp olive oil
6 cloves garlic pasted
3 stock cubes use to make 500ml stock with water (preferably Knorr brand)
40g soft pitted dates cut in slices
40g pitted prunes cut into slices
85g dried apricots cut in slices
70g skinless almonds cut into thin slices or flaked almonds
1½ tsp saffron soaked in water
2 tsp honey or to taste
1 tsp salt
Greek parsley leaves to garnish

METHOD

1. Mix the chilli powder, black pepper, paprika, ginger powder, cinnamon powder, turmeric, and salt. Use half of it to marinate into the meat. Cover and leave aside for 2-3 hours or overnight in fridge.

2. Heat the oven to 300F/150C

3. Cook the onions in half of olive oil and half of argan oil till onions are transparent. Add the remaining spice and cook on gentle heat for 3 minutes making sure the spices do not burn. Add the garlic and cook for a minute.

4. In another frying pan heat the remaining oils and add the meat to brown the outside to seal it. Add this meat to the onion saucepan.

5. Add a small amount of pulped tomatoes to the meat pan to absorb any hardened residue at the bottom of the pan, and add to the saucepan.

6. Add the remining pulped tomatoes, all the dried fruits, almonds, saffron, stock and honey to the saucepan. Bring to boil. Transfer contents to a tagine or casserole dish. Cover with lid and place in the preheated oven for 2- 2½ hours or until meat is tender.

7. Garnish with parsley, and serve with couscous or plain rice.

Moussaka

SERVES 6 /

A warming Greek dish to have on a cold wintery night with nice company of course! The beauty is that it can be made in advance and baked just before eating and so, you can be relaxed and stress free!

INGREDIENTS

1kg lamb mince
1kg potatoes peeled sliced
125g butter
4 tsp black pepper
8 tsp cumin powder
4 medium onions chopped
15 cloves garlic pasted
5 tbsp ginger paste
2 tbsp tomato paste
6 tbsp olive oil
2 tbsp oregano
2 tsp chilli powder
2 large aubergines (sliced into discs)
400g tin tomatoes pulped
5 sticks cinnamon (10cm each)
salt to taste

THE TOPPING/WHITE SAUCE
10 tbsp butter
1 cup plain flour
1200ml milk
100g parmesan cheese, finely grated
4 small eggs, beaten
2 tsp grated or powdered nutmeg
300g grated cheese (preferably mozzarella) for topping
2 rectangular oven dishes approx. 30 x 20cm
salt to taste

METHOD

1. Fry potatoes in butter till half cooked, remove, add salt to potatoes and keep the butter for later use.

2. Fry sliced aubergines in olive oil till half cooked and remove. Mix the oil with the remaining butter. Add salt to fried aubergines.

3. Fry the onions and cinnamon sticks in the olive oil and butter till onions are medium brown, then add the garlic, ginger, cumin or jeera powder, tomato paste and mince and fry till mince is browned.

4. Add salt, pepper, chilli powder, oregano and tin tomatoes and bring to boil and simmer covered for 30 minutes.

5. For the topping, melt the butter in a non-stick pan, add the flour and cook over a medium heat for one minute to cook out the flour. Gradually beat in the milk, bring to the boil, stirring, and leave to simmer very gently for 10 minutes, giving it a stir every now and then. Add salt and pepper to taste, and then the nutmeg. Cool slightly and then stir in the eggs.

6. Butter the two oven dishes and layer as following: Lay the potatoes, then aubergines, then the mince mixture, then the potatoes, then the aubergines, then the white sauce topping.

7. Cook in preheated oven at 180C/350F for 45 minutes. Add the topping grated cheese and then parmesan over it in the last 30 minutes of baking.

8. Remove and serve with garlic bread and green salad.

Note: can use 2 litre of Greek yogurt mixed with the nutmeg, eggs and salt as per recipe as a topping for the above dish. Add cheeses in the last 30 minutes of baking.

SERVES 4 /

Nihari with lamb shanks

This Indian/Pakistani dish is delicious and mouth-watering, and the lamb just falls off the bone! A dish to impress your family and guests. Can be cooked in advance

INGREDIENTS

2kg lamb shanks or lamb with a lot of bones
5 tbsp garam masala
1-2 tsp red chilli powder or to taste
4 tsp salt
4 tbsp garlic paste
4 tbsp ginger paste
1400ml water
6 medium onions chopped fine
4 tbsp fennel seeds grounded
100ml oil
4 tbsp ghee
2 tbsp dhana powder
4 bay leaves
2 tbsp white flour mixed with a little water to make into a paste
1 tsp nutmeg powder
2 tsp turmeric powder
6 cardamoms
250ml yogurt
2 large stick cinnamon
1 tbsp dried ginger powder or soont

FOR SPRINKLING ON TOP AT EATING:
½ bunch coriander leaves chopped
8cm ginger sliced very thin
3 green chillies chopped

METHOD

1. Heat the oil and ghee and fry onions till nearly brown. Remove from heat. Slot the onions out and leave aside.

2. In the oil now add garam masala, garlic, ginger, cardamom, salt, chilli powder, bay leaves, cinnamon, dhana powder, turmeric and fry for 2-3 minutes. Add the yogurt. Cook till the oil separates. Add the shanks or meat and cook for 3-4 minutes.

3. Add nutmeg, grounded fennel seeds and dried ginger and water.

4. Bring to boil and cover tight and simmer for 2 - 2½ hours or till the meat falls off the bone for the shanks or less time for the lamb. The meat must be very soft. If the mixture feels dry do add a little extra water.

5. Add the fried onions into the mixture and let it thicken. Add the flour paste slowly and stir to the required consistency. Can add less flour paste if desired consistency has been reached. Cook for 5 minutes or so on slow heat.

6. Remove from heat.

7. Serve with naan or parotha and sprinkle the coriander, ginger slices, and green chillies on top. Can squeeze a bit of lemon juice if desired.

SERVES 4 /

Paella - Spanish rice dish with fish and prawns

I had my first paella in a touristy restaurant in Spain, and was not overly impressed. I tried this version of mine made from a few recipes, and hooray! I think I got it!

INGREDIENTS

8 large raw prawns

8 bite size pieces of any fish like cod, haddock, coley, salmon, tuna steak, tilapia - boneless and skinless. You can mix the different fishes.

1 mug paella rice or Thai fragrant rice pre-soaked for 1-2 hours

4 tbsp olive oil

1 medium onion chopped

6 cloves garlic pasted

170g chopped fresh tomatoes

1½ green pepper/bell pepper chopped

90g frozen peas

2 tsp paprika powder

1 tsp turmeric

2 mugs water or less

3-4 tsp salt

1 tsp ground black pepper

2 limes-one for rice and one for decoration as wedges

4 prawns with shell cooked/grilled for decoration

2 level tsp saffron soaked in 2 tsp water sprinkle of coriander leaves and chilli flakes for decoration

METHOD

1. Heat oil in a saucepan and fry onions for 2-3 minutes. Add garlic and fry for one minute. Add tomatoes, peppers, peas, turmeric, salt ,pepper and paprika and cook for three minutes.

2. Add fish and prawns, stir, then add rice and saffron and stir gently and add half the water and simmer gently adding the rest of the water slowly only up to as much as needed. Turn the rice gently occasionally to stop it sticking and cook open.

3. Squeeze the juice of 1 lime and mix gently into the paella.

4. Decorate with rest of lime wedges, coriander leaves, chilli flakes and grilled prawns with shells on.

SERVES 2 /

Prawns - Thai coconut style

INGREDIENTS

20 large uncooked prawns in their shells-head and legs removed and deveined. Can use raw large prawns shelled too

5 tsp Thai green curry paste (p307) or enough to coat the prawns

130ml coconut milk

1 tsp haldi or turmeric

1 tsp sugar

salt to taste

15 sprigs coriander washed and chopped

3 tbsp oil

8 kaffir lime leaves very finely chopped

juice of one lime

METHOD

1. Marinate the prawns with the green paste overnight in fridge or for few hours.

2. Heat the oil in a wok and stir fry the prawns till they become pink.

3. Add salt, kaffir lime leaves and haldi and fry for a minute.

4. Add coconut milk, sugar, lime juice and cook for two to three minutes till the prawns are cooked.

5. Add coriander and serve with sticky rice or rustic bread (unsliced loaf).

SERVES 6-8 /

Spaghetti Bolognese
by Amin Shamji

My husband Amin's signature dish. Loved by the family, especially by our daughter Aalia who claims he makes it better than the Italians!

INGREDIENTS

1.25kg beef mince
40ml olive oil
20 cloves garlic pasted
7.5cm ginger pasted
6 medium size onions, sliced along the length and 2 tsp salt mixed with it
5 medium sized carrots, finely diced
1 tin of sweetcorn (165g)
7 sticks of celery, finely sliced
2 x 400g chopped tomatoes pulped
4 fresh medium tomatoes chopped
6 tbsp tomato paste
6 bay leaves
10 fresh mint leaves
10 sprigs of rosemary
2 tsp dried mix herb
2 tsp oregano
1 tbsp freshly ground nutmeg
salt and pepper to taste
splash of Worcester sauce
6 beef Knorr cubes
200ml water

METHOD

1. Place olive oil (40ml) in a large pan and fry onions until just beginning to brown.

2. Add garlic and ginger paste and stir for half a minute on low heat.

3. Add the beef, breaking it up well, and stir until well browned.

4. Add the diced carrots, celery, and sweetcorn and on low to medium heat cook the mixture for 30-35 minutes until the vegetables have softened.

5. Add (2x 400ml) tomatoes, fresh tomatoes, tomato paste, bay-leaves, mint, rosemary sprigs, oregano, mix herbs, freshly ground nutmeg, splash of Worcester sauce, freshly ground pepper, salt, and beef Knorr stock cube. Mix and cover with a lid. Leave the mixture simmering for an hour on low heat, occasionally stirring the mixture; during this simmering time, add the water from time to time.

6. Serve with spaghetti or pasta and sprinkle grated cheese on top.

Spicy (masala) fish with aubergines and potatoes

A very authentic and typical Khoja East African dish

INGREDIENTS

12 steaks (thick) red snapper/kingfish
with bone

MARINADE:
2 tsp turmeric
2 tbsp coriander powder
salt to taste
1 tsp chilli powder
1 tbsp garam masala
2 tbsp garlic paste
2 tbsp ginger paste
12 tbsp oil
3 tbsp lemon juice

VEGETABLES:
1 very large aubergine chopped into
finger size pieces (around 12 pieces
total) and deep-fried
12 small potatoes peeled and cut into
chips size pieces and deep-fried

SAUCE:
2 tbsp coriander powder
2 tbsp jeera powder
2 tsp turmeric
1 tbsp salt
juice of 1 lemon
2 tsp garam masala
1 tsp red chilli powder
10 cloves of garlic pasted
3 tbsp ginger pasted
4 tbsp oil
400g pulped tomatoes
¼ bunch coriander stalks and leaves
chopped

METHOD

1. Mix all the marinade ingredients and
   mix with the fish and leave aside for 1-2
   hours or overnight in the fridge.

2. For the sauce, heat the oil on gentle
   heat and fry the garlic, ginger, coriander
   powder, jeera powder and turmeric for
   30-40 seconds.

3. Add the pulped tomatoes, salt, chilli
   powder and the coriander stalks and
   cook gently till the mixture is of medium
   thickness. Add the lemon juice, garam
   masala and coriander leaves.

4. Shallow fry the fish and leave aside.

5. Lay the warm deep-fried potatoes and
   aubergines onto a platter and pour the
   heated sauce over it.

6. Lay the fried fish over the potatoes and
   aubergines.

7. Serve with parothas **(p275)** or rotli
   (chapatti) **(p263)**.

SERVES 4 /

Spicy (masala) leg of lamb

My mum Gulshan Babul made the best roast masala leg of lamb! It was my special request when I visited them to cook this dish for me. It was always succulent and steamy and soft. I have tried my best to get this dish to her standard, but I think I am not quite there yet!

INGREDIENTS

2kg leg of lamb
750 grams yogurt
1½ tsp black pepper
½ -1 tsp red chilli powder
1 tbsp coriander/dhana powder
1 tbsp jeera powder
1 tsp garam masala
2 tbsp garlic paste
2 tbsp ginger paste
2 tbsp tomato paste
salt to taste

METHOD

1. Mix all the ingredients except the tomato paste to make the marinade. Make some incisions into the leg of lamb and pour the marinade over the lamb.

2. Mix well into the lamb. Cover and leave to marinate overnight or for 24 hours in the fridge.

3. Preheat the oven to 160C/320F. Place lamb on oiled and lined oven tray with the marinade. Pour 6-8 tsp any oil (not olive oil) over the lamb. Cover with foil and cook for approx. 2 hours till lamb is nearly done.

4. Remove cover and cook for 20 minutes. If at this stage the stock from the lamb is getting lost add a little water to make it up. Add the tomato paste to the stock in the tray and baste the lamb. Cook uncovered again for 10 minutes or so. Make sure the stock does not burn. Add little water if needed. Check the lamb is cooked by piercing a knife into the middle of the meat and if water that comes out is clear, it is cooked. Take lamb out of the oven.

5. Cover with foil and let it rest for 10 minutes. Then cut the meat into slices and serve with vegetables, boiled new potatoes and the stock.

Steak-sweet balsamic
by Naadim Shamji

My son Naadim's version of steak when he was a student! Love it!

INGREDIENTS

1 sirloin steak 250g

MARINADE:
Marinate the steak in 4 tsp balsamic vinegar, 2-3 tsp of tomato ketchup, ½ tsp sugar, ½ tsp oregano, pinch of salt and black pepper to taste for ½ to 1 hour

METHOD

Cook the steak in a little hot oil.

Once sufficiently browned on one side, flip onto other side until sealed.

Cook to taste.

Tandoori chicken in creamy sauce

A lot of research went into developing the recipe for this popular UK dish. I consulted several books before coming to a final version. It is now a firm family favourite. It has a Bengali twist with the addition of mustard oil

INGREDIENTS

20 chicken breast boneless cubed mixed with 4 tsp salt and juice of 5 lemons and let to stand for half an hour

MARINADE:
2kg plain yogurt (not Greek yogurt)
1 tbsp hing/asafoetida
4 tbsp ginger paste
4 tbsp garlic paste
2 tbsp dhana/coriander powder
2 tbsp jeera powder
1 tbsp garam masala
4 tbsp mint sauce (Coleman's brand is fine or any brand-if you find that vinegary then use equivalent dried mint leaves throughout the recipe)
1 tsp orange food colouring powder
4 tbsp mustard oil
2 tsp red chili powder
3 tbsp tandoori powder (see right)
2 tsp sugar
250g butter

SAUCE:
300g double cream
300ml coconut milk in tin
10 green peppers chopped
2 tsp sugar
4 tsp mint sauce
5 red peppers (bell peppers) chopped
1 tsp orange food colour powder
1 tsp garam masala

Tandoori powder:
To make tandoori powder, see p339

METHOD

1. Mix the marinade except butter and pour onto the chicken that is already standing with the salt and lemon juice. Mix thoroughly and leave to marinate for at least 12 hours in fridge.

2. Preheat the oven to 200C/400F and put foil onto oven trays and altogether melt the butter and pour half onto the trays. Add the chicken.

3. Add the rest of butter on the top and open roast basting occasionally till cooked and the chicken browns on the top.

4. Pour the juices from the trays onto a large pan.

5. Grill the chicken to brown.

6. Boil the juices and add double cream, sugar, coconut milk, 10 green chopped peppers, mint sauce and orange food colour and 1 tsp garam masala . Add chicken and red peppers chopped for colour and flavour and cook for 5 minutes.

7. Serve with naan and rice and raita (p302).

SERVES 3 /

Tuna curry

A very quick, economical and easy dish to prepare, yet so tasty and exquisite. Taught to us by my mother-in-law Sherbanu Shamji. Love it!

INGREDIENTS

2 x 130g tuna in tin, drained (preferably tuna in oil. The one in brine is quite mashed)
2 medium onions chopped
8 garlic cloves pasted
3 tbsp oil
6 tbsp tomato paste
salt to taste
1 tsp chilli powder
½ cup water

METHOD

1. Fry the onions in oil until they start turning brown.

2. Add the garlic and fry for 1 minute. Add tuna, salt and the tomato paste and chilli powder. Stir fry for 2 minutes.

3. Add the water little by little.

4. Cover and leave to simmer for 5 minutes.

Serve with American or long grain cooked rice and tomato and onion kachumber/salsa **(p240)** with lemon and salt.

SERVES 4-5 /

Aubergine and chickpea vegetarian tagine

INGREDIENTS

12 long and slim aubergines (stalks chopped off but ends left intact. Cut criss-cross longitudinally just before cooking)

600g boiled chickpeas

600g pulped tomatoes

¾ cup assorted thinly sliced dried fruit e.g. apricots, sweet de-stoned dates, dried prunes and dried figs or any of the dried fruits even if it is just one sort

3 medium onions finely chopped

3 tbsp olive oil

1 tsp cumin/jeera powder

5 tsp cinnamon powder

4 tbsp harissa paste

10 large cloves garlic minced

salt to taste

½ tsp ground pepper

METHOD

1. Fry the onions in the oil in a large saucepan until the onions are translucent and browning at the edges.

2. Add garlic, harissa paste, dry spices and fry for two minutes.

3. Add the aubergines and sauté for 2-3 minutes.

4. Add salt to taste and pepper. Mix thoroughly.

5. Add chickpeas and tomatoes and half cup water. Adjust the salt.

6. Bring to boil and then simmer covered for 45 minutes or until aubergines are almost cooked.

7. Add the dried fruit and mix and cook uncovered for 5 minutes.

8. Serve with couscous or plain rice.

SERVES 3-4 /

Bitter gourd curry with jaggery (Gaur wara karela nu shaak)

The most bitter curry in Indian cuisine! An acquired taste, but why not give it a try?

INGREDIENTS

500g bitter gourd or karela
3 medium onions
4 tsp garlic paste
200g chopped tomatoes pulped
2 tsp haldi or turmeric
2 tsp jeera powder
2 tsp coriander powder
½ tsp red chilli powder
1 green chilli
2-3 tsp salt
8 tbsp oil
juice of half a lemon
3-4 tbs gaur (jaggery) to taste

METHOD

1. Finely chop the onions and chilli.

2. Top and tail the karela. Cut off skin partly of the karela, wash and halve it. Remove seeds. Then cut karelas to bite size pieces.

3. In a pan heat the oil and cook chillies and onions till onions are transparent. Add other ingredients except lemon juice and gaur.

4. Stir, then cover and cook on low heat for 20-30 minutes or till karela are soft and taste cooked. Check occasionally to see the food does not burn at bottom of pan.

5. Add the lemon juice and gaur at end and cook for 2-3 minutes.

6. Serve with rotlis (chapattis) **(p263)**.

quantity is large as it's done for festivals and parties

Biriani (East African style) with moong or masoor or vegetables with dhungar (smoke)

East African Biriani is heavier than the rest of the other birianis. A perfect and most appropriate dish to cook for any festivities and large parties. The aroma of saffron and fried onions during cooking and upon serving puts anyone into the festive mood. The smoking/dhunghar of the biriani is optional but it definitely throws a twist into this rich dish!

INGREDIENTS

2 mugs moong preferable large ones or masoor with husk washed and soaked in 4 mugs water for 1-2 hours. Then boil in this water with salt for 20-30 minutes making sure moong or masoor is just cooked and not mashed up.(Masoor may take different time to cook). May need to add more water if necessary and then strain any residual water.
OR
4kg total of assorted raw vegetables e.g cauliflower, carrots, runner beans, deep fried paneer pieces and fried potatoes the size of roast potatoes if doing vegetable biriani. Use crunchy type vegetables. Cauliflower can be cut into florets medium size. If too small the florets get mashed up. Higher proportion of paneer makes it tastier and potatoes can be eliminated totally
2 cups i.e 500ml fried onions (1kg or about 16 medium onions deep-fried in oil yields 500ml fried onions). Leave the onion oil aside. Leave a few strands of fried onions for garnish
30 cloves/laving
8 large cinnamon sticks
24 black peppercorns

30 cardamom pods slightly crushed to open the pods
1kg plain yogurt
3 x 400ml pulped tin tomatoes
8 green chillies chopped or to taste
1 tbsp red chilli powder or to taste
5 tbsp garlic paste
5 tbsp ginger paste
juice of one lemon
salt to taste
2 tbsp tomato paste
1 cup butter (250ml)
1 cup oil from the fried onions (250ml) plus 4 tbsp oil from the fried onions (set aside separately)
4 heaped tsp saffron
4 mugs basmati rice (1 mug is 350ml) washed and soaked in 8 mugs water and salt to taste
5 charcoal pieces preferably the ones that light up instantly plus 5 tsp oil-not the onion oil
5 little cups to fit the charcoal made with foil
½ tsp yellow food colour and 2 tsp saffron mixed in little water for rice
3 tbsp garam masala
1 bunch coriander washed and chopped stalks and leaves left separately

METHOD

MOONG, MASOOR OR VEGETABLE BIRIANI:

1. Mix tomatoes, tomato paste, 4 tsp saffron, chilli powder, garlic, ginger, coriander stalks, yogurt, green chillies and salt to taste in a large saucepan.

2. In another small saucepan do wagar (tempering) using the 1 cup onion oil and 1 cup butter heated and adding the cloves, cinnamon, black peppercorn, cardamom for one minute or so.

3. Pour this tempered oil into the yogurt mixture above and mix it with cooked moong or cooked masoor or raw vegetables and the fried potatoes or paneer mixture.

4. Add the 1½ cups fried onions to this mixture.

5. Cook this mixture for 10 minutes.

6. Add garam masala and lemon juice.

7. Cook the rice in another saucepan with 4 tbsp onion oil. When nearly cooked add 2 tsp saffron and the food colour mixture and roughly fold into the rice to give it an uneven colour.

8. Light the charcoals meanwhile till all are red and burning.

9. In the saucepan of the cooked moong or masoor or vegetable mixture/paneer/ potatoes add ½ cup fried onions and the coriander leaves on top and then add the cooked rice on the top.

10. Let this biriani cook very gently for 5-7 minutes to let the flavours permeate.

11. Make 5 holes in the rice and place the foil cups into them. Switch off cooker.

12. Add the burning charcoal in each cup and add 1 tsp oil in each cup. There will be a lot of smoke coming out. Quickly close the lid and place a heavy object on top to minimise loss of smoke.

13. Leave for 5-10 minutes, then remove the foil cups.

14. Can serve by folding in the moong or masoor or vegetable/paneer/potatoes mixture gently into the rice or by placing rice onto a dish topped up with moong or masoor or vegetable/paneer/potatoes mixture. Garnish with coriander leaves and fried onions. Serve with raita **(p303)** and kachumber **(p240)**.

SERVES 4 /

Cabbage and potato curry (Gobi ane bateta nu shaak)

A humble, soul comforting and economical dish to make!

INGREDIENTS

1 medium cabbage cut into thin slices
3 medium potatoes cut into fat chips sizes
2 medium onions chopped finely
300g pulped tomatoes
4 tbsp oil
juice of half a lemon
100ml water
10 cloves garlic
3 tbsp ginger paste
2 tsp dhana/coriander powder
2 tsp jeera powder
1 tsp haldi/turmeric
3 tsp salt
1 green chilli sliced
⅓ bunch coriander washed and cut, stalks and leaves separately
1 tsp garam masala

METHOD

1. Heat the oil in a large saucepan and fry the chillies and onions till onions are translucent.

2. Add garlic, ginger, turmeric, coriander powder and jeera powder and sauté for one minute.

3. Add cabbage and salt and stir for two minutes.

4. Add tomatoes, coriander stalks and water and stir till it boils.

5. Add potatoes and cook covered on simmer till potatoes and cabbage are just cooked.

6. Taste for salt and add garam masala and lemon juice and coriander leaves.

7. Let the mixture rest for five minutes. Serve with rotlis (chapattis) **(p263)** or parotha **(p275)** or lisi khichdi **(p270)**.

SERVES 4 /

Cauliflower and potato curry (Phool gobi ane bateta nu shaak)

A simple, economical and healthy dish to make

INGREDIENTS

1 medium cauliflower cut into little florets
3 medium potatoes cut into fat chips sizes
2 medium onions chopped finely
300g pulped tomatoes
4 tbsp oil
juice of half a lemon
100ml water
10 cloves garlic
3 tbsp ginger paste
1 tbsp dhana/coriander powder
1 tbsp jeera powder
1 tsp haldi/turmeric
salt 4 tsp or to taste
1 green chilli sliced
⅓ bunch coriander washed and cut, stalks and leaves separately
1½ tsp garam masala

METHOD

1. Heat the oil in a large saucepan and fry the chillies and onions till onions are translucent.

2. Add garlic, ginger, turmeric, coriander powder and jeera powder and sauté for one minute.

3. Add the cauliflower and salt and stir for two minutes.

4. Add tomatoes, coriander stalks and water and stir till it boils.

5. Add potatoes and cook covered on simmer till potatoes and cauliflower are just cooked.

6. Taste for salt and add garam masala and lemon juice and coriander leaves.

7. Let the mixture rest for five minutes and serve with rotli (chapattis) **(p263)** or parotha **(p275)** or lisi khichdi **(p270)**.

Channa daal curry (Akhi channa daal nu shaak)

SERVES 5 /

INGREDIENTS

1½ mugs channa daal presoaked overnight and then boiled in minimum water for 1½ hours or so to cook it almost
8 cloves-laving
2 cinnamon sticks 10cm each
2 medium onions chopped
1 tbsp dhana powder
1 tbsp jeera powder
1 tbsp salt or to taste
2 green chillies sliced
3 tbsp oil
5 cloves garlic minced
1 tbsp ginger paste
1 tsp turmeric (haldi)
200g pulped tomatoes
1-2 tsp garam masala
juice of ½ lemon
coriander ⅛ bunch washed and chopped

METHOD

1. Heat oil. Add onions, laving, cinnamon and green chillies. Cook till onions are golden brown.

2. Then add haldi, dhana and jeera powder, garlic and ginger and cook for ½ minute.

3. Add the tomatoes and almost cooked strained daal plus enough water to cover the daal.

4. Stir and bring to boil. Bring to simmer and cook covered till daal is cooked. Stir quite regularly to stop daal sticking to bottom.

5. Add coriander leaves, garam masala and lemon juice.

6. Serve with rice with rotlis (chapattis) **(p263)** or parotha **(p275)**.

Chickpea curry (Chana nu shaak)

SERVES 4 /
1 mug is 350ml

INGREDIENTS

4 mugs boiled brown channa/chickpeas or use 4 x 400g tins of boiled chickpeas/ channa (brown channa has more taste) - to make boiled brown channa pre- soak 1¾ mugs in water the night before and wash and cook again in water till soft and use 4 mugs of boiled channa for recipe. (1 mug dried channa yields 2½ mugs boiled channa)

1 tbsp garlic paste

1 tbsp ginger paste

1 tbsp coriander/dhana powder

1 tbsp jeera powder

1 small onion chopped

1 tsp haldi/turmeric

½ tsp red chilli powder or more

salt to taste

3 tbsp tomato paste

4 tbsp oil

juice of 1 lemon

coriander leaves to garnish

METHOD

1. Fry onion in hot oil till soft and just brown.

2. Add garlic and ginger paste and fry for a few seconds followed by dhana/ coriander and jeera powder and haldi/ turmeric - fry for 1 minute making sure spices do not burn.

3. Add tomato paste and fry for 1-2 minutes.

4. Add water (if using fresh boiled channa/ chickpeas add the water from the stock) till a thickish consistence is formed. Add salt to taste.

5. Add channa/chickpeas strained from the tin or the fresh ones and cook for 5 minutes.

6. Switch off heat. Add lemon juice and garnish with coriander leaves.

7. Serve with rotlis (chapattis) **(p263)** or parothas **(p275)** or naan.

NB this is a curry that you eat with rotli (chapatti) or parotha or naan and is not an accompaniment like channa vagaria.

Chinese chilli aubergine Schezuan

A fantastic and impressive vegetarian Chinese dish to be served as a side or a main with rice

INGREDIENTS

4 large aubergines sliced to bite size long pieces and fried in batches for 5 minutes (each batch) in hot oil till the edges brown slightly

2 medium leeks washed thoroughly and sliced thinly

10 cloves garlic minced

2 green chillies finely chopped

3 tbsp ginger paste

5 tbsp light soya sauce

2 tbsp dark brown sugar

6 tbsp oil to stir-fry

4 tbsp toasted sesame seeds

2 tbsp tomato paste

1 tsp vinegar

½ tsp red chilli powder

3 tbsp toasted sesame seed oil

1 tsp salt or to taste

METHOD

1. Pour oil into wok and heat. Once hot, fry the leeks and green chillies for 5-7 minutes.

2. Add garlic and ginger and cook for two minutes.

3. Combine the tomato paste, salt, vinegar, soya sauce, chilli powder and the dark brown sugar, and add to the wok and cook for 2 minutes.

4. Add the fried aubergines and cook for 3 minutes till the mixture is heated thoroughly making sure that the aubergines do not mash.

5. Switch off the cooker and stir in the toasted sesame seeds and sesame seed oil and mix.

6. Serve on its own or with sticky rice.

SERVES 6-8 /

Daal Masoor
Version 1

INGREDIENTS

2 mugs masoor daal (red lentils) washed and soaked in 6 mugs of water for at least ½ hour

2 green chillies chopped

3 tbsp finely chopped ginger

10 cloves garlic pasted

8 tbsp oil

1 tsp chilli powder (optional)

2 tsp jeera seeds or cumin

2 tsp rai or mustard seeds

3 medium onions finely chopped

1 heaped tsp haldi or turmeric

2 tsp dhana or coriander powder

2 tsp jeera powder

600g pulped tomatoes

⅓ bunch coriander washed and chopped (separate stalks from the leaves)

juice of one-two lemons

salt to taste

¾ tsp garam masala

METHOD

1. Boil the masoor daal in its water till soft and semi pulped.

2. In a medium saucepan start the tempering (i.e. 'wagar' or 'tarka') process. Let the oil get quite hot, then add the cumin seeds and rai. Let the ingredients pop. Then add green chillies and onions and fry till the onions start to turn golden.

3. Add haldi, dhana powder, jeera powder, garlic and ginger and cook for a minute or less.

4. Add tomatoes, red chilli powder and chopped coriander stalks and bring to boil.

5. Transfer this mixture to the boiled daal and add salt to taste.

6. Bring the daal to boil and simmer for 30 minutes or so open. Add garam masala, coriander leaves and lemon juice.

SERVES 4 /

Daal Masoor
Version 2

INGREDIENTS

2 mugs masoor daal (red lentils) washed and then strained and boiled with 3-4 mugs water till daal is soft. Can add more water if required. Blend it to a coarse mixture
1 tbsp jeera seeds
4 tbsp garlic pasted
4 tbsp ginger pasted
4 large tomatoes chopped
4 medium onions finely chopped
2-3 green chillies chopped
30 curry leaves (limbro)
1 tsp haldi/turmeric
juice of 3 lemons
salt to taste
6 tbsp oil
¼ bunch coriander–washed and chopped (separate the stalks and leaves)

METHOD

1. In hot oil add jeera seeds, let them pop. Add onions and fry till onions are transparent.

2. Then add curry leaves and fry for 30-40 seconds.

3. Then add garlic, ginger, chillies and turmeric and fry for 30-40 seconds.

4. Then add tomatoes and coriander stalks.

5. Let the mixture boil for 3-4 minutes.

6. Add the boiled daal and salt to taste.

7. Heat thoroughly and let it simmer for 10-15 minutes adding more water if needed.

8. Switch off cooker and add lemon juice and coriander leaves.

9. Serve with rice or rotlis (chapattis) **(p263)**.

Daal Moong

SERVES 8 /

This is a runny daal

INGREDIENTS

2 mugs moong daal (i.e without husk) washed and soaked for ½ hour at least then strained and boiled with 6-8 mugs water till daal is soft. Blend the daal. Can add more water if required. The consistency should be medium runny.

1 tbsp jeera seeds

4 tbsp garlic pasted

4 tbsp ginger pasted

4 large tomatoes chopped

4 medium onions finely chopped

3 green chillies chopped

30 curry leaves (limbro)

1 tsp haldi/turmeric

juice of 4 lemons

salt to taste

6 tbsp oil

¼ bunch coriander–washed and chopped (separate the stalks and leaves)

salt to taste

METHOD

1. In hot oil add jeera seeds, let them pop. Add onions and fry till onions are transparent.

2. Then add curry leaves and fry for 30-40 seconds.

3. Then add garlic, ginger, chillies and turmeric and fry for 30-40 seconds.

4. Then add tomatoes and coriander stalks.

5. Let the mixture boil for 3-4 minutes.

6. Add the boiled daal and salt to taste.

7. Heat thoroughly and let it simmer for 10-15 minutes adding more water if needed.

8. Switch off cooker and add lemon juice and coriander leaves.

9. Serve with rice or rotlis (chapattis) **(p263)**.

SERVES 8 /
Makes 10 mugs of daal

Daal sweet with peanuts (Jugu wari mithi daal)

This is my daughter Aalia's very favourite! A typical Gujarati daal dish that teases the tastebuds with its sweet, sour, hot and spicy taste that is coupled with the crunch of boiled red peanuts!

INGREDIENTS

1½ mugs toover daal washed and soaked in water for few hours. Then rinse out water and add 7 mugs of water and boil till soft. Blend to a fine puree
A small golf ball sized of dried ambli – maybe ¼ packet (tamarind) soaked in ½ mug very hot water and tamarind squeezed and water strained to be added to the daal or 2 tbsp washed and sliced kokum
3-4 green chillies chopped
2 tsp rai (mustard seeds)
2 teaspoon jeera seeds
2 sticks cinnamon 7.5cm each
2 tsp cardamom powder
2 tsp hing/aesafotida
2 tbsp pasted ginger
15 curry leaves (limbro)
2 tsp haldi (turmeric)
3 tbsp oil
600g pulped tomatoes
⅓ mug gaur (jaggery) or sugar
1 mug boiled red peanuts
¼ bunch washed and chopped coriander stalkes and leaves
lemon juice if required
salt to taste

METHOD

1. In a small saucepan start the tempering (i.e. 'wagar' or 'tarka') process. Let the oil get quite hot, then add the rai, jeera seeds, cinnamon sticks, curry leaves, green chillies and hing. Fry until the ingredients start to pop (30-45 seconds). Then add haldi and ginger and fry for half a minute and add all this to the blended daal.

2. Heat the daal mixture and add to it gaur or sugar, boiled peanuts, tomatoes, salt to taste and tamarind water or kokum.

3. Add coriander stalks only. Boil, then simmer gently open for approximately 20-30 minutes or so. Can add more water if needed.

4. Add cardamom powder and coriander leaves.

5. Add lemon juice if required.

6. Serve with rotlis (chapattis) **(p263)** and rice.

SERVES 4 /

Daal using mixed daals or with potatoes or aubergines or saragvo

INGREDIENTS

1 mug of mixed daal (equal portions - by volume not weight - of urad daal, moong daal, channa daal, masoor daal and tuver daal) (Daals are the legumes without the husk)
4 tbsp oil
1 large onion finely chopped
400g tomato pulped
5 cloves garlic pasted
1 tbsp ginger pasted
1 tsp jeera seeds
1 tsp turmeric
½ tsp black peppercorns
6 cloves
6 cardamoms
2 x 10cm cinnamon stick
⅓ bunch coriander washed and stalks and leaves chopped separately
1-2 green chillies chopped
juice of 1-2 lemons
3 tsp salt or to taste

EXTRA IF MAKING THE BELOW:
· For aubergine daal use 2 large aubergines chopped to bite size cubes or 6 small aubergines slit to open, cooked in minimum water with 1 tsp salt till nearly cooked
· For potato daal use 4 medium potatoes cut into medium slices and cooked in minimum water with 1 tsp salt till nearly cooked
· For saragwo daal use 20 x 7.5cm length top and tailed saragwo pieces with hard outer fibres partially removed. Boil in minimum water with 1 tsp salt till nearly cooked

METHOD

1. Wash the daals with water and soak in 4 mugs of water for 2-3 hours.

2. Boil the daal and simmer covered till cooked. May take up to an hour. Add more water if needed.

3. Pulp the daal and add 2 tsp salt.

4. Then in hot oil in a large saucepan do the tempering (throwing of the spices in the hot oil till they pop or give aroma) of jeera seeds, peppercorns, cloves, cardamoms and cinnamon. This takes about half a minute.

5. Add onions and green chillies and cook till onions are transparent.

6. Add garlic and ginger and turmeric and fry for ½ minute.

7. Add tomatoes and coriander stalks and cook for 4-5 minutes. Then add the pulped daal.

8. If making daal without any of the ingredients listed under 'EXTRA IF MAKING THE BELOW' in the ingredients section, add ½ to 1 mug of water as required and follow from step 10..

9. If making any of the daals with the ingredients listed under 'EXTRA IF MAKING THE BELOW', add the ingredients as listed (together with ½ to 1 mug of its stock) to the daal and follow from step 10.

10. Bring to boil. Simmer open till the ingredients are all cooked.

11. Add lemon juice and coriander leaves and serve with rotli (chapatti) **(p263)** or parotha **(p275)** and rice.

SERVES 2-3 /

Daal-Urad Punjabi style (Daal Makhani)

This Punjabi recipe is dedicated to one of my favourite aunties, Surinder Jagdish Singh. Surinder Aunty was one of my mum's closest friends, and I still keep in touch with her

INGREDIENTS

1 mug urad (with husk) pre-soaked overnight, then the water cleaned and the urad boiled in water for at least 2 hours or slightly less. Keep adding water if required but in the end the mixture should contain only little water. Add salt to taste and semi-mash the urad

2 tbsp oil or butter or ghee

2 large onion finely chopped

3 tbs garlic paste

3 tbsp ginger paste

1 green chilli chopped

1 tsp turmeric or haldi

1 tbsp jeera powder

1 tbsp dhana/coriander powder

10 sprigs coriander stalks and leaves chopped separately

2 tsp garam masala

salt to taste

4 medium tomatoes chopped

3 tbsp double cream

juice of one lemon or to taste

METHOD

1. Heat the oil or ghee or butter and fry the onions and green chillies till onions start turning brown.

2. Add the garlic, ginger, turmeric, coriander powder, jeera powder, tomatoes and coriander stalks and salt and fry till tomatoes are pulped.

3. Add the cooked urad and a little water if necessary, to bring to thick consistency. Cook covered for 5 minutes on low heat.

4. Add garam masala , double cream, lemon, and coriander leaves and switch off the cooker.

5. Serve with rotlis (chapattis) **(p263)** or rice.

Drumstick vegetable curry (Saragvo Sing nu shaak)

SERVES 3 /

Reminds me of the first time I had it as a child, at a friend's place. The seeds have to be sucked/chewed away from the fibres which are then discarded. Its an art, but the unique taste is worth the effort!

INGREDIENTS

4 long thin Saragvo Sing/Indian drumstick vegetable, top and tailed and ridged fibrous edges removed with knife cut the Saragvo stalks into 3 inch pieces
½ tsp rai/mustard seeds
½ tsp meth/fenugreek seeds
1 tsp hing/asafoetida
1-2 green chillies chopped
2 cloves garlic pasted
2 inches ginger pasted
1 tsp dhana/coriander powder
1 tsp jeera powder
1 tsp haldi
2 chopped medium tomatoes
1 tbsp channa/gram flour pasted with a little water
¼ bunch coriander-stalks and leaves chopped separately
4 tbsp oil
1½ tsp salt
juice of half a lemon

METHOD

1. Heat the oil till it just smokes. Throw in the rai and methi and let it pop. Quickly add hing, green chillies and saragvo and fry for 1 minute.

2. Add garlic, ginger, dhana powder, jeera powder, haldi, salt and sauté for 1 minute.

3. Add tomatoes, coriander stalks and cook for 2 minutes.

4. Add just enough water to half cover the saragvo and let it boil.

5. Cover and simmer till saragvo is cooked. Can take up to half an hour. Add little water at a time if needed.

6. Add the pasted channa flour and cook for 3-4 minutes on simmer.

7. Consistency should be medium thick.

8. Switch off cooker and add coriander leaves and lemon juice and serve with naan or parothas (**p275**).

SERVES 10 /

Dumpling and vegetable dry curry Gujarati style (Oondhiyo)

This is a vegetarian version of muthias/dumplings with vegetables. A complicated dish to make but well worth it for the delicious taste

INGREDIENTS

500g surti papdi or the larger Indian papdi, top and tailed

1kg green bananas (matoke) skin peeled and cut into chunks.Leave in water to stop it going dark) or 500g boiled new potatoes

500g small round aubergines

5 green chillies (or less) finely chopped

2 tbsp grated ginger

2 tbsp crushed garlic

1 cup boiled toover/bharazi/gungo or pigeon peas

5 tbsp finely chopped coriander leaves and stalks

2 tbsp white or rotli flour

20 tbsp oil

2 tsp aesafotida (hing)

1 tbsp turmeric powder (haldi)

4 tsp ajma (carom seeds or ajwain)

salt to taste

3-4 tsp sugar

lemon juice to taste

MUTHIAS:

leaves from 2 bunches methi/fenugreek washed and chopped

2½ cups besan (channa/gram flour)

2 tsp chilli powder

5 tbsp grated dessicated coconut presoaked in water and water squeezed out

salt to taste

5 tbsp oil

METHOD

MUTHIAS

1. Mix all ingredients listed under 'Muthia'. It should make a stiff dough. Only add very little water if the mixture will not hold. Otherwise avoid adding any water.

2. Form into oval dumplings about 5 cm long –may need to wet the hands slightly to stop muthias from sticking to hand.

3. Heat the 20 tbsp oil in a saucepan and fry the muthias for 2 minutes or so.

4. Leave aside and save the oil.

THEN

1. Form a paste of chilli, garlic, ginger and coriander and rub into slit aubergines (cut into four but so that the end remains intact). Leave for a few minutes.

2. In the remaining oil start the tempering (i.e. 'wagar' or 'tarka') process. Let the oil get quite hot, then add the ajma and hing. Fry until the ingredients start to pop (30-45 seconds). Then add haldi.

3. Add aubergines and papdi and cook on low heat. Cover and cook for 5 minutes.

4. Add bananas, gungo peas, flour and salt and then ½ cup water and the sugar, and stir. Cover and simmer till the vegetables are nearly done (20 minutes or so).

5. Now add the muthias and boiled potatoes (if using), and very little water (if needed) to make the muthias swell to around double the size. Keep simmering for around 10 minutes or so to allow the methi leaves to cook.

6. Add lemon juice.

The oondhiyo should be dryish with hardly any gravy. (NB the vegetables should not be overcooked otherwise they will turn mushy - so be careful of the overall cooking time).

Serve on its own.

SERVES 3-4 /

Egg Indian scambled curry (Mayai dungri nu shaak)

A fast, easy and tasty dish using the humble egg!

INGREDIENTS

10 medium eggs beaten and add ¼ tsp salt
6 medium onions sliced long
2-3 chillies chopped
6 tbsp oil
1 tsp haldi (turmeric)
2 medium ripe tomatoes chopped
4 cloves garlic minced
2 tsp dhana/coriander powder
coriander leaves 3 tbsp (optional)

METHOD

1. Heat oil. Add onions and cook till onions are soft but not brown.

2. Add green chillies, dhana powder, garlic, haldi and tomatoes. Cook for 2-3 minutes.

3. Add eggs and cook till eggs are nearly cooked. Do not stir this mixture till eggs are nearly set-few minutes only.

4. Switch off cooker.

5. Add coriander leaves.

6. Serve with rotlis (chapattis) **(p263)** and lisi khichdi **(p270)**.

Egg omelette Indian style rotli roll

Makes 2 rolls

A simple but soul-satisfying dish for breakfast. In Uganda it has become a popular street food by the name 'rolex' - literally a combination of 'roll' and 'eggs'!

INGREDIENTS

4 large eggs beaten
2 medium onions finely chopped
½ to 1 green chilli finely sliced
10 sprigs of fresh coriander chopped
2 tbsp butter or oil (butter gives a better taste)
8 pinches of salt or less
1 tsp ground black pepper (optional)
two cooking foils cut into 28 x 28cm squares
2 rotli/chapatti each 20cm in diameter. If using ready-made chapatti may need to slightly cook it on pan beforehand
non-stick frying pan with 15cm diameter at base

METHOD

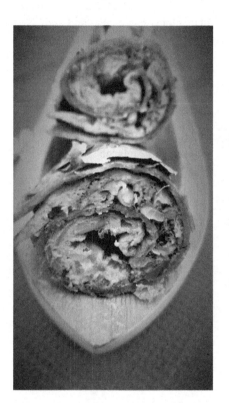

1. Add the onions, chillies, coriander, salt and black pepper to the beaten eggs.

2. Heat the frying pan with 1 tbsp butter and pour in half the egg mixture.

3. Cook the egg on one side and flip over to cook the other side.

4. Place the omelette onto the rotli and roll over the rotli and egg into like a burrito roll.

5. Then place this roll onto the cooking foil square and roll over into like a burrito roll again.

6. Twist both ends of the foil to close the roll.

7. To eat, gradually peel the foil in a circular fashion from one end of the wrap to the bottom, eating as you go along.

You can substitute the rotli with fajitas if needed. This is a good way to make this dish in advance as it keeps quite warm in the foil package!

SERVES 4 /

Flat bean or cluster bean curry (Guvar nu shaak)

My husband Amin's favourite!

INGREDIENTS

750g guvar/cluster bean/flat bean-top and tailed

2 medium onions finely chopped

400g pulped tomatoes

10 cloves garlic pasted

2 tbsp ginger paste

1 tsp turmeric

2 tsp coriander powder

2 tsp jeera powder

salt to taste

1 green chilli chopped

3 medium potatoes cut into chips size

4 tbsp oil

200ml water

fresh coriander leaves to garnish

METHOD

1. Heat the oil in a pan and add the onions and cook till onions are translucent.

2. Add garlic, chillies and ginger and cook for 30 seconds.

3. Add the turmeric, coriander and jeera powder and cook for 30 seconds.

4. Add tomatoes, salt, water and the guvar and bring to boil.

5. Bring to simmer and cover cooking for about an hour checking if more water is needed to let the curry not burn.

6. Add potatoes and cook on simmer covered for ½ hour or till potatoes are cooked.

7. The curry should be semi-dryish.

8. Serve with rotlis (chapattis) **(p263)** or parothas **(p275)** or lisi khichdi **(p270)**.

Green moong curry (Moong nu shaak)

My friend Tazim Esmail gave me an insight into this delicious recipe

INGREDIENTS

1½ mugs green moong presoaked overnight or for 3-4 hours, washed and strained and then boiled in minimum water without covering for ¾ hour or so to cook it almost
8 cloves laving
2 cinnamon sticks 10cm each
2 medium onions chopped
1 tbsp dhana/coriander powder
1 tbsp jeera powder
1 tbsp salt or to taste
2 green chillies sliced
¼ tsp red chilli powder (optional)
3 tbsp oil
5 cloves garlic minced
1 tbsp ginger paste
1 tsp haldi/turmeric
200g crushed tomatoes
1-2 tsp garam masala
juice of half large lemon
1 tsp sugar
coriander ¼ bunch washed and chopped

METHOD

1. Heat oil. Add onions, laving, cinnamon and green chillies.Cook till onions are golden brown.

2. Add haldi, dhana and jeera powder, red chilli powder, garlic and ginger and cook for 1 minute. Add the tomatoes and sugar and the strained moong plus enough water to cover the moong.

3. Stir and bring to boil. Bring to simmer and cook uncovered till moong is cooked.

4. Stir quite regularly to stop moong sticking to bottom.

5. Add corinder leaves, garam masala and lemon juice.Serve with rice and rotlis (chapattis) **(p263)**.

SERVES 4 /

Green pepper curry (mircha nu shaak)
by Mrs Semey

Mrs Kamrunissa Semey, my mother-in-law's friend, made this curry and we loved it. It's simple yet so tasty

INGREDIENTS

3 tbsp oil

3 medium onions finely chopped

4 large green/red peppers (bell peppers) diced

1 tbsp coriander powder

1 tbsp jeera powder

1 tsp haldi (turmeric)

½ tsp red chilli powder

4 tsp ginger paste

4 tsp garlic paste

1 tbsp salt

300g pulped tomatoes

1 tbsp tomato paste

3 tbsp sweet ambli sauce (tamarind sauce) or juice of one lemon and 2 tsp sugar

METHOD

1. Heat oil in saucepan and fry onions till they start to go golden brown.

2. Add garlic and ginger paste and fry for a minute on medium heat.

3. Add all the dry spices except chilli powder and cook for a minute.

4. Add tomato paste and green/red peppers and cook for 2-3 minutes.

5. Add tomatoes, salt and red chilli powder and tamarind sauce and cook for 15-20 minutes slightly covered.

6. Serve with rotlis (chapattis) **(p263)** or parothas **(p275)**.

SERVES 4 /

Ivy gourd curry (Tindora nu shaak)

Tindoras look like mini cucumbers and its crunchy nature makes it a very appealing vegetarian curry

INGREDIENTS

750g tindora/ivy gourd cut at the ends and longitudinally into quarters
2 tsp rai/mustard seeds
1 tsp methi/fenugreek seeds
10 tbsp oil
1 tbsp hing/asafoetida
1 tbsp coriander/dhana powder
1 tbsp jeera powder
1 tsp turmeric/haldi
1 tsp red chilli powder
20 curry leaves
salt to taste
300g pulped tomatoes
2 tsp sugar
1 tsp garam masala
½ cup water
¼ bunch fresh coriander stalks and leaves chopped separately
juice of one lemon

METHOD

1. Heat the oil in a pan and when oil is hot do wagar (tempering) of rai and methi in the pan. Let the seeds pop and immediately add the curry leaves and hing and cook for 30 seconds.

2. Add garlic and ginger, dhana and jeera powder and turmeric and cook on medium heat for 30 seconds.

3. Add tomatoes, chilli powder, water, salt and sugar and coriander stalks and cook for 5 minutes.

4. Add tindora, bring to boil and cook simmered and covered till tindora are cooked.

5. Add garam masala, chopped coriander leaves and lemon juice and serve with rotlis (chapattis) **(p263)** or puri **(p259)** or lisi khichdi **(p270)**.

SERVES 4 /

Kidney bean and aubergine curry

INGREDIENTS

3 tbsp oil
2 medium size onions, longitudinally sliced
1 tbsp garlic pasted
1 tbsp ginger pasted
2 green sliced chillies or ½ tsp chilli powder
2 tsp jeera powder
2 tsp dhana/coriander powder
1 x 400g chopped tomatoes OR 4 ripe tomatoes chopped
1 ½ tbsp of tomato paste
1 tin (400g) red kidney beans in water
handful of chopped fresh coriander leaves
2 tsp salt
½ tsp black pepper
1 medium size aubergine cut into 12 pieces

METHOD

1. Into a medium size cooking pan, add oil and heat. Once hot, add onions with ½ tsp salt until the onions are light brown.

2. Add to the above, paste of garlic, ginger and chillies and continue frying at low heat for ½ minute and then add jeera and dhana powder and stir, followed by chopped tomatoes, tomato paste and fresh coriander. Add 1½ tsp salt or to taste. Continue heating this mixture for 20 minutes at low heat with lid on until all the ingredients become a thick sauce. Stir regularly to avoid the sauce sticking.

3. Add aubergine pieces and cook at low heat for 35-40 minutes with lid on. Add freshly grounded pepper. Add water intermittently from the red kidney bean tin, and stir regularly. At the end of this period, the aubergines will become soft and cooked.

4. Add red kidney beans to the above and cook for a further 5-10minutes. You may add a bit of water to make the curry light.

5. Sprinkle a handful of coriander leaves for extra flavouring.

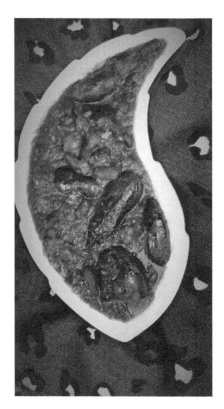

SERVES 3 /

Kidney bean curry

My husband Amin's recipe

INGREDIENTS

1 x 400g good quality red kidney beans
in water, napolina brand preferably
1 tbsp vegetable oil
3 medium size onions finely sliced
1 tsp jeera seeds
1 tbsp garlic pasted
1 tbsp ginger paste
½ tsp turmeric powder
1½ tsp dhana/coriander powder
1 tsp jeera powder
1 x 400g pulped tomatoes
2 tbsp tomato paste
1 bay leaf
salt to taste
2 green chillies
handful of chopped fresh coriander

METHOD

1. In a medium size cooking pot, place the vegetable oil and heat. Once hot, add jeera seeds, bay-leaf and stir.

2. Once the seeds start to splutter, add finely chopped onions and add a bit of salt to speed up frying until onions is golden brown.

3. At this point add sliced green chillies, followed half minute later with garlic paste and ginger paste and half a minute later with turmeric powder, jeera and dhana powder, tomatoes and tomato paste. Continue heating this mixture at low heat until all tomatoes have dissolved in the pot. This takes about 20 minutes. Add water, maybe ½ cup, to keep the mixture fluid.

4. Add the kidney beans to the pot and add maybe ½ cup of water plus salt to taste.

5. Simmer mixture for 15-20 minutes and finally add handful of finely chopped coriander leaves and stalk to add extra flavouring to the curry. At this point switch off heat.

6. Serve with rotlis (chapattis) **(p263)** or rice.

SERVES 4-5 /

Okra (Lady finger) curry (Bhinda nu shaak)

Absolutely loved by many. A must in any vegetarian thali!

INGREDIENTS

600g bhinda (okra) washed, dried, top and tailed and cut into quartered and cut into 5cm length

2 very large onions or 4 medium onions sliced long and thin

8 cloves of garlic peeled and minced

4 inches of peeled and grated ginger

6 tbsp oil

2-3 green chillies sliced

1 tsp turmeric

100g pulped tomato

2 tsp jeera powder

2 tsp coriander powder

salt to taste

1 handful of washed and chopped coriander leaves

METHOD

1. Fry the onions and chillies in hot oil till onions are soft but not brown.

2. Add bhinda and sauté for 4-5 minutes. Cover and cook for ½ hour or so on low heat. Do not add water.

3. Then add garlic, ginger, turmeric, jeera powder, coriander powder and salt. And chilli powder if required. Fry for 2-3 minutes. Add the tomatoes and cook uncovered on simmer till the bhindas are cooked.

4. Garnish with coriander leaves. Serve with rotlis (chapattis) **(p263)** or parothas **(p275)**.

Makes 20 masala dossas 20cm in diameter or 12 masala dossas 25cm in diameter or 6 masala dossas 35cm in diameter

Masala dossas including dossa, stuffing and South Indian Daal sambhal

Now who does not like Masala Dossa? My husband Amin Shamji certainly did when I introduced it to him on our second date in 1982! This dish was still not known to many in the UK and there were only a handful of restaurants that made them. To impress him I took him to a small dingy restaurant in a basement in London and he was bowled over! By the way he was also an incredibly talented cricketeer then (pun intended). He has not left my side since then and we got engaged within two months

INGREDIENTS

DOSSAS/PANCAKES:
2 mug basmati rice
1 mug urad daal (without husk)
½ tsp sodium bicarbonate
½ tsp citric acid for crispiness
salt to taste
cast iron pan

METHOD

1. Wash and soak the rice and daal separately for 4-5 hours. Strain and blend till very fine separately in a blender. Mix the blended rice and daal in a metal dish and add the sodium bicarbonate. The mixture should be thickish. Cover.

2. Leave to ferment preferably in the airing cupboard or warm place for 24 hours or more.

3. Then add water to bring up to a medium consistency.

4. Add salt and citric acid.

5. Heat the cast iron pan. Grease a cast iron pan using an oiled half onion. Add sufficient batter to make a dossa of the size required. Using a ladle, pour the mixture into the middle of the pan. Quickly spread into a round disc of the required size. Do not cook on the other side.

6. Take the dossa out and add one portion potato stuffing, and then roll. Have with coconut chutney and South Indian daal/sambhal.

INGREDIENTS

POTATO STUFFING FOR THE DOSSAS:
2kg potatoes - King Edwards or other- do not use waxy potatoes. Boil the potatoes and cut into cubes or semi mash them. Add salt to taste
6 tbsp oil
2 large onions chopped
8 tsp urad daal
4 tsp rai/mustard seeds
1 tbsp haldi/turmeric
2 tsp asafoetida/hing
½ bunch coriander chopped - leaves and stalks separated
1 handful limbro/curry leaves
juice of one large lemon
2 green chillies chopped
salt to taste

METHOD

1. In hot oil add the urad daal, rai, and cook for 40-50 seconds, letting the rai pop.

2. Add limbro and hing and haldi and fry for another 30 seconds.

3. Add onions and fry till onions becomes soft but not brown.

4. Add potatoes and coriander stalks and lemon juice and stir-fry till mixture is thoroughly heated. Adjust salt.

5. Cook for 3-4 minutes. Turn off cooker and add coriander leaves.

INGREDIENTS

SOUTH INDIAN DAAL/SAMBHAL:
1 mug toover daal washed, pre-soaked for 2 hours or so, then strained. Add 2 mugs water and boil. Once daal is soft, do not drain, then blend. Should be medium runny consistency. Can add more water during boiling if required. Tamarind sauce made by boiling ¼ packet tamarind pulp in 1 mug of water for 10 minutes and strain the mixture.
salt to taste
½ tsp haldi/turmeric
400g of pulped tomatoes
2 green chillies chopped
½ tsp red chilli powder
2 small onions chopped
½ bunch coriander stalks and leaves - chopped and separated
4 tbsp oil
2 tsp rai/mustard seeds
2 tsp jeera seeds
1 tsp asafoetida/hing
1 handful of limbro/curry leaves
6 cloves garlic sliced

METHOD

1. Heat 4 tbsp oil. Then add the mustard seeds, jeera seeds and let them pop for 30 to 40 seconds.

2. Add curry leaves, hing, garlic cloves, turmeric, green chillies and cook for a minute or so.

3. Add this mixture to the daal.

4. To the daal add salt to taste, pulped tomatoes, red chilli powder, onions, coriander stalks, tamarind sauce and cook for 15 to 20 minutes (do not cover).

5. Add coriander leaves to garnish.

Serve with the dossas and coconut chutney **(p289)**.

SERVES 8-10 /

Paneer and pea curry (Matar paneer)

A fantastic recipe from my dear friend Jyotsna Samji aka 'Jo'. Jo was my dear friend and classmate in Mombasa, and we we later became flatmates as newly-arrived students in London. She met my cousin Altaf Samji who was besotted by her, and they are happily married with two wonderful children

INGREDIENTS

1½kg frozen peas (preferably good quality e.g petit pois)

500g paneer cut into 2.5cm by 1cm pieces

6 tbsp of peeled ginger chopped fine

1½ mugs dessicated coconut

6 tbsp oil

600g of pulped tomatoes

water 1 mug or less

125ml double cream

2 tsp haldi/turmeric

2 tsp garam masala

3 green peppers/bell peppers cut into little pieces

salt to taste

4 green chillies chopped

oil for deep frying

METHOD

1. Deep fry the paneer till lightly browned. Drain. Leave aside.

2. In the oil cook the dessicated coconut, ginger and garam masala and green chillies till the coconut is slightly browned.

3. Add haldi.Then add tomatoes and salt. Cook for 5 minutes. Add the peas and water. When nearly cooked add the paneer and green peppers and cook for a further 3-4 minutes.

4. Add the double cream and cook for 1 minute.

5. Serve with naan or parothas (p275).

SERVES 3 /

Paneer and spinach curry (Saag paneer)

Pump up those muscles like Popeye the Sailor did with ingesting spinach! This iron rich spinach, together with the option of calcium rich paneer is a perfect way to healthy eating

INGREDIENTS

250g paneer cut into bite-size cubes (2.5cm x 1cm) and lightly fried till just turning golden brown

900g frozen leaf spinach or fresh spinach

5 tbsp cooking oil plus 3 tbsp butter

4 tbsp garlic paste

5 tsp ginger paste

2 tsp haldi (turmeric)

5 tsp jeera powder (cumin powder)

5 tsp dhana powder (coriander powder)

salt to taste

400g pulped tomatoes

4 tbsp tomato paste

3 green chillies (optional)

1 tsp red chilli powder (optional)

⅓ cup water if needed later

2 tsp garam masala

METHOD

1. Heat the oil and butter in a pan and add the green chillies and fry for ½ minute. Add garlic paste, ginger paste, haldi, jeera powder, dhana powder and the tomato paste. Cook for just one minute.

2. Add the pulped tomatoes, semi-fried paneer, spinach and salt.

3. Cook covered at simmer for 45 minutes or so until the spinach is soft and thoroughly cooked. Add the water if the curry gets too dry during cooking. Taste for salt and add the red chilli powder if using. Add garam masala.

4. Stir serve with naan.

SERVES 4 /

Paneer and sweetcorn curry

A quick and light vegetarian dish to make

INGREDIENTS

800g boiled sweetcorn
200g paneer cut into bite-size cubes (2.5 x 1cm) and lightly fried till just turning golden brown
400g pulped tomatoes
2 tbsp garlic pasted
2 tbsp ginger pasted
2 tsp hing/asafoetida
20 curry leaves
½ green chilli chopped
1 tsp coriander powder
1 tsp jeera powder
1 tsp turmeric/haldi
1 ½ tsp salt
6 tbsp oil
juice of ½ lemon
15 sprigs fresh coriander stalks and leaves chopped separately
2 tsp fennel powder or crushed fennel seeds (optional)
150ml water
½ tsp sugar

METHOD

1. Heat the oil in a pan and add curry leaves and hing and fry for half a minute.

2. Add green chilli, garlic, ginger, coriander powder, jeera powder, turmeric and cook for a minute.

3. Add the tomatoes, coriander stalks, salt and sugar and cook for 2 minutes.

4. Add the water, sweetcorn, fried paneer and fennel powder if using and cook for 10 minutes on simmer.

5. Add the juice of ½ lemon and serve with rotlis (chapattis) **(p263)** or rice.

Note: the paneer can be substituted with 15 medium mushrooms quartered and added at step 4 instead

Potato, aubergine and pea curry (Ringna, bateta ane matar nu shaak)

SERVES 6 /

INGREDIENTS

1 very large aubergine cut into large bite size cubes

350g potatoes cut into large pieces

350g lb frozen peas

2 large onions finely chopped

12 cloves garlic pasted

2 tbsp ginger paste

1½ tsp turmeric

1 tbsp coriander powder

1 tbsp jeera powder

400g tomatoes pulped

1 tbsp salt

¼ bunch fresh coriander stalks and leaves chopped separately

2 green chillies

6 tbsp oil

400ml water

1 tbsp tomato paste

1 tsp garam masala

METHOD

1. Heat the oil in a pan and fry the onions till they are golden brown.

2. Add chillies, garlic, ginger, turmeric, coriander and jeera powder and cook for a minute on medium heat.

3. Add tomato paste and fry for a minute. Then add tomatoes, salt and coriander stalks.

4. Add the aubergines and water and cook for 15 minutes.

5. Add potatoes and peas and bring to boil. Then simmer and cook till all vegetable are cooked.

6. Add garam masala and coriander leaves and serve with rotlis (chapattis) **(p263)** or chhuti khichdi **(p271)**.

SERVES 4-6 /

Potato and aubergine stuffed dry curry (Ringna bateta bharela nu shaak)
by Roshan Babul

I used to love this dish as a child and yearned for it as an adult. So I asked my biological mum Roshan for the recipe over the phone. She guided me on the method for this complicated and skilled dish. After a couple of trials I cracked it and composed my recipe as below!

INGREDIENTS

12 small potatoes peeled

10 small aubergines round-cut most of the tail

2 tbsp coriander powder

2 tbsp jeera powder

2 tsp haldi/turmeric

1 tbsp salt

½ tsp citric acid

2 tsp garam masala

1 tsp red chilli powder

10 cloves of pasted garlic

3 tbsp pasted ginger

8 tbsp oil (4 tbsp for cooking and 4 tbsp for sauce)

3 tbsp tomato paste

4 tbsp water plus 1 tbsp salt

¼ bunch coriander washed and finely chopped

METHOD

1. Mix the 3rd to 11th ingredients to make a paste.

2. Criss cross the potatoes and aubergines with a sharp knife and stuff the vegetables with paste using up to ⅔ of the paste total. Leave the ⅓ paste aside.

3. Heat 4 tbsp of oil in a wide saucepan and place aubergines and potatoes. Add the 4 tbsp water and 1 tbsp salt with minimum disturbance. Baste vegetables with this liquid

4. Cover the saucepan with an inverted lid. Add cold water onto the lid and leave to simmer so that the vegetables cook in their own steam (the water on the lid prevents this steam escaping). Keep changing the water on the lid with cold water when it gets hot.

5. Baste the vegetables at intervals adding little water if necessary. Continue to monitor till vegetables are cooked. May take up to an hour.

6. In another saucepan make a sauce by heating the 4 tbsp oil and add the ⅓ left over paste. Cook for one minute. Add tomato paste and cook for one minute. Add coriander stalks, 2 mashed potatoes from the cooked vegetables, and any residual liquid from the vegetables and cook for one minute.

7. Add this sauce to the vegetables and fold in gently and serve with parothas **(p275)** or naan or rotlis (chapattis) **(p263)**.

Potato curry (Bateta nu shaak)
Version 1

A Gujarati type curry using tomato paste

SERVES 4 /

INGREDIENTS

1kg boiled potatoes cut to cubes and 2 tsp salt added and mixed and let to rest for 10-15 minutes
20-30 curry leaves (limbro)
2 tsp haldi/turmeric
3 tsp dhana/coriander powder
2 tsp jeera/cumin powder
4 tbsp tomato paste
250ml water
2 tsp hing/asafoetida
2 tsp rai/mustard seeds
1 tsp methi/fenugreek seeds
1 whole bulb garlic pasted (this is a whole bulb i.e about 10 cloves of garlic)
1-2 tsp red chilli powder or to taste
4 tbsp oil
2 tsp sugar
salt to taste
¼ bunch coriander stalks and leaves chopped separately
1 tsp garam masala

METHOD

1. Heat the oil and when it just starts to smoke add the mustard and methi seeds, let it pop for 30 seconds or so, add the curry leaves and leave for 30 second, then add the hing, dhana powder, jeera powder and haldi, leave for 30 seconds and add the garlic. Cook for 30 seconds, add the tomato paste, cook for 30 seconds and then add the sugar and chilli powder. Add the potatoes and coriander stalks and sauté for 2-3 minutes.

2. Add water and salt to taste and let the mixture simmer for 5-7 minutes. Add garam masala and coriander leaves. Serve with puri or rotlis (chapattis) **(p263)** or lisi khichdi **(p270)**.

SERVES 4 /

Potato curry (Bateta nu shaak)
Version 2

This is also a red Gujarati potato curry, and uses pulped tomatoes, whereas the version 1 uses tomato paste and water

INGREDIENTS

1kg potatoes peeled and cut to cubes
20-30 curry leaves (limbro)
2 tsp haldi/turmeric
1 tbsp dhana/coriander powder
2 tsp jeera powder
400ml tomato pulped
2 tsp hing/asafoetida
2 tsp rai/mustard seeds
1 tsp methi/fenugreek seeds
1 whole bulb garlic pasted (this is a whole bulb i.e about 10 cloves of garlic) or 3 tbsp garlic paste
1-2 tsp red chilli powder or to taste
4 tbsp oil
2 tsp sugar
1 tbsp salt
¼ bunch coriander stalks and leaves chopped separately
1 tsp garam masala

METHOD

1. Heat the oil and when it just starts to smoke add the mustard and methi seeds, let it pop for 30 seconds or so, add the curry leaves and leave for 30 seconds, then add the hing, dhana powder, jeera powder and haldi, leave for 30 seconds and add the garlic. Cook for 30 seconds. Add the potatoes, salt, chilli powder and coriander stalks and sauté for 2-3 minutes.

2. Add tomatoes and cook covered on low heat till potatoes are cooked adding a little water if needed only. Add sugar.

3. Add garam masala and coriander leaves. Serve with puris or rotlis (chapattis) **(p263)** or lisi khichdi **(p270)**.

Potato curry (Bateta nu shaak)
Version 3

SERVES 4 /

This is a dryish potato curry with a coconut twist in it

INGREDIENTS

1kg potatoes
4 tbsp oil
½ tsp rai/mustard seeds
1 tsp jeera seeds
10 curry leaves
1-2 green chillies (optional)
1 tbsp tomato paste
salt to taste
½ tsp chilli powder (optional)
½ tsp jeera powder
½ tsp haldi or turmeric
lemon juice to taste
¼ bunch coriander leaves washed and chopped
3 tbsp desiccated coconut soaked in water for 5 minutes and then the water squeezed out

METHOD

1. Peel and cut the potatoes into 3cm cubes. Boil till nearly cooked. Drain well.

2. Heat oil, and add the mustard seeds, cumin seeds, curry leaves and green chillies and let the seeds pop.

3. Immediately add tomato paste, salt, chilli powder, haldi and jeera powder and sauté for a minute. You can add a little bit of water if needed to get a sauce. Add the rehydrated desiccated coconut and cook for 2 minutes.

4. Add cooked potatoes and continue cooking for 2-3 minutes.

5. Add lemon juice and coriander leaves.

6. Serve with naan or rotlis (chapattis) (p263).

SERVES 2 /

Potato curry (Paida bateta nu shaak)
Version 4

My mother-in-law Sherbanu Shamji would delight us with this simple but addictive potato curry!

INGREDIENTS

6 tbsp oil
4 medium potatoes peeled and cut into discs (paida)
2 green chillies sliced
1 tbsp garlic minced
1 tbsp ginger paste
1 tsp dhana/coriander powder
1 tsp jeera powder
1-2 tsp salt
juice of half lemon
1 tsp garam masala

METHOD

1. In hot oil add green chillies, then add the potatoes and fry for 1-2 minutes.

2. Add 3-4 tsp water, salt and cook covered for 6-7 minutes on low heat or until the potatoes are nearly cooked.

3. Add garlic, ginger, dhana and jeera powder and cook open till potatoes are cooked and the mixture is dryish.

4. Add garam masala and lemon juice. Mix.

5. This is a very simple potato curry and should be eaten with rotlis (chapattis) **(p263)** or puri **(p259)**.

SERVES 2 /

Radish leaves curry (Mooli Bhaji nu shaak)

I had this dish for the first time made by my mother-in-law, Sherbanu Shamji, and absolutely loved it!

INGREDIENTS

4 bunches red mooli (radish) with lots of leaves washed thoroughly as it can have grit

4 tsp coriander/dhana powder

4 tsp jeera powder

8 tbsp oil

8 tsp ginger pasted

8 tsp pasted garlic

½ tsp red chilli powder

4 large tomatoes chopped

8-10 tsp channa flour sifted

2 tsp salt

1 tsp turmeric/haldi

1-2 green chillies chopped (optional)

METHOD

1. Chop all the leaves from the mooli and thinly slice only 15 radishes finely. The rest of the radishes can be used elsewhere.

2. Heat the oil in a saucepan and add garlic, ginger, green chillies and the dry spices. Cook for ½ a minute and add the tomatoes and cook for 3-4 minutes.

3. Add the leaves, salt and the sliced mooli (radish).

4. Cook covered for half an hour or so till leaves are well cooked. Keep stirring in between.

5. Add the channa flour and stir thoroughly to make sure it is well mixed.

6. Cover and simmer for 10 minutes checking mixture does not stick to bottom.

7. Serve with rotlas **(p267)** or rotlis (chapattis) **(p263)** or lisi khichdi **(p270)**.

SERVES 4 /

Red cowpea curry in coconut sauce (Nariyal waru lal chori nu shaak)

INGREDIENTS

1 mug dried red chori beans/adzuki beans/red cow peas pre-soaked overnight in water and washed with water next day and boiled till cooked in water (can take up to two hours!). This will yield 3 mugs of boiled beans (do not add salt during boiling as it delays cooking. Add the salt after it is cooked)
2 medium onions finely chopped
4 tsp garlic paste
4 tsp ginger paste
1 tsp haldi/turmeric
1 tbsp dhana/coriander powder
1 tbsp jeera powder
50ml water from boiled beans
salt to taste
200ml coconut milk from the tin
2 large ripe tomatoes chopped finely
juice of two lemons
15 sprigs coriander stalks and leaves chopped separately
3 tbsp oil
1-2 green chillies finely chopped
1 tsp garam masala

METHOD

1. Heat the oil and fry the onions till they turn golden brown.

2. Add the garlic, ginger and green chillies and cook for 30 seconds.

3. Add the haldi, dhana powder and jeera powder and cook for 30 seconds.

4. Add tomatoes, coriander stalks and salt to taste and cook for 5 minutes.

5. Add the strained beans and 50ml of stock from the beans and cook for 10 minutes. Check the salt.

6. Add the coconut milk and cook for 5 minutes.

7. Add garam masala, lemon juice and coriander leaves and let it rest for 5 minutes.

8. Serve with rotlo **(p267)** or parotha **(p275)** or rotlis (chapattis) **(p263)** or rice.

SERVES 4 /

Ridged gourd curry (Ghisoda or turia or turai nu shaak)

There is a lovely crunch to this vegetable

INGREDIENTS

1kg ghisoda/turiya/turai/ridged gourd. Ridges almost cut leaving the outer green crunchy coating and then cut into small bite size cubes
3 medium potatoes cut into same size as the ghisoda
1 tbsp rai/mustard seeds
2 tsp methi/fenugreek seeds
4 tbsp oil
2 tsp hing/aesafotida
2 tbsp coriander powder
1 tbsp jeera powder
2 tsp turmeric
30 curry leaves
4 tsp salt
400g pulped tomatoes
2½ tsp sugar
1 tsp red chilli powder
½ cup water
juice of one lemon (optional)

METHOD

1. Heat oil in the pan and do wagar (tempering) of rai and methi by throwing them into the oil and letting them pop.

2. Immediately add curry leaves, hing, turmeric and coriander and jeera powder and cook for 30 seconds.

3. Add the ghisoda and cook for 3 minutes.

4. Add the tomatoes, salt, sugar and chilli powder and ½ cup water and bring to boil.

5. Simmer and cook covered for 15 minutes.

6. Add the potatoes and bring to boil and then cook covered on simmer till all the vegetables are cooked.

7. Add lemon juice if needed.

8. Serve with rotlis (chapattis) **(p263)** or lisi khichdi **(p270)**.

SERVES 4/

Spanish omelette

A lovely and hearty omelette to enjoy

INGREDIENTS

750g or three large potatoes peeled and thinly sliced

8 tbsp butter plus 2 tbsp extra

3 medium red onions chopped fine

10 garlic clove minced

1 green pepper and 1 red pepper diced fine (bell peppers)

2 medium tomatoes chopped fine

200g cooked sweetcorn

8 large eggs or 12 medium eggs

10 tbsp chopped fresh parsley or 2-3 tsp smoked paprika

salt to taste

1 tsp pepper or to taste

enough grated parmesan or cheese to cover the top of omelette

METHOD

1. Fry the potatoes in 8 tbsp butter till nearly cooked. Add onions and fry for 3-4 minutes.

2. Add garlic, peppers, tomatoes, sweetcorn, salt and pepper and cook for 2-3 minutes.

3. Add parsley or smoked paprika and mix.

4. Add beaten eggs to the mixture and shake gently. Cook on medium to low heat until underneath is cooked through.

5. Add 2 tbsp butter on top and let it melt.

6. Add cheese on top and place under medium grill for 5-7 minutes till omelette is cooked. Alternatively cook in a preheated hot oven for 10 minutes or so or till cooked.

7. Cut into wedges and serve.

Thai vegetable curry

SERVES 3 /

A spicy and elementally fragrant curry

INGREDIENTS

½ cauliflower cut into bite size florets

3 medium carrots cut to bite size large cubes

1 red pepper cut to bite size squares

2 medium onions cut to bite size squares

2 medium sweet potatoes with skin on cut to bite size large cubes

6 medium mushrooms cut into quarters

salt to taste

1 tsp sugar

10 kaffir lime leaves (veins removed)

1 tsp turmeric

juice of 1-2 limes

50ml schezuan sauce (p 304)

4 tbsp oil

600 to 800ml coconut milk

METHOD

1. Heat the oil in pan and add all the vegetable except cauliflower and red pepper and fry for 2-3 minutes.

2. Add turmeric and cauliflower, salt, kaffir lime leaves and red pepper and fry for a minute.

3. Add sugar, coconut milk and Schezuan paste and bring to boil.

4. Cook on simmer until vegetables are nearly cooked.

5. Add lime juice and serve with sticky rice.

SERVES 4 /

Vaal or lima bean curry (Vaal nu shaak)

My mother-in-law's speciality!

INGREDIENTS

3 mugs of boiled Vaal (this bean is available in Indian stores) or butter beans or lima beans
1 tsp hing/asafoetida
2 tbsp channa/gram flour made into a runny paste with water
4 tsp garlic paste
4 tsp ginger paste
salt to taste
1 tsp red chilli powder
2 tsp coriander powder
2 tsp jeera powder
1 tsp turmeric/haldi
200ml water
2 tsp sugar
2 medium tomatoes finely chopped
1 tsp garam masala
4 tbsp oil

METHOD

1. Heat the oil in a pan and add the garlic and ginger and cook for half a minute.

2. Add the coriander powder, turmeric, jeera powder and hing and cook for half a minute.

3. Add tomatoes, salt and sugar and cook till tomatoes are pulped.

4. Add the vaal, water and the red chilli powder and cook for 10 minutes.

5. Slowly add the channa flour paste and keep mixing into the pan.

6. Cook for a further 5 minutes adding more water if required. The curry should be semi-dryish.

7. Add garam masala and serve with rotlis (chapattis) **(p263)** or naan or parotha **(p275)**.

SERVES 4 /

Valor (Indian runner bean) curry (Valor nu shaak)
by Alka Shah

This dish was created with the expert guidance from our dear family friend Alkaben Shah!

INGREDIENTS

750g valor/Indian runner bean/field bean- top and tailed and strings removed
3 medium potatoes cut into same size as fat chips
½ of large aubergine cut into small size pieces
¾ tsp ajma (carom seeds)
½ tsp hing/asafoetida
2 tsp coriander/dhana powder
3 tsp jeera powder
¾ tsp turmeric/haldi
4 medium tomatoes chopped
1 tbsp salt
1½ tsp sugar
1 tsp red chilli powder
1 mug water
3 tbsp oil
½ tsp garam masala

METHOD

1. Heat the oil in the pan and add the ajma seed and let them pop. Reduce heat.

2. Immediately add the dhana and jeera powder, hing and turmeric and cook for ½ minute.

3. Add valor and aubergines and cook for 2 minutes.

4. Add tomatoes, salt, sugar, red chilli powder and water and cook for 15 minutes on simmer covered.

5. Add the potatoes and cook covered on simmer till all the vegetables are cooked.

6. Add garam masala.

7. Serve with rotlis (chapattis) **(p263)** or lisi khichdi **(p270)**.

SERVES 4 /

Yogurt runny curry Gujarat style (Kadhi)

Delicious with any khichdi

INGREDIENTS

500ml sour yogurt (not Greek yogurt).
If you only have non-sour yogurt,
lemon juice can be added to the dish at
the end of cooking
600ml water
¼ mug of channa flour pasted with little
water till smooth
5 cloves/laving
2 tsp jeera seeds
2 green chillies
20 limbro or curry leaves
1 tsp hing/asafoetida
3 cloves minced garlic
5 tsp butter
1-2 tsp oil
2 tsp sugar
salt to taste
(do not use any haldi/turmeric)
handful of chopped coriander stalks
and leaves

METHOD

1. Blend together with a hand blender the yogurt, water and the pasted channa flour in a large saucepan.

2. Add salt, sugar, garlic and coriander stalks.

3. Heat the butter and oil in a pan and do wagar (tempering) of cloves, jeera seeds, hing, limbro and green chillies and let the seeds pop.

4. When the seeds have popped add to the yogurt mixture and heat all on high heat and stir continuously without stopping in one direction till the kadhi starts to boil.

5. Then lower the heat and simmer gently uncovered and stop stirring.

6. Simmer for approximately 10 minutes.

7. Add coriander leaves and lemon juice if needed. Serve with khichdi.

Yogurt runny curry Punjabi style with pakoras (Kadhi-Punjabi style with pakoras)

This recipe is dedicated to my mum's dear Punjabi friend Mrs Surinder Singh

SERVES 4 /

INGREDIENTS

500ml yogurt
600ml water
¼ mug channa flour or besan or gram flour
5 cloves (laving)
1 tbs jeera seeds
1 tbsp garlic paste
1 tbsp ginger paste
2 green chillies slices
1 large onion sliced fine
4-5 sprigs coriander
½ tsp haldi or turmeric
salt to taste
20 limbro leaves or curry leaves
juice of half a lemon
2 tbsp butter
8 punjabi pakoras/fritters (p90)

NB - this kadhi can also be eaten with khichdi, but omit the pakodas if doing so.

METHOD

1. Add a little water to the channa flour and make into a smooth paste and add to yogurt and water. Blend all with a whisk or blender. Add salt, haldi and garlic.

2. Heat the butter in a small saucepan and add jeera and let it pop. Quickly add the cloves, limbro, ginger and chillies and cook for a minute or less. Add onions and fry till onion is transparent.

3. Add to the yogurt mixture. Mix. Heat, and stir in one direction (do not stop) with a wooden spoon till the kadhi boils. This process stops the kadhi from cracking!

4. You can stop stirring. Let the mixture simmer for 5 minutes. Add the pakoras.

5. Switch off cooker and add coriander leaves and lemon juice. Serve on its own.

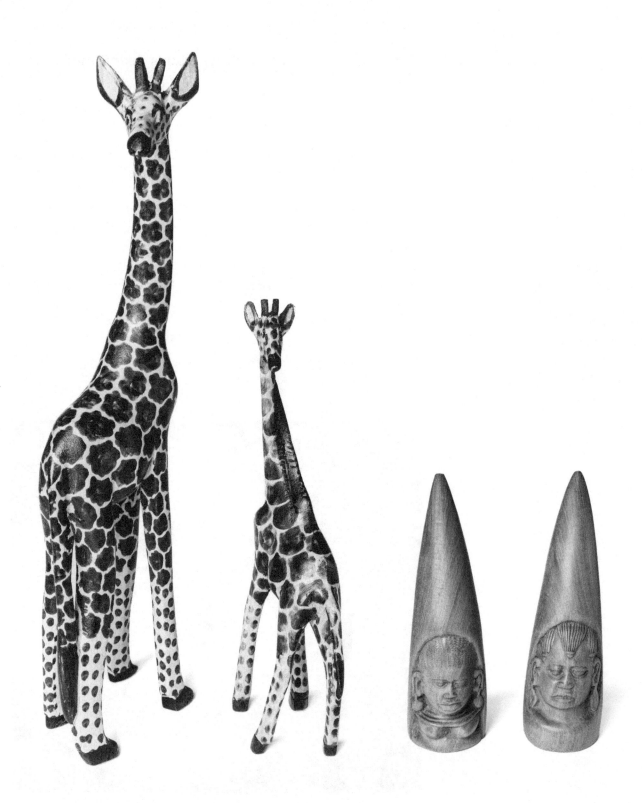

SOUPS

SERVES 4 /

Chicken and sweetcorn soup

This was my son Naadim's weekly takeaway treat for many years after his evening piano lessons. This is our homemade version

INGREDIENTS

1½ **mugs of cooked chicken breast**
1½ **mugs of sweetcorn frozen or tinned**
2 **inches grated or pasted ginger**
salt to taste
enough broth to cover the chicken and sweetcorn plus a little extra on top (use broth from boiling the chicken flesh or use water and 2 stock cubes - preferably Knorr)
3 **tbsp cornflour**
2 **tsp sugar**
2 **sprigs of chopped spring onion**
2 **tbsp toasted sesame seed oil**
egg white from one egg

METHOD

1. Boil the sweetcorn in the broth and semi blend it when soft.

2. Add the cooked chicken and ginger and sugar and simmer for a few minutes.

3. Paste the cornflour with little cold water and add to the mixture.

4. Add the spring onions and cook for 2 minutes.

5. Turn off cooker and add the sesame seed oil.

6. Whisk the egg white and add to the saucepan over a fork, stirring the soup in circular motion to get the stringy effect.

Lemongrass soup with chicken

Makes 8 medium bowls of soup

This soup was described as elemental and fragrant by my son Naadim. It is a light soup and a perfect starter for a heavy main meal

INGREDIENTS

2 large chicken breast cut into thin slices

12 fresh runner beans topped and tailed and cut longitudinally or equivalent in frozen (approx. 2 mugs full) or 2 mugs of top and tailed fine beans-boil in minimum water till soft

1½ tsp salt

750ml water (made up with the strained water from the boiled runner or fine beans)

2 inches ginger finely grated

5 medium lemon grass bulbs the soft inside bits chopped finely discard the stalky bits

40g rice stick noodles or udon noodles grated rind of ½ lime

¼ tsp sugar

1 tbsp thai fish sauce (nam pla)

¼ bunch coriander stalks and leaves chopped

1 red chilli finely sliced (or to taste)

juice of 1 lime or more

METHOD

1. Gently boil the chicken slices in 750ml water together with the salt, udon noodles or rice stick noodles, ginger, sugar, lemon grass, coriander stalks and fish sauce.

2. When nearly cooked add the lemon rind and runner beans or fine beans. Boil for 3-4 minutes.

3. Then add lime juice and the coriander leaves, chilli slices and adjust the seasoning.

4. Let the soup rest for 5 minutes. Serve.

SERVES 8 /

Chinese hot and sour soup

For those who love soups with a bite

INGREDIENTS

2 mugs dried Chinese mushrooms e.g shitake mushrooms - these should be washed and left to soak for at least ½ hour in warm water and then chopped retain the water and use as part of water quantity

2 litres water (use the mushroom water as part of quantity)

3-4 chopped chillies or 2 tsp chilli oil or to taste

¼ mug of soya sauce

¼ mug of toasted sesame seed oil

¼ mug clear/normal vinegar

1 mug mixture of chopped carrots and peas

1 small can of finely slivered bamboo shoots

1 packet tofu cubed or small packet of thin bite size sliced paneer

¼ mug cornflour pasted with a little water

½ mug spring onions chopped

salt to taste

METHOD

1. Bring the stock/water to boil.

2. Add mushrooms, peas, carrots, bamboo shoots and soya sauce and simmer for 10 minutes or more if required.

3. Add tofu/paneer, vinegar, pasted cornflour and stir into soup.

4. Adjust salt taste if required and cook for 3-4 minutes.

5. Add spring onions, toasted sesame seed oil and chopped chillies to taste.

SERVES 4 /

French onion soup
by Naadim Shamji

According to his sister Aalia, Naadim makes better French Onion Soup than the French! This was a remark made after sampling the soup a few times in France at different restaurants!

INGREDIENTS

500g onions thinly sliced
5 tablespoons butter
1 tablespoon white flour
1 litre stock (can be made by adding 2 knorr vegetable stock cubes to the water - do not use Oxo cubes)
salt and pepper to taste
1 bay leaf
6 slices French bread or sliced baguette
75g cheddar cheese finely grated

METHOD

1. Fry the onions gently in the butter till evenly browned all over stirring frequently to stop burning.

2. Stir in the flour and cook for a minute (but do not allow to burn), gradually add the stock and bring to boil.

3. Season well and add bay leaf. Cover and simmer for about 50 minutes.

4. Remove bay leaf and adjust seasoning.

5. Lay slices of bread on baking sheet and cover with grated cheese.

6. Allow the cheese to melt under warm grill.

7. Ladle the soup into bowls and serve with the bread slices on top.

Italian bean soup

A filling and hearty soup for a large gathering

INGREDIENTS

5 medium carrots diced
3 large onions chopped
15 cloves garlic sliced
10 celery sticks sliced very fine
800g tin tomatoes pulped or equivalent of vine tomatoes.
8 tbsp olive oil
salt to taste
white pepper to taste 1-2 tsp
5 bay leaves
10 sage leaves or more
3 mugs boiled butter beans plus its water
1 mug boiled barlotti beans plus its water
1 mug boiled black eye beans plus its water
1 mug boiled Vaal beans plus its water (beans can be varied if wanting to use other types)
total water from boiled beans is approximately 4 mugs
5-6 medium potatoes diced
juice of 1-2 lemons (optional)
1-2 tsp chilli powder (optional)

METHOD

1. Heat oil in large saucepan and sauté all vegetables for 7-10 minutes together with the sage and bay leaves. Add garlic and sauté for 2-3 minutes.

2. Then add all the beans (including the water), salt, tomatoes and pepper and cook for 15-20 minutes on slow heat. Adjust water if need more. Switch off cooker. Adjust salt, pepper 15 minutes after switching off cooker as the salt mixes into the vegetables and the flavouring may need adjusting. Add the lemon juice and chilli powder if desired.

SERVES 4 /

Mushroom soup

Once you have made this homemade version you will never go for the tinned option

INGREDIENTS

250g any white mushrooms wiped and chopped
250ml stock made with water and 1 knorr vegetable stock cube
1 small peeled sliced onion
2 tbsp butter
4 tbsp plain/white flour
250ml milk
salt and pepper to taste
2 tbsp double cream
chopped parsley to garnish

METHOD

1. Place the mushrooms and onions in a pan with the stock. Bring to boil, cover and simmer for 20-30 minutes until tender. Liquidise the mixture coarsely.

2. Melt the butter in a pan and add the flour and cook for 1 minute. Take off the heat and add a little milk and stir very quickly to make a creamy mixture. Heat the pan again for 1-2 minutes and take off the heat and add more milk and whisk. Keep doing this till all milk is used and a creamy texture is formed.

3. Gradually add the pureed mushroom mixture to this pan and season to taste with salt and pepper.

4. Bring to boil, cover and simmer for 5-10 minutes.

5. Just before serving add the cream and reheat but do not boil.

6. Garnish with parsley.

7. Serve with crusty bread.

SERVES 4-5 /

Pea soup

A simple and humble soup to satisfy a hungry family

INGREDIENTS

25g butter
12 spring onions roughly chopped
1 small potato peeled and roughly diced
2 clove garlic minced.
350g frozen peas preferably petit pois
600ml chicken stock
salt and pepper to taste
150ml fresh double cream

METHOD

1. Melt the butter in a large saucepan.

2. Add the spring onions, potato and garlic.

3. Cover with lid and sweat for 10 minutes.

4. Add the peas, stock, salt and pepper, bring to boil and simmer for approximately 15 minutes.

5. Remove from heat and liquidise.

6. Pass through sieve into a clean saucepan.

7. Reheat the soup.

8. Add the cream and heat through, correcting the seasoning.

9. Serve in warm bowls with hot crusty bread.

SERVES 4-6 /

Pumpkin or butternut squash Thai soup

We had this marvellous soup on a cold winter's night when exploring the Xmas lights at Eltham Palace (London)

INGREDIENTS

1kg pumpkin or butternut squash peeled, seeds removed and cubed
2 tbsp oil
1 large onion chopped
300ml water
300ml coconut milk
salt to taste
6 lemon grass stalks of which the soft part in the bulb is finely peeled and chopped, rest is discarded
10 fresh kaffir lime leaves or 20 dried leaves. The hard vein removed and leaves finely chopped
8 tsp finely chopped ginger
2 tsp sugar

METHOD

1. Heat the oil and fry the onions till the onion is transparent.

2. Add ginger and fry for a minute.

3. Add pumpkin/butternut squash cubes, lemon grass chopped bulbs, kaffir lime leaves and the water.

4. Add salt to taste. Bring to boil and simmer covered till pumpkin/butternut squash is soft.

5. Puree the mixture coarsely and then add the coconut milk plus sugar.

6. Simmer for two minutes and serve.

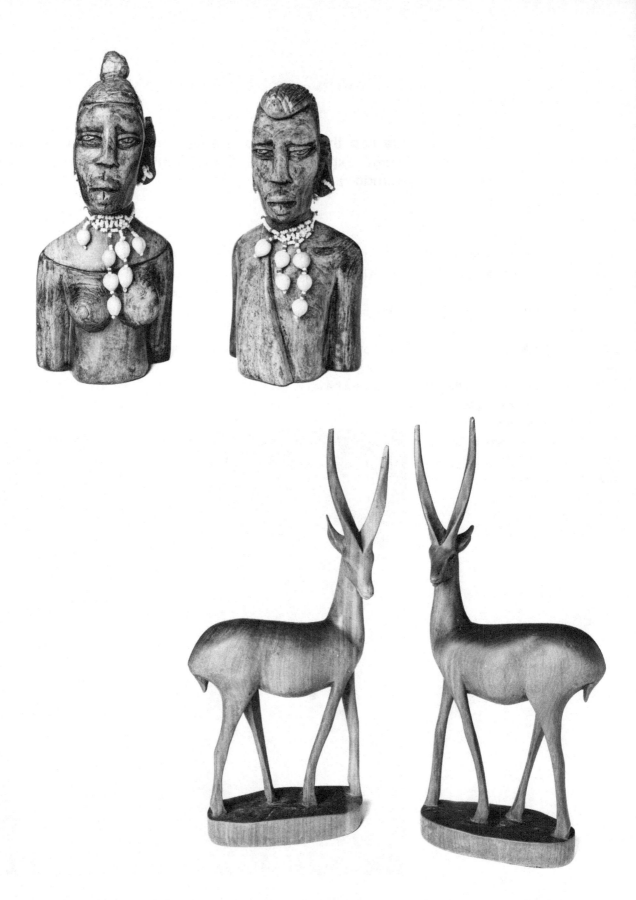

SALADS

Non Vegetarian

234/ Caesar salad with chicken
235/ Thai salad and dressing with fish sauce

Vegetarian

236/ Caesar salad
237/ Coleslaw-Indian style
238/ Couscous salad
239/ Greek salad
240/ Indian Salsa (Kachumber)
241/ Mediterranean salad
242/ Mixed bean salad
243/ Okra (Bhindi) and aubergine salad
244/ Olive salad
245/ Potato salad-Indian style
246/ Rocketty, nutty, fruity cheese salad
247/ Thai salad and dressing
248/ Zathar spice salad

Caesar salad with chicken

A delicious and filling salad to eat on its own. One can substitute the chicken with boiled eggs or grilled halloumi

SERVES 10 /
for starters

INGREDIENTS

CHICKEN:
2kg boneless chicken breasts cut into thin strips

MARINADE:
250ml extra virgin olive oil
30 cloves garlic crushed
8 tsp paprika powder
8 tsp salt
4 tbsp oregano
125ml vinegar
juice of 2 lemons

GARLIC CROUTONS:
15 cloves garlic crushed
150ml extra virgin olive oil
10 thick slices of white bread, the edges cut and the slices cut into crouton sizes

SALAD:
4 large romaine lettuce or 8 small gem lettuce, washed and torn into bite size pieces

CAESAR DRESSING:
400ml of mayonnaise
150ml lukewarm water
6 cloves garlic crushed
8 tsp freshly grated parmesan cheese

CHEESE:
4 tbsp grated parmesan cheese

METHOD

1. Mix the marinade ingredients and use to marinate the chicken pieces. Best to leave it overnight in the fridge.

2. Make the garlic croutons by mixing the olive oil and garlic and spreading it on an oven tray. Preheat the oven to about 180C/350F. Spread the bread cubes onto the tray and mix lightly. Put the tray into the oven for about 20-25 minutes or until the croutons turn light brown. Remove and let the croutons cool.

3. Make the Caesar dressing by mixing the mayonnaise and water – whisk if necessary. Add the garlic and parmesan and mix. Can add more water if the dressing is too thick.

4. To cook the chicken use a griddle pan. Heat the pan till very hot and cook the chicken in batches till cooked. Let it cool.

5. Spread the lettuce onto a large plate, top it up with chicken, croutons, parmesan cheese and finally the Caesar dressing.

Thai salad and dressing with fish sauce

SERVES 6 /

A lovely and refreshing salad to any Thai meal

INGREDIENTS

SALAD:
One small red cabbage finely sliced
3 large carrots grated
3 tbsp fresh mint chopped
3 tbsp basil chopped
3 tbsp fresh coriander chopped
2 tbsp toasted sesame seeds

THE DRESSING:
juice of two limes
1-2 tbsp fish sauce depending upon
how strong you want
1 tbsp honey
2 tsp sesame seed oil
1 tbsp grated ginger

METHOD

1. Make the dressing by mixing all the dressing ingredients.

2. Mix the vegetables and herbs of salad ingredients.

3. Add the dressing to the salad just before serving. Mix.

4. Sprinkle the toasted sesame seeds on top.

Caesar salad

You can also have the salad with boiled eggs or grilled halloumi

INGREDIENTS

GARLIC CROUTONS:
15 cloves garlic crushed
150ml extra virgin olive oil
10 thick slices of white bread, the edges removed and sliced into crouton shapes

SALAD:
4 large romaine lettuce or 8 small gem lettuce, washed and torn into bite size pieces

CAESAR DRESSING:
400ml of mayonnaise
150ml lukewarm water
6 cloves garlic crushed
8 tsp freshly grated parmesan cheese

CHEESE:
4 tbsp grated parmesan cheese

METHOD

1. Make the garlic croutons by mixing the olive oil and garlic and spreading it on an oven tray. Preheat the oven to about 180C/350F. Spread the bread cubes onto the tray and mix lightly. Put the tray into the oven for about 20-25 minutes or until then croutons turn light brown. Remove and let the croutons cool.

2. Make the Caesar dressing by mixing the mayonnaise and water – whisk if necessary. Add the garlic and parmesan and mix. Can add more water if the dressing is too thick.

3. Spread the lettuce onto a large plate. Top it up with croutons, parmesan cheese and finally the Caesar dressing.

Coleslaw-Indian style

Spice up that coleslaw to go with any Indian bites or barbeques

INGREDIENTS

2 mugs finely sliced white cabbage
1 medium onion finely minced or sliced
1 large carrot grated
juice of one lime
salt to taste
3 tbsp mayonnaise and 3 tbsp yogurt mixed
3 tsp nigella seeds/kalonji/onion seeds
2 tsp turmeric

METHOD

Mix all and serve.

Couscous salad

A lovely way to prepare this refreshing Morrocan salad on a hot summer's day

INGREDIENTS & METHOD

Make couscous according to packet instructions using 500g of dry couscous. Leave to cool, and separate with fork
1 bunch cleaned and chopped mint leaves
1 bunch Greek parsley cleaned and chopped
1 packet (200g) feta cheese cubed
1 bunch spring onion chopped
I mug roasted pine nuts or cashews or sunflower seeds or pistachio nuts
I-2 finely chopped red pepper or 2 bottled roasted peppers chopped
juice of 3 to 4 limes
3-4 chopped preserved yellow lemons (optional)
salt to taste
½ tsp chilli flakes (optional)
3 cloves garlic minced
½ mug olive oil
½ mug black olives chopped
mix all and adjust flavours and taste accordingly

Greek salad

INGREDIENTS

2 gem lettuce or equivalent in volume of iceberg lettuce coarsely cut
1 cup of cherry tomatoes cut into halves
1 cup of pitted and drained black olives cut into halves
½ a cucumber deseeded and chopped into little cubes
15 mint leaves coarsely cut
1 large red onion cut into rings
½ packet (100g) of feta cheese cut into little cubes
enough French dressing to coat the salad

METHOD

1. Lay the lettuce in a big bowl followed by onions, cucumber, cherry tomatoes, black olives and feta cheese.

2. Sprinkle the mint leaves on top.

3. Add enough French dressing (in the recipe book) to coat the salad just before serving.

Indian Salsa (Kachumber)

SERVES 4 /

I call this the Indian salsa! Perfect with rice dishes like biriani, pilau, akni etc

INGREDIENTS

2 medium onions finely chopped
3 medium tomatoes finely chopped
½ cucumber finely diced
2 tsp salt
juice of 2 large lemons

METHOD

Mix everything into a bowl.

Mediterranean salad

SERVES 6 /

This salad was created for my daughter Aalia to take to a picnic when she was young. It was an instant hit!

INGREDIENTS

3 large aubergines sliced thinly longitudinally

3 large red onions sliced long and thin

3 large green/red peppers (bell peppers) cut longitudinally and thinly

1 mug mixture of any olives pitted

1 packet feta cheese (200g) or similar size halloumi cheese (halloumi cheese to be sliced thin, oiled and grilled)

1 tsp chilli flakes

1 tbsp oregano

1 lemon sliced very thin (optional)

salt to taste

10 sun dried tomatoes thinly sliced

DRESSING:

30ml juice of lemon or lime

90ml extra virgin olive oil

salt to taste

½ tsp black pepper

1 tsp sugar

METHOD

1. Oil the peppers, aubergines and onions with extra virgin olive oil and griddle or grill till cooked and slightly burnt at edges. Cut the aubergine slices into smaller pieces.

2. Make the dressing up in a jar and shake till it is mixed.

3. Add the rest of the ingredients to the grilled/griddled vegetables, mix and add the dressing and serve.

Mixed bean salad

This is a healthy salad with an array of colours and flavours using assorted beans

INGREDIENTS

3x 400g tins of any beans like barlotti, butter beans, red kidney beans, haricot beans, black eye beans, chick peas etc or equivalent of home-cooked boiled beans. The beans to be strained
juice of 1 large lemon
grated rind of one large lemon
4 tbsp of any herb like basil, dill, parsley etc
2 spring onions finely chopped
2 stalks of celery sticks finely sliced
1 small red onion very finely chopped
2 cloves of garlic pasted
½ tsp chilli flakes (optional)
2 tsp Dijon mustard
salt to taste
olive oil to coat the salad

METHOD

Mix all the above and pour in enough olive oil to coat the salad. Adjust the salt.

Okra (Bhindi) and aubergine salad

This unusual soft and crunchy salad is a fusion of Indian and Chinese flavours

SERVES 4 /

INGREDIENTS

1 large aubergine cut to small cubes
250g okra/ladies' fingers/bhindi top and tailed and sliced into bite size pieces
1 medium onion cut to small cubes
2 large spring onions chopped
10 sprigs of coriander stalks and leaves chopped separately
3 tbsp oil
8 cloves garlic minced.
1 tsp chilli flakes
1 tbsp salt
2 tbsp toasted sesame seeds
3 tbsp encona Thai sweet chilli sauce
oil for deep frying

METHOD

1. Deep fry aubergines and bhindi separately and collect in a dish and let it cool.

2. Fry the onions till soft in the 3 tbsp oil and then add the garlic and fry for a minute and add to the mixture.

3. Add the rest of the ingredients and mix thoroughly. Serve.

SERVES 4 /

Olive salad
by Amin Shamji

A perfect salad for a picnic

INGREDIENTS

400g drained queen green pitted olives
100g drained Kalamata olives preferably with stone
200g drained pitted black olives
4 cloves garlic thinly sliced
2 x 10cm long gherkins finely chopped
1 teaspoon thinly sliced jalapeno peppers or less or few chilli flakes
6 thinly sliced sun-dried tomatoes
1 slab chopped feta cheese 200g
½ lemon with skin very thinly sliced into very small pieces
1 griddled and chopped or ready-made smoked red pepper or equivalent of griddled aubergines chopped
1 teaspoon oregano
juice of half a lemon
Enough olive oil to coat the salad and a little extra

METHOD

Mix everything and serve with baguette.

Potato salad-Indian style

SERVES 4 /

These moreish Indian potatoes get to half the volume as I am cooking, as they are totally irresistible

INGREDIENTS

1kg potatoes boiled and peeled and cut into small roast potato sizes and 3 tsp salt added to the boiled potatoes few minutes before stir frying
1 tsp turmeric/haldi
4 tsp sesame seeds
30 curry leaves
1 tsp hing
4 tbsp oil
1 tbsp pasted garlic
2 green chillies
juice of one lemon
5 tbsp dessicated coconut pre-soaked in little water to rehydrate it
15 sprigs fresh coriander, stalks and leaves chopped separately

METHOD

1. Heat the oil in a wok and add sesame seeds and brown them slightly.

2. Add curry leaves, garlic, green chillies, coriander stalks, turmeric and hing and cook for 30 seconds.

3. Add the dessicated coconut and cook for 30 seconds.

4. Add the lemon juice, stir and then add the salted potatoes and mix thoroughly.

5. Cook for few minutes till the potatoes are thoroughly heated up.

6. Add the coriander leaves.

SERVES 4 /

Rocketty, nutty, fruity cheese salad

A colourful and interesting salad

INGREDIENTS

120g Rocket/Arugula leaves
4 long red peppers(mild) griddled with oil and cut to bite size pieces
4 heaped tbsp toasted nuts like pecan semi crushed or walnut semi crushed or cashews semi crushed or pine nuts
250g goat's cheese or any fruity cheese with cranberries or apricots etc
4 tbsp fresh (de-stoned) cherries, halved OR dried figs cut into small pieces OR fresh pomegranate seeds (optional)
French dressing with vinegar to coat the salad (p290)

METHOD

Assemble all the ingredients in a nice decorative way and coat with just enough dressing before serving.

Thai salad and dressing

A lovely and refreshing salad to any Thai meal

INGREDIENTS

One small red cabbage finely sliced
3 large carrots grated
3 tbsp fresh mint chopped
3 tbsp basil chopped
3 tbsp fresh coriander chopped
2 tbsp toasted sesame seeds

THE DRESSING:
juice of two limes
1 tbsp honey
2 tsp sesame seed oil
1 tbsp grated ginger

METHOD

1 Make the dressing by mixing all the dressing ingredients.

2 Mix the vegetables and herbs of salad ingredients.

3 Add the dressing to the salad just before serving. Mix.

4 Sprinkle the toasted sesame seeds on top.

Zathar spice salad

INGREDIENTS

500g cherry tomatoes washed and halved

diced flesh of 2 avocado (add lemon juice to stop the avocado from darkening)

20 green olives

a handful of coriander leaves chopped

salt to taste

olive oil to coat the salad

1 tsp grated lemon rind

zathar spice to coat the ingredients (p335)

METHOD

Mix the 7 ingredients and add enough zathar spice (p339) to coat the salad.

RICE, PASTA, FLATBREADS, PASTRIES

Non Vegetarian

252/ Cornish pasty
253/ Creamy chicken pasta
254/ Mince stuffed shallow fried flatbread
(Kheema parotha)
256/ Pastries - Chicken or Lamb mince curry puffs
and sausage rolls

Vegetarian

257/ Boiled egg pilau (Mayai pilau)
258/ Coconut rice with kalonji seeds (onion seeds)
259/ Deep fried mini puffed bread (Puri)
260/ Deep fried puffed bread (Puri) for bhel puri
261/ East African deep fried bread (Mandazi
or Mahamri)
262/ Fenugreek flatbread (Methi parotha)
263/ Indian flatbread (Rotli)
264/ Maize or cornmeal flatbread (Makke ki roti)
265/ Maize or cornmeal porridge (Ugali)
266/ Middle Eastern rice
267/ Millet flour flatbread (Rotlo)
268/ Parotha using leftover lisi khichdi
269 Potato stuffed flatbread (Aloo parotha)
270/ Rice and moong salty porridge (Lisi khichdi)
271/ Rice with lentils or daal (Chhuti khichdi)
272/ Samosa pastry (par)
274/ Shallow fried flaky flatbread (Parothas-flakey)
275/ Shallow fried flatbread (Parotha)
276/ Spanish saffron rice
277/ Sweet and savoury egg fried bread (Mitha
pau and Tikha pau)
278/ Sweet rice (Jardo or Mithu khaau)

Cornish pasty

Makes 10 large pasties

We visited Cornwall with my husband's niece Salima Yunus nee Manji and her family for a few days in September 2018 and sampled endless Cornish Pasties with delicious scones with clotted cream, jam and hot tea! After that holiday none of us dared step onto the scales!

INGREDIENTS

SHORTCRUST PASTRY:
300g butter cold and grated. (Can put the butter in the freezer for a short time beforehand)
750g plain/ white flour
2 pinches of salt
260ml cold water

STUFFING:
850g top rump steak cut into small pieces
100g swede peeled and cut into small cubes
300g potatoes peeled and diced into small cubes
250g carrots diced into small cubes
350g onions peeled and diced into small cubes
salt and black pepper to taste
1 egg beaten for glazing

METHOD

1. Sift the flour and salt into a large bowl and mix in the grated butter. Then stir in cold water and mix thoroughly with your fingers.

2. Knead briefly till the dough is smooth and pliable.

3. Wrap the dough in clingfilm/stretch-and-seal. Can chill longer if required.

4. Mix the meat, potatoes, carrots, swede and onions and add the salt and black pepper.

5. Divide the dough into ten portions and roll out each one individually till the diameter is 17cm.

6. Divide the mixtures between the circles piling it on one side of each. Then brush the edges of the pastry with water and bring the other halves over the filling so the edges meet.

7. Press together and crimp the edges.

8. Place the pasties on an oiled baking tray and chill for an hour or longer covered with foil.

9. Preheat the oven to 180C/350F (or if fan assisted, 160C/320F).

10. Remove the pasties from the fridge, brush with beaten egg and make three small slits on top of each one.

11. Bake for an hour until richly golden. Serve hot.

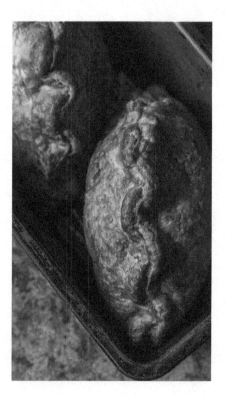

SERVES 6 /

Creamy chicken pasta

A lovely pasta dish with an Indian twist!

INGREDIENTS

5 medium chicken breasts cut to bite size pieces
1 tbsp salt
400g pasta preferably penne as this does not break easily
5 tablespoons garlic paste
3 tbsp oregano
2 tsp black pepper
5 tbsp olive oil
600g pulped tomatoes
1 tbsp vinegar
1 tsp haldi/turmeric
2 tbsp dhana/coriander powder
2 tbsp jeera powder
100ml boiling water or more if needed
4 green peppers/bell peppers diced
1 tsp paprika
1 tsp red chilli powder (optional)
2 tbsp tomato paste
250ml fresh double cream
2 tsp sugar

METHOD

1. Marinate the chicken in half the garlic and 1 tsp salt and leave for 2-3 hours or overnight.

2. Heat the oil and fry the rest of the garlic for ½ minute.

3. Add the haldi, dhana and jeera powder, and cook for one minute. Add tomato paste and cook for a minute. Then add tomatoes, rest of salt, oregano, sugar, black pepper, paprika, chilli powder and chicken and bring to boil. Let it simmer gently for about 15 minutes or so. Add vinegar, double cream and green peppers and cook for 2-3 minutes.

4. Meanwhile cook the pasta in salt and water according to the packet instructions. Cook the paste a le dente (not overcook). Then add the strained pasta and 100ml of boiling water into the chicken mixture and stir gently to mix thoroughly. Check for salt if more is needed.

5. Let the dish rest for a few minutes and serve with salad or garlic bread.

Mince stuffed shallow fried flatbread (Kheema parotha)

Makes 6 square parothas

A tricky flatbread to make but well worth it! This dish takes me back to the alleyways of Mombasa and the food stalls of Zanzibar. Queuing for your turn to be served this sizzling hot special parotha was well worth the wait. It has left wonderful lasting memories

INGREDIENTS

MINCE MIX:
500g lamb/beef mince good quality
juice of one lemon
salt to taste
5 cloves of garlic pasted
1 tbsp ginger paste
1 tsp garam masala
2 green chillies chopped
6 medium onions finely chopped
10-12 sprigs of coriander washed and chopped

REST OF THE INGREDIENTS:
6 cups white/plain flour
2 tsp salt
6 small eggs
oil and ghee to fry

METHOD

1. Cook the mince on a heated wok and add the lemon juice and salt to taste. Stir fry till all the juices have evaporated.

2. Add garlic, ginger, green chillies and stir well and cook for 10-15 minutes or till mince is cooked.

3. Take the wok off the heat and let the mixture cool down.

4. Add onions and mix. Add coriander and garam masala and mix. Let the mixture cool.

5. Make the dough by mixing the flour and salt using lukewarm water to make a pliable dough. Knead for 5 minutes. Cover the mixture, and let the dough rest for a minimum of 15 minutes

6. Make dough into six discs and roll out onto a floured board as thin as possible.

7. Divide the meat mixture into six portions, and place each portion into the middle of each disc.

8. Add one egg over each meat mixture just before frying.

9. Before cooking, you will need to fold the pastry into a sealed square. To do this, fold one side of the parotha into the centre, then fold the opposite side so that it overlaps in the middle. Do the same for the other two sides of the parotha so that you end up with a neat square. Press on the folds to seal.

10. Dry cook each parotha at a time on a frying pan on each side. Then turn over and add 2 tbsp oil and 2 tbsp ghee onto side and roll the frying pan to let it spread all over.

11. Turn the parotha and cook again. Repeat for the rest of the parothas.

12. Remove and serve with raita (**p303**) or yogurt.

Makes 24 triangular chicken or lamb mince pastries (or 12 sausage rolls)

Pastries - chicken or lamb mince curry puffs and sausage rolls

These delicious pastry dishes we call curry puffs and sausage rolls, are very moreish and control has to be exercised to stop picking on them as they come out of the oven!

INGREDIENTS

500g chicken mince or lamb mince (or 12 sausages if making sausage rolls)
2 or less green chillies finely minced
6 large garlic cloves minced
2 tbsp ginger minced
2 medium onions finely chopped
salt to taste
4 tbsp chopped coriander leaves
Juice of 1 or two lemons
2 tsp garam masala
1 tsp jeera or cumin powder
4 tbsp oil
4 x 320g puff pastry ready rolled sheets defrosted overnight or as per instructions on packet
(Each sheet gives 6 squares for the chicken or lamb mince. Therefore total is 24 squares) (for sausage rolls cut each pastry sheet into 3 rectangles making a total of 12 rectangles)
2 eggs beaten

METHOD

1. Heat oil and stir in chicken or lamb mince, oil, salt, garlic, chillies, ginger, and stir fry till chicken or lamb mince is almost cooked mashing the meat to mix it well.

2. Add garam masala , jeera powder, and onions and cook till meat is cooked.

3. Add lemon juice and coriander leaves.

4. Let the mixture cool.

5. Roll out the pastry as instructed and cut into 24 squares altogether.

6. Add mixture into half of the triangle (avoiding the edges) per square and fold over to make a triangle.

7. Seal edges with end of a fork tightly. Lift the triangle and press again at edges to seal securely.

8. Lay the pastries on lightly oiled oven trays and brush with beaten egg on top. Keep distance between pastries to allow for expansion.

9. Bake in a preheated oven at 160C/320F for 25 minutes or so. Serve with salad or tomato chutney.

10. To make the sausage rolls use 12 sausages and remove the skin. Place each sausage into the middle of the rectangle (a total of 12 rectangles) and fold the pastry over from both sides and seal. Place each sausage onto an oiled tray with the folded side down, making diagonal slits and brushing the surface of each roll with the beaten eggs.

11. Cook as above method.

Boiled egg pilau (Mayai pilau)

SERVES 6 /

A very East African coastal dish using coconut milk in the rice

INGREDIENTS

2 mugs basmati rice washed and pre-soaked for 1-2 hours
4 tsp salt
4 large tomatoes chopped
2 medium onions chopped
6 cloves
10-12 black peppercorns
3 cinnamon sticks 12cm long
1 tsp turmeric
6 cloves garlic minced
2 tbsp ginger pasted
2 green chilies chopped
300ml coconut milk
⅓ bunch washed and chopped coriander leaves
1 mug water
10 boiled eggs
10 tbsp oil

METHOD

1. Heat the oil in the saucepan and add cloves, cinnamon and peppercorns and fry for 1 minute. Add onions and green chillies and fry till onions are softened and translucent.

2. Add turmeric, garlic and ginger and fry for ½ minute. Add tomatoes and cook for 3-4 minutes.

3. Add the strained rice, 1 mug water, salt and eggs. Bring to boil and simmer covered till nearly all the water is absorbed.

4. Add the coconut milk and coriander leaves and mix gently but thoroughly.

5. Cook covered on very gentle heat till rice is cooked. If need to add more water do in exceedingly small proportions to make sure rice does not get soggy.

6. Switch off the cooker and let the rice rest to let the grains cook in its own steam.

7. Serve with yogurt or kachumber **(p240)**.

Coconut rice with kalonji seeds (onion seeds)

SERVES 5 /

INGREDIENTS

2 mugs jasmin fragrant rice washed and pre-soaked for about an hour
2 tbsp kalonji/onion/nigella seeds
50-60 curry leaves/limbro
5 tsp ginger paste
1 tbsp salt
400ml coconut milk
¾ mug water
2 tbsp oil
2 tsp sugar
¼ bunch coriander washed and chopped

METHOD

1. In a saucepan heat the oil till it is just smoking. Throw in the kalonji and let it splutter for 30-40 seconds.

2. Add limbro and ginger and cook for 30 seconds or so.

3. Add the sieved rice and cook in the pan for a couple of minutes stirring all the time.

4. Add water, salt and sugar and bring to boil and simmer covered till water is absorbed.

5. Add the coconut milk and coriander leaves and stir thoroughly but gently.

6. Bring to boil and simmer very gently making sure rice does not burn at the bottom. Add more water if needed very little at a time. It is best to place an iron griddle at the bottom of the pan on the heat to make sure rice does not burn.

7. Serve with any Thai curry.

Deep fried mini puffed bread (Puri)

A good puffed-up flat bread to be eaten with dry curries or on its own

Makes 12 puris

INGREDIENTS

2 cups rotli/chapatti flour medium
4 pinches salt
4 tbsp oil
flour to dust
oil for deep frying

METHOD

1. Mix the flour, salt and the 4 tbsp oil into a crumbly mixture.

2. Add lukewarm water to make into a pliable dough and knead for 3-4 minutes.

3. Rest for ½ hour or so.

4. Make 12 portions and flatten to discs ready to roll and add flour on both side.

5. Roll out each puri to 7-8cm diameter on dusted rolling board.

6. Deep fry in medium to hot oil by dropping each puri and pressing it down to allow it to puff up.

7. When the bottom side is golden brown turn over and cook again on the lower side till golden brown. The lower side take longer as that part is thicker than the top side.

Deep fried puffed bread (Puri) for bhel puri

Makes 50 puris with a 6cm diameter cutter

INGREDIENTS

2 cups white/plain flour
½ cup normal temp water
1 tsp salt
2 tbsp oil
oil for deep frying

METHOD

1. Mix the salt and oil with flour. Then add the water slowly and make into a stiffish dough. Knead for a few minutes.

2. Separate into two balls and roll out on a floured board to two rotlis discs – not too thin nor too thick. Thin makes the puris flat and thick does not make it crispy.

3. Use the cutter to cut out the puris. Re-roll the remainder dough and cut out the puris again.

4. Repeat with the second rotli.

5. Fry the puris in medium to hot oil. As you place each puri dunk it in the oil with the ladle for it to puff. Turn round and fry the other side.

6. Let it cool and stuff with bhel to make bhelpuris.

East African deep fried bread (Mandazi or Mahamri)

Makes 12 Mandazis

This is a lovely yeasty smelling deep fried African bread eaten for breakfast and is also known as mahamari. Can be eaten on its own or with coconut marage (kidney beans) or bharazi (gungo peas/pigeon peas)

INGREDIENTS

(1 cup is 250ml)

A. ¼ cup lukewarm water
   ½ tsp sugar
   ¾ tsp dried yeast
B. 1½ cup plain white flour (can mix ¾ plain white and ¼ strong white flour by volume to get a tougher texture)
   ½ cup sugar
   2 tsp crushed cardamom seeds
C. 40ml coconut milk approximately

METHOD

1. Mix all ingredients of A in a cup and leave for the yeast to froth for 10 minutes or more.

2. Mix A and B and slowly add coconut milk (C) into the dough making sure it ends up in a pliable dough, give and take a few ml of the coconut milk.

3. Knead on a floured board for 10 minutes or so. May need to use oiled hands in case the dough sticks to the hand.

4. Cover the dough in a bowl and let it rest overnight in a warm place or till the dough rises maybe twice the size.

5. Separate the dough into three parts and roll each piece on the palms. Then on a floured board roll out into a circular shape about 15cm diameter and cut into 4 triangles. Repeat with the rest.

6. Let the mandazis rise again for an hour or so in a warm place. The optimum temperature range for yeast fermentation is between 32-35C (90-95F). Every degree above this range depresses fermentation.

7. Deep fry the mandazis in hot oil and serve with marage (coconut kidney beans) or bharazi (coconut gungo/pigeon peas).

Fenugreek flatbread (Methi parotha)

Makes 4 large or 8 small parothas

The methi in these parothas gives it its characteristic aroma. Make sure you wash your hair after cooking these yummy flatbreads!!

INGREDIENTS

2 cups rotli/chapatti flour (medium type)
¼ cup channa/gram flour
¼ cup bajra flour (millet flour)
6 tbsp oil
methi leaves washed and chopped from two bunches
2 tsp salt
2 tbsp garlic
2 tbsp ginger
2 tsp haldi (turmeric)
4 tsp dhana/coriander powder
4 tsp jeera powder
3 chopped green chillies
oil for frying

METHOD

1. Mix all and bind into a dough adding little water at a time. Knead for 3-4 minutes and leave for 10-15 minutes or more.

2. Divide into 8 portions (for small parothas) or 4 portions (for large parothas) and make into balls. Then roll on dusted board to the size required. For large parothas roll out to 20cm diameter discs and for small parothas roll out to around 15cm diameter discs.

3. On a heated tawa or frying pan dry cook the parotha/discs on both sides. Then turn the third time and pour in 4 tbsp oil and cook. Turn again and cook. Add more oil if required.

4. Serve with raita (p303) or yogurt.

Indian flatbread (Rotli)

Makes 8 rotlis (chapattis)

INGREDIENTS

2 cups rotli/chapatti flour medium
4 tbsp oil
4 pinches salt
butter to coat the cooked rotlis / chapattis
flour to dust

METHOD

1. Mix the flour and oil on a big bowl and make into a crumbly mixture. Slowly add lukewarm water and keep mixing and kneading till the dough becomes pliable and is slightly sticky but peels off the fingers when pulled away. (May need about 200ml of water approximately).

2. Knead for 3-4 minutes and let it rest covered for at least 20 minutes or so. Make 8 balls and flatten slightly and pat in flour on both sides.

3. Roll into rotli to 18cm diameter on dusted board and cook on tavri/pan as follows: Place the uncooked rotli on the heated pan, when slightly cooked, turn on the other side. When slightly cooked turn again and keep pressing on the rotli till it starts puffing up. Cook evenly and turn on the other side to cook if necessary. Take out of the pan and dab a little butter on the rotli.

4. Repeat.

Maize or cornmeal flatbread (Makke ki roti)

This is a Punjabi flatbread that requires a lot of skill to make!

Makes 8 rotis

INGREDIENTS

2 mugs fine cornmeal
2 mugs coarse cornmeal
2 tsp salt
2 tbsp ghee melted
4 tbsp white/plain flour
2¼ mugs lukewarm water approximately
ghee to rub over cooked rotis

METHOD

1. Mix all the ingredients using water slowly to get to a pliable consistency. May need slightly less or more water.

2. Knead the dough for 5 minutes and let it rest covered for one hour.

3. Knead again for few minutes and make 8 portions.

4. Roll each portion into a ball.

5. Heat an iron griddle and pat the portion flat using wet hands and place on the griddle. Spread this portion with your hand to about 12cm disc. Keep it on medium heat.

6. Let the bottom side set and carefully tease the edges with a sharp knife and lift the roti.

7. Turn the roti over and cook the other side till done.

8. Remove from heat and smear ghee generously over the roti and serve with sarso ka saag (mustard spinach curry) or any spinach curry.

Maize or cornmeal porridge (Ugali)

SERVES 4 /

This is *the* East African staple food item. It is a traditional accompaniment to African curries like spinach curry, fish and coconut curry or runny lamb curry. In consistency, it is similar to a thick porridge. Normally little balls are made as one is eating, and a small hole is made in it to scoop up the curry before being consumed

INGREDIENTS

1 cup white maize flour
2½ cups water
1 tsp salt

METHOD

1. Boil the water in a large saucepan with the salt.

2. Add maize flour slowly and stir continuously removing any lumps for 5-7 minutes.

3. Switch off the cooker and let the ugali rest for 2-3 minutes.

4. Serve with coconut fish curry or spinach curry or lamb curry.

SERVES 4 /

Middle Eastern rice

INGREDIENTS

1½ mugs American parboiled rice
2 large handfuls of chopped Greek
parsley leaves
5 cloves of garlic slivered
1 tsp turmeric
salt to taste
2 tbsp olive oil
3 mugs of water

METHOD

1. Wash the rice twice , strain and pre-soak in 3 mugs of water for 1-2 hours.

2. Heat the oil in a pan and fry the garlic for 1 minute on medium heat. Add turmeric and fry for 15 seconds.

3. Add the rice with its water and salt. Bring to boil and then reduce heat and cook the rice till it is nearly ready.

4. Add the parsley leaves and mix in very gently and cook till rice is ready.

5. Serve with meats etc and tzatziki **(p312).**

Millet flour flatbread (Rotlo)

Makes one rotlo

This flatbread is traditionally eaten by Indian farmers as they work hard in the fields. Millet has a low GI index value, and thus stays longer in the gut, making you sated for longer. The bonus is that it is also very tasty, although my son calls it 'carpet'! Lovely to have with dryish curries, masala fish, yogurt and bhurto

INGREDIENTS

2 tsp white/plain flour
1 mug bajra (millet) flour (1 mug is 350ml)
½ tsp salt
2 tsp ghee or butter or oil
(ghee or butter to spread on cooked rotlo)

METHOD

1. Mix all the 4 items above and make a pliable dough by adding cold water slowly. The dough should not be too soft otherwise it is difficult to make the rotlo.

2. Knead the dough for 2-3 minutes.

3. Using wet hands, make rotlos /discs using both palms, turning the rotlo and repairing the edges as the rotlo rolls on the palms to about 20cm diameter.

4. Make sure the rotlo does not give into gravity!

5. Quickly place the formed rotlo on a hot iron griddle and let it set before turning it around. You can use a knife and a big spatula to turn the rotlo.

6. Cook on the other side the same way and turn it briefly to cook on the third side.

7. Remove from griddle and spread a lot of ghee or butter to the hot rotlo.

8. Serve.

Parotha using leftover lisi khichdi

Make use of that leftover lisi khichdi!

Makes 8 parotha

INGREDIENTS

1 mug cooked lisi khichdi (p270)
12 cloves garlic pasted
10 tsp ginger paste
3 green chillies finely chopped
½ tsp haldi/turmeric
2 tsp salt
5 tbsp kasuri methi (dried methi leaves)
or 5 tbsp chopped fresh coriander
gram /channa/flour (besan) ½ mug
chapatti flour medium 1½ mug
2 tbsp oil
2 tsp dhana/coriander powder
oil for frying

METHOD

1. Mix the flours, salt and 2 tbsp oil and make into a crumbly mixture.

2. Mix the rest of the ingredients into the khichdi and mix well.

3. Add the mixed flours little by little into the khichdi mixture and knead well for 3-4 minutes. The mixture will be sticky yet you should be able to roll it on a floured ball. If need be, you can add a bit more chapatti flour to make the mixture less sticky.

4. Leave to rest for half an hour.

5. Separate dough into 8 pieces and make discs and pat flour on both sides ready to roll.

6. Roll out each parotha on floured board to 14cm diameter discs.

7. Heat a frying pan on medium heat and place parotha on it.

8. Cook on one side for 2 minutes, then on the other side for one minute, turn over and pour in 1 tbsp oil and swirl the pan and cook for 30 seconds.

9. Turn the parotha to the other side and cook for 30 seconds or till cooked.

10. Serve with yogurt or pickles.

Potato stuffed flatbread (Aloo parotha)

Lovely to have on a cold wintery day

Makes 4 parothas

INGREDIENTS

DOUGH:
1½ cup white/plain flour
4 tbsp oil
½ tsp salt

STUFFING:
4 medium sized potatoes boiled and nearly mashed
2 tsp salt
2 finely chopped green chilli
10 sprigs of coriander finely chopped
1 tbsp jeera powder
¼ tsp citric acid (optional)

EXTRA:
oil to fry ghee to fry

METHOD

1. Mix all the ingredients for the stuffing.

2. Make the dough with enough water to make into a pliable dough and knead for 3-4 minutes. Divide the dough into 4 balls and roll each ball into 10cm diameter on floured board.

3. Divide the stuffing into 4 portions and make ball shape.Place the one portion stuffing onto the rolled dough and fold over the ends and press to enclose the stuffing. Reshape this into a ball and dust the folded edges with a lot of flour.

4. Turn the ball with this folded side resting onto the rolling patlo/board (rolling surface). Using a rolling pin make into parothas/discs to about 16 cm diameter. Repeat with the rest of the dough.

5. Onto a heated griddle or frying pan. Dry cook each side. Turn over the third time and add 3 tbsp oil plus 1 tbsp ghee. Cook.

6. Turn over again and cook. Serve with raita **(p303)**.

SERVES 6 /

Rice and moong salty porridge (Lisi khichdi)

This khichdi is called Lisi khichdi as it is smooth and porridgy. It is different to Chhuti khichdi which has more rice and is fluffy and fragrant

INGREDIENTS

1½ mugs split 'moong daal (also known as 'chilka') (this is the split daal with husks on)
½ mug Basmati rice
2 tsp salt
6 mugs water
6 tbsp butter

METHOD

1. Mix the daal and rice and wash with water a few times. Strain.

2. Add the 6 mugs of water and pre-soak for 2-3 hours.

3. Heat this mixture in a large pan to allow frothing and expanding of the khichdi.

4. Bring to boil removing froth all the time.

5. Then bring to simmer and when the water is nearly absorbed into the mixture, cover and cook on low heat for approximately an hour stirring occasionally gently.

6. The khichdi should be cooked and soft to bite. Stir the mixture into a thick porridge like consistency and add salt and butter.

7. Let the khichdi rest for 5 minutes.

Rice with lentils or daal (Chhuti khichdi)

SERVES 4 /

The moong can be replaced with boiled daals like channa or masoor

Chhuti khichdi is more fluffy and separate compared to Lisi khichdi which is thicker and like a thick porridge

INGREDIENTS

2 tbsp oil

2 medium sticks cinnamon

8 cardamoms

6 cloves

1 tsp cumin/jeera seeds

3 tsp garlic paste

½ tsp turmeric

1 mug washed and strained moong daal pre-soaked in water for 1-2 hours

1½ mug basmati rice washed and pre-soaked in water for 1-2 hours

salt to taste

5 mugs water

METHOD

1. Strain the rice and daal.

2. Heat oil in pan and add the cinnamon, cardamom, cloves and cumin seeds and fry for 2 minutes.

3. Add garlic and turmeric and cook for 30 seconds.

4. Add rice and daal and mix thoroughly and sauté for a minute.

5. Add water and salt to taste. Bring to boil removing any froth that appears.

6. Simmer and cook covered till rice and daal is cooked. May need to stir gently intermittently during cooking.

7. Let the khichdi rest for 5 minutes.

8. Serve with kadhi or aubergine, potato and pea curry or yogurt.

Samosa pastry (par)

Makes 32 pars (pastry envelopes)

INGREDIENTS

SAMOSA PAR:
2½ mugs white/plain flour (a mug is 350ml)
1½ tsp salt
nearly ⅔ mugs water
for the oil and flour mixture to rub between rotlis /chapattis - mix 3 tbsp oil with 2 flat tbsp white flour and mix thoroughly

METHOD

1. Mix the flour and salt and add water slowly to make a pliable dough which is slightly harder than rotli dough. Knead for 3-4 minutes and leave aside for few minutes.

2. Break the dough into 16 small balls and roll each one in palm and flatten into discs.

3. Roll out each disc into rotlis /discs of 10cm diameter each.

4. Rub oil and flour mixture on top of rotli, and place another rotli on top of it and rub likewise. Repeat this process until you have a stack of 4 rotlis. Do not rub this mixture on the top of the very last rotli.

5. So you will have 4 stacks now. Add flour on top and bottom rotli of a stack and roll out till the stack is 22cm in diameter. You will find the bottom rotli to be smaller as you turn. Keep turning over and roll again changing the sides till top and bottom rotlis are almost 22cm in diameter.

6. Heat a frying pan or iron griddle (tawa) and roast the rolled out rotli stack on one side till it just bubbles. Turn over and do the same on the other side. Carefully peel out each thinned rotli and keep it covered. If rotli does not peel try heating it further and hope for the best!

7. Repeat with the rest of the stacks.

8. Cut the uneven edges of the thin peeled rotlis and cut into half by cutting on the diameter.

9. This makes 32 pars or pastry envelopes total.

10. Cover in slightly damp tea towel for use straight away or wrap in cling film first, then foil and then plastic bag and leave in fridge for a day or two or deep-freeze for future use.

11. To defrost leave out for 2-3 hours or so before use.

12. To make the pastry sealing paste, mix white flour with little water at a time till it is quite thick paste. Should look like a thick porridge!

13. To fold the pars/pastry envelopes use the paste and fold in accordance with the diagrams on next page.

Shallow fried flaky flatbread (Parothas-flakey)

A light and flaky version of parothas by my mum Roshan Babul

Makes 6 small parothas

INGREDIENTS

2 mugs plain white flour
½ mug rotli flour medium
2 tsp salt
4 tbsp oil
2 eggs whisked
paste of 2 tsp oil and 2 tsp white/plain flour
12 tbsp oil for cooking or more

METHOD

1. Mix the first 5 ingredients and add enough lukewarm water to make into pliable dough.

2. Knead for 3-4 minutes and let the dough rest for minimum 10 minutes.

3. Roll out a large rotli (circular)as thin as possible on a dusted board and add the oil and flour paste over it and spread all over.

4. Roll the disc into like a Swiss roll and cut into 6 equal sizes. Flatten each piece and flour each side before rolling out.

5. Roll each piece like you would to make a rotli about 15cm in diameter.

6. To cook the parothas, heat a frying pan and toast the parotha on both sides till slightly browned.

7. Flip over and this time add the 2 tbsp oil at the edges and swirl the pan for the oil to be absorbed. Cook till puffy and slightly browned.

8. Turn over and cook for a minute or so adding more oil if needed. Repeat with each parotha.

9. Serve with a curry or yogurt or pickle or raita (p303).

Shallow fried flatbread (Parotha)

Makes 4 parothas

INGREDIENTS

2 cups plain/white flour
1 cup rotli/chapatti flour medium
1 tsp salt
6 tbsp oil
ghee and oil to fry parothas
flour for dusting

METHOD

1. Mix the flour and oil on a big bowl and make into a crumbly mixture. Slowly add lukewarm water and keep mixing and kneading till the dough becomes pliable and is slightly sticky but peels off the fingers when pulled away.

2. Knead for 3-4 minutes and let it rest covered for at least 20 minutes or so.

3. Break dough into 4 portions and make balls. Slightly flatten into discs and coat with flour on both sides. Roll into parothas/discs to 20cm diameter on a dusted board.

4. Cook on a round iron griddle or a pan on one side for a minute or two, then turn and do the same, but when turning third time add 2 tbsp oil and 2 tbsp ghee to the pan and cook. Turn again and cook parotha evenly.

5. Take out of the pan and serve.

SERVES 3-4 /

Spanish saffron rice

This is a well flavoured Spanish rice dish - a vegetarian version of Paella

INGREDIENTS

4 tbsp olive oil

1 large or 2 medium onions finely chopped

3 bay leaves

4 cloves garlic pasted

200g fresh tomatoes chopped

1 green or red pepper or half of each chopped (bell pepper)

½ tsp haldi/turmeric

½ tsp ground black pepper

1 tsp sugar

⅓ tsp saffron soaked in 1 tsp or so of water

1½ mugs water

salt to taste

1 mug Thai fragrant Jasmin rice

METHOD

1. Wash and pre-soak the rice for 1-2 hours. Then drain the rice.

2. Heat olive oil in the saucepan and fry onions till soft but not brown.

3. Fry bay leaves for 2-3 minutes.

4. Add tomatoes, green pepper, garlic, turmeric, sugar, black pepper, soaked saffron with its water. Fry for 3-4 minutes till tomatoes are soft.

5. Add rice and fry for 2-3 minutes. Add water and salt. Bring to boil, cover and simmer very gently till rice is cooked. May need to gently turn the rice once during cooking. Add little water at a time if needed. Take off the heat.

Sweet and savoury egg fried bread (Mitha pau and Tikha pau)

A very hearty breakfast dish to wake one up and make the world go round!

Makes 3 slices of bread

INGREDIENTS

3 slices white bread or seeded bread (seeded bread gives a nice crunch)
4 tsp sugar if making Mitha pau (sweet) or 4 tsp ground black pepper and ½ tsp salt if making Tikha pau (savoury)
4 eggs beaten up
oil for shallow frying

METHOD

1. Add the sugar or black pepper and salt to the beaten eggs and soak the sliced bread in the egg.

2. Shallow fry the soaked bread in minimum oil and cook on both sides.

3. Serve hot.

4. Can add a few drops of vanilla essence to Mitha pau mixture before frying.

Sweet rice (Jardo or Mithu khaau)

A sweet rice dessert dish. Kids love it!

INGREDIENTS

2 mugs basmati rice washed and soaked for half an hour in water and then strained

⅔ mug sugar

60g butter

3 tbsp oil

2 medium sticks cinnamon

5 cardamoms slightly crushed

5 cloves (laving)

1 heaped tsp saffron soaked in 2-3 tsp water

4 mugs water

¼ tsp orange food colouring powder dissolved in 4-5 tsp water

METHOD

1. Heat the oil in a saucepan and add the cinnamon, cardamom and cloves and let it sizzle for about a minute.

2. Add the strained rice and cook for a minute or two.

3. Add the water, colour and saffron and mix.

4. Bring the rice to boil, cover and simmer very gently till nearly cooked.

5. Add the sugar and stir carefully to mix the sugar or the rice will break.

6. Add the butter and mix carefully again gently and cover and cook slowly till rice is cooked.

7. Leave to rest for 5 minutes.

8. Serve garnished with slivered almonds and crushed pistachios.

Tinga-Tinga is a painting style that originated in East Africa. In this painting you will find humour, sarcasm, naivety and plenty of colour. This painting was created using bicycle paint on canvas for the tourists to take back home in a rolled-up packaging. This painting is from my daughter Aalia's collection and I would like to share it with you.

CHUTNEYS, SAUCES, DIPS, PICKLES, DRESSINGS & PASTES

Arrabiata sauce

A spicy tangy sauce that can be used as a pasta sauce

INGREDIENTS

1 x 400g tin tomatoes pulped
3 tbsp oil
2 tbsp tomato paste
4 tsp cajun spice
salt to taste
4 cloves garlic paste
chilli powder to taste

METHOD

1. Heat the oil and add the pulped tomatoes and salt and fry for 5 minutes on simmer.

2. Add tomato paste, garlic, chilli powder and Cajun spice and simmer for another 4 minutes and switch off cooker.

Baba ghanoush

A favourite of my family and at parties

SERVES 8 /

INGREDIENTS

3 large aubergines
3 large garlic cloves crushed
pinch of paprika
juice of 2 large lemons
100ml tahini paste
salt to taste
2 tsp chopped mint or flat leaf parsley
for garnish
3-4 black olives for garnish
1 tbsp olive oil to top up
pitta bread or crudités to serve

METHOD

1. Remove stalks of aubergine and pierce aubergine all over with knife and oil the skin.

2. Using 2 skewers per aubergine at each end rotate the aubergine over the gas flame for 4-5 minutes or till aubergine is cooked inside and smoke is being emitted from the slits. Do the rest of the aubergines.

3. Wash the aubergines under cold water and peel the skin off. Mash the aubergines and leave in a bowl.

4. Add garlic, salt, paprika, lemon juice and tahini paste and blend coarsely.

5. Turn into serving bowl and top with olive oil. Garnish with the mint or parsley and black olives.

6. Serve with pitta bread or crudités.

Black bean sauce

INGREDIENTS

1 tbsp salted and fermented black beans rinsed in water and slightly mashed (can be purchased from Asian food stores)

2 tbsp orange juice or 1 tbsp rice vinegar mixed with 1 tbsp water can use less if you do not want the sharpness

1 large clove finely chopped garlic

1 tbsp light soya sauce

2 tsp sesame seed oil

2 tsp brown sugar

1 tsp finely grated ginger

½ tsp cornflour

METHOD

Mix all the above and add to any stir fries and let it cook for 1-2 minute. Can add more water if sauce is too thick.

This sauce should be enough for one marinated chicken breast plus one green pepper and one medium onion chopped if used in a stir fry.

Carrot pickle in tomato paste chutney
Version 1

INGREDIENTS

4 tbsp oil

1 tbsp crushed coriander (dhana) seeds

4 tsp tomato paste

2 tsp haldi (turmeric)

2 tsp dhana/coriander powder

2 tsp jeera powder

½ tsp red chilli powder

salt to taste

4 cloves minced garlic

lemon juice to taste

2 medium sized carrots peeled and thinly sliced

little water to bring to a medium consistency

METHOD

1. Heat the oil and add the crushed coriander seeds and cook for half a minute.

2. Add the tomato paste and cook for a minute. Switch off heat.

3. Add haldi, dhana powder, jeera powder, garlic and red chilli powder and salt to taste.

4. Add a little bit of water to bring to medium consistency with the lemon juice to taste.

5. Let the mixture cool and add enough thinly sliced carrots to coat with the mixture.

6. Adjust salt to taste.

Carrot pickle
by Navroz Shamji - Version 2

This recipe was shared with me by Navroz Shamji, my husband's cousin's wife

INGREDIENTS

3 large carrots cleaned and cut into long bite size pieces
2 tbsp tomato paste
2 tbsp tomato ketchup
4 tbsp oil
½ tsp citric acid
½ tsp salt
4 tbsp oil
3 tbsp achar masala (available from Indian shops)
½ tsp garlic
½ tsp ginger paste

METHOD

Mix all-need no cooking!

Carrot pickle
Version 3

My husband Amin's masi/aunt, Amina Meghji, gave him a cooking lesson on this recipe. It is a hit wherever we take it or serve it!

INGREDIENTS

8-10 medium sized carrots, washed and cut into 4cm -6cm slices and salted with 30ml salt and dried over 2 days (carrot slices evenly spread on cloth in a tray) optional - 3 small raw mangoes cut into slices and stone removed together with any fibrous bits attached to the mango stone and cut as above for carrots and same instructions followed as for carrots

9 cloves of garlic and made into paste

a quarter tsp haldi/turmeric

1 tsp of chili powder

8 tbsp tomato paste

1-2 green chili longitudinally cut

1½ tsp dhana/coriander powder

100ml oil

METHOD

1. Gently heat oil to medium heat and add garlic paste. Fry it for half minute and then add haldi.

2. Take the pan off from heat and add tomato paste, dhana powder, chili powder and green chili. Stir and put back pan on heat gently cook for 2-3 minutes.

3. Let the mixture cool for 10 minutes.

4. Add to the above sauce the carrots and mangoes prepared and stir until sauce is evenly spread in with the rest of carrots and mangoes.

Serve with your dish be it lamb akni etc.

Carrot and mango pickle
by Gulshan Babul Version 4

My dear mum Gulshan was immensely popular for making this quick pickle

INGREDIENTS

3 green chillies sliced lengthwise
5 small raw mangoes de-stoned and fibrous tissue around stone removed, and flesh cut into thin slices with skin still on (available from Indian stores. Make sure they are raw. The small mangoes have soft stones which can be picked out easily. If using large mangoes, the stone will be harder to extract, and therefore you will need to carefully peel around the stone)
5 large carrots peeled and cut into julienne or matchsticks shape and size
3 tbsp tomato paste
3 tbsp tomato ketchup
6 tablespoons vinegar (preferably the clear type)
1 tbsp salt
½ teaspoon red chilli powder or less optional

METHOD

Mix all the ingredients into a large bowl and the pickle is ready to eat. Can be stored in the refigerator for a week or so.

Coconut chutney

Makes nearly 2 mugs chutney

INGREDIENTS

1 mug desiccated coconut preferebly fine (make sure it is not sweetened coconut)
1 tsp salt or to taste
juice of 2 limes/lemons
15 sprigs of washed coriander leaves chopped
1-2 green chillies chopped
½ mug water

METHOD

1. Soak the coconut in the ½ mug water for 15-20 minutes.

2. Then mix all the ingredients, and blend.

French dressing with lemon juice

Makes 400ml dressing

INGREDIENTS

150ml lemon juice
250ml olive oil
1 tbsp salt
1 tbsp sugar
1 tbsp Dijon mustard

METHOD

Mix all the ingredients into a jar and shake vigorously till the mixture is a fine emulsion.

Shake the jar every time before serving.

French dressing with vinegar

Makes 400ml

INGREDIENTS

150ml vinegar
250ml olive oil
1 tbsp salt
1 tbsp sugar
1 tbsp Dijon mustard

METHOD

Mix all the ingredients into a jar and shake vigorously till the mixture is a fine emulsion.

Shake the jar every time before serving.

Ganthia chutney
by Amin Shamji

Makes 15 tbsp of chutney

INGREDIENTS

100g Phulli ganthia or Fafra ganthia
(available from Indian stores)
2 green chillies finely chopped
8-10 stalks fresh coriander chopped
1 tsp sugar
4 tbsp lemon juice
130ml water
¼ tsp salt
pinch of green food colouring powder

METHOD

1. Blend the first 4 ingredients in a blender to a nearly fine mixture.

2. Add the lemon juice and salt and stir in the water to make it into a thick consistency paste. Add green food colouring powder. You can add more water to make the chutney less thick.

Lovely with fried mogo and bhajias.

Garlic, tomato and chilli oil chutney

Makes 8 tbsp chutney

INGREDIENTS

3 dried big red chillies thinly sliced
10 cloves garlic finely chopped
8 tbsp oil
4 tbsp tomato paste
½ tsp salt

METHOD

1. Heat oil to medium heat and throw in garlic and cook till garlic just starts to get light brown.

2. Add chillies and cook for ½ minute.

3. Add tomato paste and salt and cook for 3-4 minutes.

4. Serve with khichi or parotha **(p275)** or dhokra **(p100)** or puri **(p259)**.

Green chutney (Gujarati style)
by Jyotsna Samji

Makes 10 tbsp chutney

This is a tasty chutney that my dear friend Jyotsna is very popular for. Scoop it with ganthias, and feast

INGREDIENTS

1 bunch coriander coarsely chopped
2 green chillies chopped
1 tsp salt
juice of one lemon
1 tbsp sugar
4 tsp crushed ganthia
4 tsp crushed raw peanuts
½ green /bell pepper roughly chopped

METHOD

Mix all and blend adding very little water
only if needed.

Green chutney and raita

INGREDIENTS

GREEN CHUTNEY:
3 bunches coriander cleaned and chopped with stalks and leaves
1 whole bulb garlic peeled and chopped
10 green chillies, roughly chopped
juice of 6 limes
2 mugs water
6 tsp salt

RAITA:
500ml yogurt
½ cucumber

You can freeze the green chutney for use later by placing the chutney into an ice cube tray, and leaving to freeze. When frozen, you can remove each cube and store in a container in the freezer

METHOD

GREEN CHUTNEY:
To make this chutney, blend all ingredients listed under *GREEN CHUTNEY* in the ingredients section

RAITA:
Add 2-3 tablespoons of the green chutney to the yogurt, plus a little salt. Grate the cucumber, and remove any excess water by squeezing the cucumber using your hands. Add the mushy cucumber to the yogurt and serve.

Guacamole
by Aalia Shamji

Lovely recipe by my daughter Aalia

INGREDIENTS

1 ripe avocado medium size-semi-mashed
juice of ½ lime
¼ tsp salt
2-3 drops of tabasco sauce (or ½ green chilli minced if tabasco is unavailable)
1 clove garlic minced
5 sprigs of coriander finely chopped
¼ medium red onion finely minced
3-4 cherry tomatoes quartered

METHOD

Mix all.

Kokum chutney

Makes 8 tbsp chutney

INGREDIENTS

60 pods of kokum (very similar to tamarind and available from Asian stores)
6 tbsp water

METHOD

1. Soak the pods in enough water and slide your finger in the cut up centre to remove any grit.

2. Blend the cleaned pods with the water.

3. Serve with tikha chilla (**p68**).

Lemon achar
by Mrs Rohila

I once worked with a lovely lady called Mrs Rohila. She was originally from my hometown, Tanga, and we spent many hours reminiscing about the good old days. She also shared with me this lovey sweet and sour lemon pickle recipe

INGREDIENTS

1.5kg or 40 yellow limes from Indian shop top and tailed, cut up, flesh removed. Flesh chopped very fine and rind cut into very thin slices
500g sugar
4 tsp salt
1 tsp black ground pepper
2 tsp haldi/turmeric
6 cloves

METHOD

1. Mix all the ingredients in a clean bowl.

2. Transfer to a clean and sterile bottle (clean the bottle with kettle boiled and cooled water and wipe with clean kitchen towel).

3. Leave out for a week or so and keep rotating and mixing the contents in the bottle.

4. Store in fridge.

5. Pickle should be ready to eat in another 3 weeks or so after the rind has softened.

Makes two large bottles

Lemon pickle (Limbu, garmar, amba hardar ane adu)

INGREDIENTS

1.5kg small fragrant yellow limes (from Indian shops)
1kg amba hardar (root vegetable available from Indian stores)
30 cloves (laving)
125g guvar/flat bean top and tailed and washed (optional)
1kg garmar (root vegetable available from Indian stores)
500g ginger
turmeric enough to coat all the cut ingredients
250ml salt

METHOD

1. Pre-soak the garmar in slightly salted water for 3-4 hours or overnight and then scrape the skin. The skin can get dark upon scraping. Cut to small lengths of 7cm. Keep in water as it gets dark. Perhaps do this vegetable last.

2. Peel and cut ginger to small discs and coat in salt and turmeric.

3. Cut lemons into quarters and add 250ml salt, and enough turmeric to coat each lemon.

4. Squeeze some lemons to release juice.

5. Scrape the amba hardar and cut into small bite-size pieces. Coat the amba hardar and garmar with sufficient turmeric.

6. Into a large bowl, mix the garmar, lemons, amba hardar, guvar, cloves and ginger.

7. Pour the lemon juice on top and mix every few hours at room temperature. Cover the bowl when not mixing.

8. Source two large sterile bottles. Transfer the mixture into the bottles and leave in the fridge for two days. If it appears the mixture is not entirely covered by liquid, add more lemon juice as approximate.

9. Every few days, for 3-4 weeks, shake the bottle and turn the bottle upside down and upright again. Eat when pickle is soft.

Mango and jaggery sweet pickle (Gaur keri nu anthru)

My mother-in-law's specialty

INGREDIENTS

14 small raw mangoes stone removed and fibre around it removed. Cut to small bite size pieces with skin still on. Add 3 tsp salt and 1 tsp haldi (turmeric) and leave to dry on a tray with cloth underneath for 2-3 days

6 large carrots cleaned and cut into long bite size pieces. Add 3 tsp salt and leave to dry on tray with cloth underneath for 2-3 days. Do not over-dry the carrots

WAGAR OR TARKA OR TEMPERING:

4 tsp variari (fennel seeds)

10 elchi (cardamoms)

5 large stick taj (cinnamon)

4 tsp dhana seeds (coriander seeds)

½ mug oil

1 mug gaur (jaggery) cut into very small pieces

4 tbsp Achar powder (bought in Indian shops)

METHOD

1. When carrots and mangoes are ready do wagar/tempering as below.

2. Do tempering by heating oil in a large saucepan and add the cinnamon, cardamoms, fennel and coriander seeds and fry for 2-3 minutes.

3. Let the oil cool slightly and add the gaur and let it melt.

4. When the mixture is still warm add the Achar powder and the carrots and mangoes and stir. Let it cool.

5. Cover and leave outside for 2-3 days. Store in bottle and leave in the fridge.

SERVES 4 /

Maru style chutney
by Gulbanu Manji

A lovely version of Maru's style chutney by my sister-in-law Gulbanu Manji, also known as 'Gulibai'

INGREDIENTS & METHOD

1 green pepper (bell pepper)
1 red pepper (bell pepper)
½ cucumber
1 large carrot
juice of two lemons
salt to taste
1 tbsp tomato ketchup (be careful as more ketchup will make it too sweet)
coarsely chop all the veg and blend without ketchup
add ketchup and mix well
have with crispy bhajias

Mixed vegetable pickle (Katakia nu anthru)
by Roshan Babul

I used to love this pickle as a child. So I asked my biological mum Roshan Babul, who resides in Edmonton (Canada), to guide me over the phone in making this pickle. After a few moments, eureka! I finally got the recipe written down. It is a fusion of Chinese and Indian influences

INGREDIENTS

500g carrots peeled and cut into very small cubed pieces

500g white cabbage very thinly sliced or cauliflower washed and cut into very small florets

25 top and tailed (if necessary) French beans or fine beans washed and cut into very small slices (do not use runner beans as these are quite hard)

6 green chillies cut into thin slices

4 tbsp semi grinded rai /mustard seeds or readymade split rai/mustard

700ml vinegar (plus 2 tbsp extra)

8 tsp salt

4 tsp sugar

3 tbsp water

1 tbsp haldi/turmeric

METHOD

1. Mix all the vegetables and chillies in a bowl and add 4 tsp salt, haldi and 2 tbsp vinegar. Place in a sieve and let the juices drip out. Leave for 2 hours.

2. In a saucepan add the 700ml vinegar, 3 tbsp water and 4 tsp sugar and heat and boil for 3-4 minutes. Then leave to cool.

3. After the 2 hours place the vegetables in a bowl and add the split mustard seeds and 4 tsp salt and mix.

4. Add these vegetables into a sterilised jar (by cleaning inside of jar with boiled and slightly cooled kettle water and drying the inside thoroughly with a kitchen towel).

5. Top up the vegetables with cooled vinegar mixture and shake the jar.

6. Leave outside and shake the jar routinely (to make sure pickle does not go off) for 2-3 days till vegetables become softish. Then refrigerate and shake jar occasionally. The vinegar will be sharp to begin with but will mellow with time.

Pesto

INGREDIENTS

4 tbsp toasted pine nuts

3 garlic cloves chopped

a large bunch of basil leaves at least 50g cut

salt to taste - caution, parmesan can add saltiness too

120ml virgin olive oil

3 tbsp freshly grated parmesan

pinch of black pepper

METHOD

Blend all without the parmesan. Add parmesan at end.

Raita

INGREDIENTS

l litre natural yogurt
10 stalks coriander chopped finely
1 clove garlic finely minced
half a green chilli finely minced
(optional)
a quarter grated and squeezed
cucumber (to take excess water out)
salt to taste

METHOD

Mix all and let it cool in the fridge.

Serve with pitta bread or as a dip.

SERVES 4-5 /

Schezuan haka sauce to make various dishes

A sauce to give a Chinese twist to various dishes

INGREDIENTS

50ml of Schezuan Sauce (p302)
2 tbsp tomato paste
4 tbsp oil
4 cloves garlic pasted
4 tbsp sesame seed oil
4 tbsp dark soya sauce
1 tbsp sugar
6 tbsp water
20 sprigs coriander chopped

METHOD

1. Fry the tomato paste and garlic in hot oil for a minute.

2. Add the rest of the ingredients except coriander and cook for 2-3 minutes.

3. When cool add the coriander.

NOTES:
For serving 4-5 people.

1. To make Schezuan Haka mogo deep fry 25 sticks 10cm long x 2.5cm thick of boiled mogo, remove and add the above quantity of Schezuan Haka sauce to the mogo. Mix. Place the mogo in an oven dish and bake in hot oven for 20-30 minutes till mogo crispens on the outside.

2. To make Schezuan Haka Paneer marinate 2 slabs of cubed paneer 2.5cm long by 1 cm thick (total around 400g) in 4 cloves of pasted garlic and 4 tbsp dark soya sauce for at least 2-3 hours. Deep fry the paneer till it browns on the edges. Remove from heat. Stir fry 3-4 green peppers /bell peppers cut to bite size pieces in a wok in little oil. Remove and mix with Paneer and Schezuan Haka sauce of above quantity.

3. Mix the above Schezuan Haka sauce quantity with appropriate quantity of stir fried rice with vegetables or noodles with vegetables.

Schezuan sauce

Makes 300ml

INGREDIENTS

15 small red Thai birds eye chillies very finely minced
3 tbsp finely chopped garlic
4 tsp grated ginger
2 tbsp finely chopped onions
250ml water
1 tbsp cornflour mixed with 2 tbsp water
1 tbsp vinegar
1 tbsp sugar
3 tbsp oil
salt to taste

METHOD

1. Heat the oil in a saucepan and add garlic, ginger, chillies ,onions and cook for ½ a minute.

2. Add water and then add cornflour paste and mix. Add vinegar, sugar and salt and bring to boil.

3. Leave to cool. This sauce can be frozen.

Taco sauce

Used in fajitas, nachos etc

INGREDIENTS

1 x 400g tin tomatoes pulped
3 tbsp oil
2 tbsp tomato paste
4 tsp Cajun spice
salt to taste

METHOD

1. Heat the oil and add the pulped tomatoes and salt and fry for 5 minutes on simmer.

2. Add tomato paste and Cajun spice and simmer for another 4 minutes and switch off cooker.

Tamarind (Ambli) sauce

Makes 750ml Ambli sauce

INGREDIENTS

200g packet of dried tamarind/ambli
800ml of water
300ml of boiling water
plus another 100ml of boiling water
1 tbsp salt
1 tsp chilli powder
4 tbsp sugar or more for extra sweetness
1 tbsp roasted jeera powder

METHOD

1. Tear the dried ambli into pieces and place in a saucepan with 800ml of water.

2. Bring to boil and let it simmer for 30 minutes periodically using masher to soften the pulp.

3. Take it off the heat and sieve in a drainer/sieve and press to maximise sieving of pulp.

4. Place the strained pulp back into the saucepan with 300ml boiling water and repeat the process.

5. Place the strained pulp into the pan with 100ml boiling water and repeat the process.

6. Discard the pulp now and bring all the total liquids to boil in another pan.

7. Add the salt, sugar, chilli powder and roasted jeera powder and stir to make sure it is all dissolved.

8. Let the mixture cool. The yield is less than the liquid put in due to loss from boiling and sieving.

9. Can be left in the fridge for 2 months or can be frozen.

To the ambli sauce one can add fresh chopped coriander and onions before serving with items like kachori, samosas and fried mogo etc.

Thai dressing

INGREDIENTS

Juice of two limes
1 tbsp honey
2 tsp sesame seed oil
1 tbsp grated ginger

METHOD

Mix all.

Note:
Non-vegetarians can add
1-2 tsp fish sauce/Nam pla

Thai green curry paste

INGREDIENTS

6 medium hot green chillis or less
2 stalks lemon grass-peel the bottom of stem and chop the soft bits inside and use that
2 tablespoons coriander stalks and leaves
1 tsp jeera powder
2.5cm ginger pasted
2 shallots finely chopped
1 tsp coriander (dhana) powder
2 tsp garlic paste
1 tsp black peppercorns
1 tsp zest of lemon
1 tsp lime juice

METHOD

Blend all.

Thai Massaman curry paste

INGREDIENTS

1 tsp coriander/dhana powder
½ tsp jeera powder
8 fresh red chillies or less
4 shallots chopped
2 tsp garlic paste
1 tsp ginger paste
2 lemon grass peeled and the soft bits chopped and used, discard hard bits
10 black peppercorns
½ tsp clove powder
1 tsp salt
1 tsp sugar
4 coriander stalks
1 tsp haldi or turmeric
2 tbsp oil

METHOD

Blend it all.

Note:
Non-vegetarians can add
½ tsp shrimp paste-optional

Thai red curry paste

INGREDIENTS

1 tsp dhana/coriander powder
½ tsp jeera powder
8 fresh red chillies or less
4 shallots chopped
2 tsp garlic paste
1 tsp ginger paste
2 lemon grass peeled and the soft bits chopped and used, discard hard bits
3 kaffir lime leaves fresh or 6 of dried ones (veins removed)
10 black peppercorns
a good pinch of cinnamon powder
1 tsp salt
4 coriander stalks
1 tsp haldi or turmeric
2 tbsp oil

METHOD

Blend it all.

Note:
Non-vegetarians can add
½ tsp shrimp paste-optional

Tikha ganthia chutney (Tanga style)

Makes about 4 tbsp chutney

INGREDIENTS

4 tbsp (heaped) tikha ganthia blended coarsely
2 tsp oil
1 tsp haldi/turmeric
¼ tsp green chilli finely chopped
¼ tsp red chilli powder
2 tsp sugar
½ tsp ajma/carom seeds/ajwain
juice of half a lime
½ tsp salt
water as required

METHOD

1. Heat the oil and throw in the carom seeds and cook for 30 seconds. Switch off heat and add haldi and stir.

2. Mix the rest of the ingredients except water and add the above to the mixture.

3. Slowly add water to make the chutney to a thickish consistency.

4. Serve with fried mogo or any type of bhajias or pakodas.

Tomato and onion chutney

INGREDIENTS

6 medium tomatoes
1 medium onion
20 coriander stalks
2 green chillies
juice of 2 limes or lemons
salt

METHOD

1. Roughly chop the first 4 ingredients and add the salt and lemon /lime juice. Do not add any water.

2. Blend coarsely and serve.

Can be used with bhajias, dhokri, BBQ food, etc.

Tomato chutney - Indian style

INGREDIENTS

1kg ripe tomatoes very finely chopped
4 green chillies finely chopped
8 cloves garlic finely chopped
3 tbsp oil
¼ bunch fresh coriander finely chopped
stalks and leaves separated
1 tsp chilli powder
salt to taste

METHOD

1. Cook the garlic in medium hot oil in a large saucepan for ½ minute.

2. Add green chillies and cook for a minute.

3. Add tomatoes, salt, red chilli powder and coriander stalks and cook for 5 minutes.

4. Add coriander leaves and leave to cool.

Tzaziki

A Middle Eastern yogurt, cucumber and mint dip

INGREDIENTS

250ml Greek yogurt
3 tbsp lemon juice
6 tbsp finely chopped mint leaves
½ cucumber grated and water squeezed out
2 large cloves of garlic pasted
salt to taste

METHOD

Mix all the ingredients.

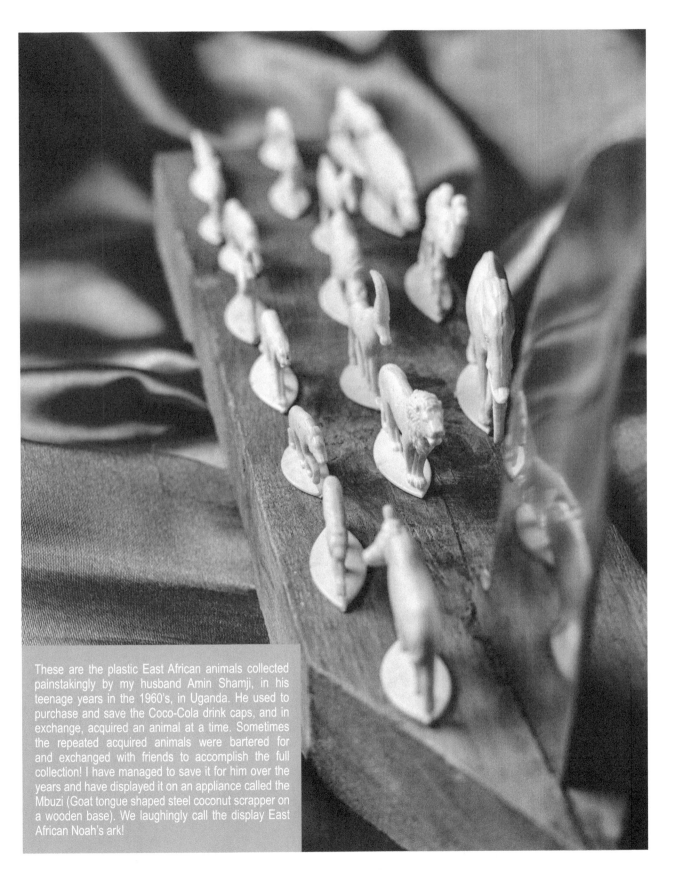

These are the plastic East African animals collected painstakingly by my husband Amin Shamji, in his teenage years in the 1960's, in Uganda. He used to purchase and save the Coco-Cola drink caps, and in exchange, acquired an animal at a time. Sometimes the repeated acquired animals were bartered for and exchanged with friends to accomplish the full collection! I have managed to save it for him over the years and have displayed it on an appliance called the Mbuzi (Goat tongue shaped steel coconut scrapper on a wooden base). We laughingly call the display East African Noah's ark!

These family heirlooms were bought in India in the 1950s by my mother-in-law. My father-in-law's name Ismail Shamji has been etched onto these appliances in Gujarati"

SWEETS & DESSERTS

SERVES 8-10 /

Bulghar wheat dessert (Lapsi)

An Indian bulghar wheat dessert best served warm

INGREDIENTS

1 cup butter

2 cups coarse lapsi or bulghar wheat

2 cups milk

3 cups water (add a little more if required)

1¾ cups sugar

3 tbsp fennel seeds

¾ cup sliced almonds

2 tsp ground cardamom/elchi seeds

2 tsp saffron

2 tsp ground nutmeg

½ cup dessicated coconut (rehydrated with water and then excess water removed)

a pinch of orange food colour powder

METHOD

1. Heat the butter in a saucepan and add fennel seeds and fry for ½ minute.

2. Add lapsi and sauté till it becomes medium brown but not burnt (may take 5-6 minutes).

3. Add water and milk. Bring to boil and simmer for 5 minutes.

4. Add sugar and cook for 5 minutes.

5. Add almonds, ground cardamom, nutmeg, saffron, food colour and rehydrated coconut and cook for another 6-8 minute on low heat.

6. Switch off cooker. Cover with lid. Let it rest 10 minutes.

7. Serve.

Faludo/Creamy mousse - Ismaili style

SERVES 12 /

INGREDIENTS

12gm china grass washed and soaked for 10 minutes (available from Indian and Asian stores) (Exact measure is very important)
1400ml semi skimmed or 2% milk
410g evaporated milk (preferably Nestle's Carnation brand)
400g condensed milk (preferably Nestle's Carnation brand)
½ tsp ground cardamom seeds
3-4 pinches of saffron
Ground almonds and pistachios enough to garnish

METHOD

1. Drain the china grass and boil in a large saucepan containing 250ml of water.

2. Stir until the china grass has dissolved (some bits may remain undissolved).

3. Add the milk and boil for 15 minutes stirring all the time.

4. Add the evaporated and condensed milk into the pan and stir continuously for another 8 minutes or so.

5. Remove from heat and let it cool slightly.

6. Strain the mixture into a heatproof bowl and discard the strained bits.

7. Add cardamom seeds and mix gently.

8. When setting, add the ground almonds, pistachios and saffron onto the Faludo.

9. Keep in a cool place or refrigerate and serve cold.

SERVES 8 /

Mango milky ice cream (Mango kulfi)

A delicious dessert after a hot spicy meal on a hot summer's day

INGREDIENTS

600ml fresh double cream

350ml mango pulp (available in tins from Indian stores)

4 tbsp runny honey

8 metal receptacles/cone shaped containers 150ml each

METHOD

Mix the ingredients thoroughly and transfer into the 8 containers and freeze.

Milky vermicelli (Doodh wari sev or Kheer khurmo)

My mother-in-law used to make this dish especially for her grandson Naadim

SERVES 4 /

INGREDIENTS

500ml water
⅔ cup sugar
¼ tsp yellow food colour or less
70g butter
250g sev/vermicelli-normally comes coiled (vermicelli-do not use the very fine hair like vermicelli) Break to very small pieces
4 big pinches of saffron
½ tsp cardamom powder
4 big pinches nutmeg powder
½ cup evaporated milk
1 tbsp custard powder added to 500ml of milk
plus another 200ml evaporated milk
finely grated pistachios and almond slivers to garnish

METHOD

1. Boil sugar, water and food colour to light syrup for about 2 minutes.

2. In another saucepan, melt butter and add broken vermicelli/sev and sauté in butter on medium heat until light golden brown in colour.

3. Add the light syrup, saffron, cardamom and nutmeg to the vermicelli.

4. Continue cooking on a low heat covered for some time until almost all the water has evaporated. This can take up to ½ hour or more.

5. Add the ½ cup evaporated milk just before end of cooking time.

6. Add the 500ml of milk with the custard powder to the above ready sev and cook on low heat for 3-4 minutes. Then add 200 ml evaporated milk and keep stirring for 3-4 minutes and serve hot.

7. Garnish with pistachios and almond slivers.

Peanut and Almond brittle (Jugu and almond paak/chikki)

I have had the commercial versions, but nothing can beat this homemade version

Makes 40 pieces of 7.5cm X 7.5cm

INGREDIENTS

1½kg small red peanuts roasted and skinned (roasting instructions below in notes. Can use Almonds. See notes below)
1kg jaggery or gaur broken into pieces
1 tbsp oil
2 oiled oven trays 30 x 35cm
2 mugs oiled from outside to press the hot mixture on the trays

METHOD

1. Heat the jaggery in the oil in a large saucepan, stirring continuously until all the melted jaggery is medium to dark brown and just begins to smoke. This may take 5-7 minutes or even more.

2. Quickly add the peanuts and mix thoroughly as the mixture begins to set.

3. Very quickly transfer this mixture onto the 2 oiled trays.

4. Using a mug that is oiled on the outside press the mixture to spread evenly on the trays.

5. Quickly then cut 20 square pieces from each tray using a sharp knife. Make sure the mixture is still warm when doing it otherwise the mixture will crumble.

6. Separate the pieces when cooled.

NB to cook the peanuts, bake in an oven at 200C/400F in two trays 30 x 35cm for 30 minutes or so (depending upon your oven) turning the peanuts occasionally. Let the peanuts semi-cool and rub the peanuts in palms of hand to remove the skin. Toss the tray in air gently and discard the skins.

One can substitute peanuts for the same weight of ALMONDS with skin on. Follow the same baking method but do not remove the skin and follow as above.

SERVES 8 /

Rice pudding (Kheer)

The kewra water gives this sweet dish a Pakistani flavour, whereas the rose water gives it more of an East African taste

INGREDIENTS

1 mug (350ml) arborio rice or risotto rice or short grain rice or paella rice
3 litres milk
100g butter
½ mug sugar (or less to taste)
4 pinches saffron
6 tbsp kewra water or 2 tsp rose essence (essence is stronger than rose water)

METHOD

1. Heat the milk in a heavy-duty large saucepan.

2. Stir rice and cook till about an hour uncovered. Keep stirring to stop mixture burning at bottom.

3. When rice is all cooked add the sugar and butter and cook for 5 minutes stirring.

4. Switch off the cooker and add the kewra water or rose essence and saffron.

5. Serve with puris or on its own hot or cold.

Semolina Pudding (Seero or Sooji halwa)

SERVES 20 /
Or for 160 as offering for religious event

The following is my mother-in-law's famed seero recipe. Seero is a traditional Ismaili offering served as part of religious ceremonies in the Ismaili community. It has now been re-mastered by my son and her grandson Naadim - a budding chef!

INGREDIENTS

1kg semolina course
1kg sugar
2 litres milk
1¼ litres water
1kg butter
2 tsp saffron strands
pinch of yellow food colouring

METHOD

1. Melt the butter. Cook the semolina in the butter and stir till the semolina starts going light brown and you can smell the cooked semolina. If you undercook the semolina the seero will be sticky and if overcooked then it will be crumbly and tasteless. Therefore this bit is very important.

2. Meanwhile warm the milk, water, sugar and the saffron in a saucepan but do not boil. It is to dissolve the sugar.

3. Add the warmed milk mixture to the semolina (take care as it may splutter. It is a good idea to use a deep saucepan and a long handled stirrer) .It will form a lumpy mass. Keep stirring.

4. Add the yellow colouring and keep stirring and cook for 4-5 minutes.

5. Switch off the cooker and close the lid on the saucepan and let the seero rest for 5 minutes for all the semolina grains to fluff up.

6. Serve sprinkled with crushed almonds and pistachio nuts.

SERVES 4 /

Sweet vermicelli (Sev)

A traditional buttery pasta-like dessert. Also served at festivities and weddings. Moreish. Hmmm

INGREDIENTS

500ml water
⅔ cup sugar
¼ tsp yellow food colour or less
70g butter
250g sev/vermicelli - normally comes coiled (vermicelli - do not use the very fine hair like vermicelli) break to very small pieces
4 big pinches of saffron
½ tsp cardamom powder
4 big pinches nutmeg powder
½ cup evaporated milk
finely grated pistachios and almond slivers to garnish

METHOD

1. Boil sugar, water and food colour to light syrup for about 2 minutes.

2. In another saucepan, melt butter and add broken vermicelli/sev and sauté in butter on medium heat until light golden brown in colour.

3. Add the light syrup, saffron, cardamom and nutmeg to the vermicelli.

4. Continue cooking on a low heat covered for some time until almost all the water has evaporated. This can take up to ½ hour or more.

5. Add evaporated milk just before end of cooking time.

6. Serve garnished with the almonds and pistachios.

Thick yogurt dessert (Shrikhand)

A very Gujarati sweet starter

INGREDIENTS

500g Greek yogurt (can use normal yogurt but it will yield less as there is more water but can still use below quantities)
3 tbsp sugar
¼ tsp ground cardamom/elchi
⅛ tsp ground nutmeg/jaifer
2 tbsp chopped almonds and pistachios (slightly roasted tastes good)
10 strands saffron/kesar

METHOD

1. Strain the yogurt by placing it in the centre of a muslin cloth. Tie opposite corners and put a long ladle between the knots to make it like a hammock. Position the ends of the ladle between the handles of a tall saucepan and let the water drip out. May take minimum 1½ hours. The more it stand the more it drips.

2. Take the strained yogurt (curd) out of the cloth and place in a bowl. Add the sugar and mix well, and tie it up in the muslin cloth as before, and position as before to drip. The sugared water will drip but only do it for ½ hour or so.

3. Place the sugared curd into a bowl and add the cardamom, nutmeg, and saffron and mix well.

4. Decorate with the almonds and pistachio.

5. Enjoy with puris.

Normal yogurt will yield ¼ volume for shrikhand only. Greek yogurt will be a bit more.

Passion fruit juice, a landmark of East African drinks!"

DRINKS & BEVERAGES

SERVES 6 /

Cardamom tea (Elaichi chai)

INGREDIENTS

1 litre water
1 litre semi skimmed milk
7 heaped teaspoons of crushed cardamom powder (whole pods of cardamom powdered)
7 teabags
50ml of evaporated milk

METHOD

1. Boil the water, cardamom powder and teabags for 3-4 minutes.

2. Then add the milk and let it boil for another 5 minutes or so. The tea can overflow very easily at this stage so reduce heat if that happens.

3. Add the evaporated milk and re-boil for 30 seconds.

4. Switch off the cooker and strain the tea into a teapot.

5. Serve with lots of sugar. This tea has to be quite sweet.

Lemon ice tea

Makes one full mug

I had this tea in India on a hot blazing day and it was most refreshing. What a wonderful discovery!

INGREDIENTS & METHOD

Brew one teabag in a mug with minimum boiling water

remove the teabag

add 8-10 tsp of sugar (yes that is the right amount!) and mix thoroughly

add juice of 1½ limes

top up the mug with crushed ice and water and mix

pour into a glass and drink with a straw

Mojito mocktail

Makes one tall slim glass 250ml drink

INGREDIENTS

½ lime-cut into 4 slices
2 tbsp brown sugar
25 fresh mint leaves chopped
sparkling water or soda water 250ml
2-3 cubes ice crushed

METHOD

Pound the mint leaves, lime and sugar in a pestle and mortar. When quite pounded add to the glass. Add the sparkling water and 2-3 cubes crushed ice.

Serve with a straw on a very sunny and hot day!

(For a short-cut version pound the mint leaves and lime in pestle and mortar and add to the glass. Top up with sparkling lemonade and ice).

(Also, you can make up the syrup by dissolving two volumes of sugar to one volume of water and boil for a few minutes. Then store in fridge. Make the drink by pounding the mint and lime, add the sparkling water and top up with syrup (to taste. Add the ice).

Moroccan tea

Makes 4 moroccan teacups 150ml each

My first experience of this wonderful drink was in Marrakesh, Morocco. The orange flower water added to this tea gives it its special oumph!

INGREDIENTS

50 garden mint leaves or equivalent pulped in pestle and mortar (or 20 mint leaves from Turkish shops)
2 drops orange flower water (not orange essence) of good quality (optional)
⅓ tsp loose tea leaves or 1 teabag
6 tsp sugar

METHOD

Preheat the teapot with boiling water. Discard the water. Add the mint leaves and tea leaves into the pot and pour in 600ml of boiling water. Let it brew for 2-3 minutes. Add the orange flower water and sugar and stir. Leave for 2-3 minute and pour tea from a height into the cup to get the froth.

SERVES 1 /

Rose and almond mocktail

INGREDIENTS

10ml rose syrup (preferably Rubicon rose syrup)

10ml almond syrup (preferably Natura almond syrup - available from specialist Italian shops)

160ml soda water or fizzy water

2-3 ice cubes

few pomegranate seeds to garnish

METHOD

Mix all and serve.

SERVES 1 /

Salted yogurt drink (Chhaas or Lassi)

A cold glass of Lassi cools the mouth and settles the stomach after a spicy meal

INGREDIENTS

125ml of yogurt
125ml of water
¼ tsp roasted jeera powder grinded
salt to taste

METHOD

Mix all and blend and serve cold.

Rose milkshake (Ismaili Sherbet)
by Naadim Shamji

SERVES 300 /
Makes 300 serving of 150ml each

This is an authentic East African Ismaili Khoja celebratory drink with rose flavoring. It is also one of my son Naadim's most popular recipes! He made sherbet for a large religious celebration in Kent (UK), for his cousin Aliza Vellani's wedding in Vancouver (Canada) and his cousin Aleem Jaffer's wedding in Edmonton (Canada)! At each event the drink was a super hit! I was an immensely proud mum and his assistant, trying extremely hard not to interfere!

INGREDIENTS

27 litres of whole milk
25 evaporated milk cans (390ml each)
8 condensed milk cans (290ml each) (use 10 cans to make it sweeter)
3 tubs of Walls vanilla ice cream (2 litre containers each)
120ml vanilla essence
50ml rose essence
6ml red food colouring (10ml to make it pinker)
Takmaria (basil seeds) soaked in water as required (recipe right)
Badam pista (almond and pistachio coarsely ground) as required (recipe right)

METHOD

1 Mix all and keep really cold except badam pista and takmaria

2 Serve with badam pista ground and takmaria as required by each person

TAKMARIA FOR 120 PEOPLE:
Use 1 tsp swollen takmaria (basil seeds) for each serving.

Not everyone likes takmaria in sherbet.

To make swollen takmaria add 800ml water to 20 tsp takmaria seeds and soak for 10 minutes or so. Makes 120 tsp swollen takmaria.

BADAM PISTA FOR 120 PEOPLE:
Use 1 tsp badam pista for each serving.

50g almonds (badam) whole and 25g (pista) pistachio whole and shelled makes 200ml when ground. The ratio is 2:1 of almonds and pista by weight.

200ml of ground badam pista yields 40 tsp.

Need 600ml of badam pista for 120 tsp (1 tsp per person).

SPICES

Cajun spice

INGREDIENTS	METHOD
1 tbsp garlic powder 1 tbsp onion powder 2 tsp white pepper 2 tsp black pepper 1 tsp cayenne pepper 2 tsp dried thyme ½ tsp dried oregano	Mix the spices and store in container in freezer

Makes approx. 4 tbsp powder

Makes 20 tsp. Each teaspoon serves 2 mugs of tea

Chai masala

INGREDIENTS	METHOD
1 tbsp ground cardamom powder ½ tsp ground cinnamon powder 4 tbsp ground dried ginger (soont) 2 tsp ground nutmeg 1 tsp ground black pepper 2 tsp ground cloves	Mix all the ingredients and store in airtight container

Jeera powder roasted

INGREDIENTS	METHOD
Roast half a cup of jeera seeds on a baking tray in a preheated oven 150C/300F for 10 minutes or until some smoke comes out of the jeera seeds	Cool and grind to a powder. Can be frozen.

Makes half a cup

Garam masala

INGREDIENTS	METHOD
25 cardamoms 6 x 2.5cm long cinnamon sticks 3 tbsp fennel seeds 1 tbsp black peppercorns 25 cloves 12 star anise 2 tsp nutmeg ground	1. Place all the ingredients except the nutmeg on a baking tray and cook in a preheated oven at 150C/300F. 2. Cook for 7 minutes and let it cool. 3. Grind and add the nutmeg and mix. 4. Can be stored in the freezer.

Makes 15 tbsp of powder

Tandoori powder

INGREDIENTS

To make tandoori powder roast 1 part methi/ fenugreek seeds,1 part coriander/dhana seeds and 2 parts jeera seeds and grind together

Zathar spice

INGREDIENTS	METHOD
½ mug of roasted sesame seeds 3 tbsp dried oregano 3 tbsp of dried thyme 3 tbsp ground sumac berries 2 ttsp salt	Mix all and store in airtight container.

This is a Middle Eastern sprinkle to be spread on salads etc

Gujarati curry powder for vegetarian dishes

INGREDIENTS

60g coriander seeds
30g cumin/jeera seeds
20g fenugreek/methi seeds
25g channa/gram flour
25g garlic powder
20g paprika powder
20g turmeric powder
20g garam masala
5g ground dried curry leaves
5g asafoetida hing powdered
5g ginger powder
5g red chilli powder
5g yellow mustard powder
5g ground black pepper

METHOD

1. Dry roast the first three ingredients till you can smell the aroma of the spices. Grind them to a powder.

2. Add the remaining ingredients to the above and mix well.

3. Store in an airtight container and use for vegetarian Gujarati dishes.

Makes 250g or 50 teaspoons of powder

Wireless Iron

This is my precious East African stamp collection dating many years. Some of these were passed on to me by my dear grand uncle from my mother's side, Hassanali Premji Samji Boghani (whom I called Nanabapa).

Another treasured collection of my old East African notes to share

These old East African coins are from the treasure box of my parents' and my own collection!

GLOSSARY

The ingredients here are listed mainly in their English names followed by the common Indian names. However, in some cases the ingredients have been listed with their Indian names by which they are commonly known e.g. jeera seeds.

A

Almond or badam is a seed and is used in savoury and sweet dishes.

Amba hardar is a root available from Indian stores and is used in pickles. It has the fragrance of mango and adding it to a lemony pickle gives it the raw mango taste.

Asafoetida or asafoetida compound or hing is a gum from a giant fennel. It has a strong and pungent smell. It is a good substitute for onion or garlic.

Aubergine or ringna or baigan or eggplant or brinjal is one of the best vegetables of the world! It can be cooked in many ways, e.g., fried, baked, pureed, stuffed, marinated, stewed, used in curries etc. It has a creamy texture and soaks up any flavour you put in!

Amchoor is dried mango powder.

B

Bhaji is normally referred to as spinach.

C

Caraway seed has a nutty flavour with a combination of aniseed, dill and mint. The seed can be easily confused with jeera seed which tastes entirely different.

Cardamom or elchi or elaichi is a pod with seeds inside used for savoury and sweet dishes. The two main varieties are the green or white, which is the most commom variety and the black cardamom (elcho) which is larger and dark brown and has a smoky smell that makes it more suitable for savoury dishes.

Carom seed or ajwain or ajma is used in Indian cuisine. It has a bitter pungent taste.

Chapatti or rotli flour or atta is pale brown in colour and is a slightly gritty flour that is made by milling whole wheat flour. There are three grades: wholemeal, medium and white flour. White flour is also called maida and there is no bran in it.

Chilli or mirch or mircha or pepper is a fruit used for flavour and adding heat to a dish. There are many varieties with varied intensities. Dried chilli is used to make chilli powder. Kashmiri chilli powder is a milder version whereas cayenne chilli powder is 8 times hotter than normal chilli powder. Jalapeno pepper (a very hot chilli) in vinegar is used in fajitas nachos, pizza etc.

Cinnamon or taj or dalchini or cassia (Chinese cinnamon) is a spice obtained from the inner bark of a cinnamon tree. It has an aromatic flavour.

Coconut or nariyal is the fruit of the coconut palm. The water inside is called coconut water or juice. Coconut can be eaten raw and can be used in cooking.

Coconut milk is made from coconut and has the consistency of cow's milk whereas coconut cream is a much richer and creamier version. Pure creamed coconut is a block of condensed coconut cream and pieces of it can be used to add flavour to and to thicken the dish.

Desiccated coconut is the dried version of grated coconut.

Coriander or cilantro or dhana or dhania is a member of the parsley family. Coriander leaves are used as a herb. Coriander seeds are used whole and as a powdered spice.

Cornmeal or maize flour or ugali flour is a flour made from ground maize/corn. It can be of a fine or a coarse consistency. Very finely ground cornmeal is called cornflour. In Swahili cornmeal is called ugali flour. In Hindi it is called makke ke atta and in Gujarati it is called makai-no-lot. Polenta is a form of cornmeal.

Cowpea is a legume whose variety includes black eyed beans or chora and adzuki beans or red cowpeas or red chori.

Cream: Single cream is also known as light cream and the nearest to it is half and half. Double cream is also known as heavy or whipping cream. Clotted cream is famously used with scones and jam for the delightful Cornish treat.

Curry leaf or limbro or kaddi patta is a leaf used to flavour various Indian recipes.

Citric acid or limbu na phool or nimbu na phool is the crystalline ingredient used as a lemon substitute in Indian cooking.

D

Daal is a term used for dried split pulses without husk. Daal is often known in Indian cuisine as lentils but it can be extended to peas, chick peas, kidney beans,etc. In cooking however, a pulse not split and with husk is still called by its name only e.g. moong. If the recipe uses split and husked pulse then it would be called daal e.g. moong daal. Normally these daals are used for runny soups called daals to be eaten with rice. There are many types of daals which include moong, tuver, channa, urad, masoor etc. Confusing!?

E

Eno is a crystalline powder that is a mixture of sodium bicarbonate and citric acid. When it gets mixed with water it forms bubbles and hence it is used as a raising agent. Therefore, in cooking it is used just before steaming or baking. Eno can be purchased from pharmacies or Indian stores.

Evaporated milk is concentrated milk usually found in tins whereas condensed milk is concentrated milk but with sugar added to it.

F

Fish sauce or nampla is a liquid made by fermentation of fish in salt. It has a distinctive flavour and is used in Thai cooking.

Five spice powder is used in Chinese cooking and is a combination of cinnamon, fennel seeds, star anise, Sichuan peppercorns and cloves.

G

Ganthia are deep fried Indian snacks made from chickpea flour. There are many versions for example tikha ganthia, papdi ganthia and fafda ganthia etc.

Garam masala is a blend of powdered spices mainly of cinnamon, cloves, mace, peppercorn, coriander seeds, cumin seeds and cardamom pods.

Garlic or lasan is a species of the onion family. Each segment of the garlic bulb is called a clove.

Garmar is a root used in making pickles and is available from Indian stores.

Ghisoda or turai or turiya is a ridged gourd available from Indian stores.

Ginger or adrak or adu is a rhizome. Powdered ginger is known as soont.

Ghee is clarified butter.

Guvar or cluster bean or flat bean is a legume. It needs to be topped and tailed before use.

Gram flour or besan or channa flour or chickpea flour is a flour made of ground chick peas.

Gungo pea or pigeon pea or bharazi is a type of legume.

J

Jaggery or gaur is unrefined cane or palm sugar and can be purchased from Indian stores.

Jeera or cumin seed is used extensively in Indian cooking. Jeera powder is ground jeera seeds.

K

Karela or bitter gourd is an edible fruit which has the most bitter taste amongst all vegetables and is renowned for its health benefits especially in managing diabetes.

Kewra water is an extract that is distilled from pandamus flowers. It is used to flavour spiced rice dishes like biriani or sweet dishes like kheer.

Kokum is a fruit related to mangosteen.

It is quite sour and is used in curries and in making chutneys. Best to clean it in water to remove the grit. Available from Indian stores.

Kasuri methi is dried methi (fenugreek) leaves.

M

Methi or fenugreek: Methi leaves and seeds are both used in cooking. Methi seeds have a pungent smell and are normally used for tempering dishes. Methi leaves are cooked for a short period of time in oil to impart its pungent flavour. Kasuri methi is dried methi leaves and can be added to the cooking when suggested.

Mogo or cassava or yucca or manioc is a long tuberous starch root that is used in East African, Latin American and Caribbean cuisine. Mogo can be eaten boiled, grilled, fried and in stews.

Matoke is a green banana from the East African Highlands. To cook it, carefully peel and boil or bake it. It can be eaten mashed and can also be added to stews.

Mooli or daikon or radish is a mild flavoured winter radish root that has leaves too. There is the white long root variety or the red shorter variety. The leaves can be cooked to make a curry.

Millet flour or bajra is a gluten free alternative to wheat and is used in Indian cooking to make rotlas (flatbreads), muthias (dumplings) etc.

Mango or Keri or Amba is a stone fruit. Raw mango is used in pickles. Sweet mango which is creamy, is used in desserts whereas dried mango powder amchoor is used to add tartness to a dish.

Mustard seeds or rai: The three most popular varieties are black, brown and white. In Indian cooking black and brown varieties are most popular. The seeds are mainly used in tempering dishes for flavour. Split mustard seeds are used for pickling dishes.

Mace is the covering of the nutmeg seed.

N

Nutmeg or jaifer or jayphal is a big seed that is ground and used mainly in sweet dishes or chai (tea) masala.

Nigella seed or kalonji or onion seed or kala jeera is a seed that has a very nutty pungent flavour and is used in pickles, tempering dishes and on top of naan bread.

O

Okra or ladies fingers or bhinda or bindi is an edible seed pod.

P

Paneer is fresh Indian cottage cheese common to the Indian subcontinent. It is a non-aged and non-melting cheese.

Peppers: Here we are defining bell peppers or sweet peppers. They are mild and come in various colours e.g. red, green, yellow, orange, white and purple.

Pawa or flat rice or poha is rice parboiled before flattening. This allows its faster cooking.

Peppercorns or Mari: These come in various types. The common ones are black or white. They can be used whole in cooking or be used powdered as a condiment. The white peppercorn has a stronger flavour.

Pistachios or pista is a member of the cashew family.

R

Rice is the seed of the grass species. It is a cereal grain widely consumed worldwide especially in Asia and Africa. There are 40,000 varieties of cultivated rice. The varieties include long grain e.g., basmati rice; medium grain e.g., jasmine rice; and short grain e.g., arborio rice. Brown rice is rice with husk on and is a healthier option. In Indian cooking basmati rice is considered as the top brand variety.

Rice flour is made from ground rice and is used in making rice noodles, South Indian pancakes called dosa and in making Gujarati dishes like hondwo and khichi etc.

Rose essence, rose syrup and rose water: Rose water is a rose flavoured water made by steeping rose petals in water. Rose essence is a more concentrated form of rose water. To make 15ml of rose water from rose essence add 5ml of rose essence to 10ml of water. Rose syrup is a syrup made with rose water and sugar.

Rocket leaves or rucola or aragula has a very peppery flavour and has a bite to it.

S

Saffron or kesar is the most expensive spice derived from the stigma and styles of the flower crocus sativus.

Saragva sing or drumstick is the green pod vegetable available from Indian stores.

Semolina is purified wheat middlings of durum wheat. There are two varieties, coarse and fine.

Sev or vermicelli: Vermicelli is a type of pasta similar to spaghetti but thinner.

Sesame seed Sesame seed or til or tal has a nutty flavour when roasted and is excellent when sprinkled on dishes. Sesame seed oil (toasted) is made from the toasted sesame seeds and is used extensively in Chinese cooking.

Shahi jeera is a seed used in Mughlai cooking. It tastes similar to cumin but it is much milder.

Soont is dried ginger powder. It has a pungent smell and is also used to make chai/tea masala.

Surti papdi is a type of bean in a pod that has to be topped and tailed and eaten whole.

Sweetcorn or makai is a variety of maize with high sugar content.

Spring garlic is the green leaves of garlic.

T

Tahini is a condiment made from toasted hulled sesame seeds and is used in Middle Eastern dishes like humus, baba ghanoush and halva.

Takmaria or tukmaria or basil seeds: These seeds swell up in water and are used in sweet Indian drinks like Ismaili sherbet and faluda.

Tamarind or ambli or imli is a fruit. It can be sweet or tart. Dried tamarind comes in packs and is used to make tamarind sauce called ambli or imli.

Tomato paste is made by cooking tomatoes for a long period of time and then it is pasted.

Tomatoes pulped is tomatoes in a tin or ripe fresh tomato that are pulped.

Turmeric or haldi or hardar is a spice from the turmeric plant root, a relative of the ginger plant. Turmeric has been recommended as the super food and is claimed to fight cancer, depression and to ease the pain of arthritis.

V

Variari or fennel seed or saunf is an aromatic seed that is used to flavour curries, breads, desserts etc.

Valor is an Indian vegetable that is similar to runner bean. It needs to be topped and tailed before cooking.

Vaal is a bean that is similar in taste to butter bean but it is smaller in size. It can be purchased from Indian stores.

W

White flour also known as plain flour or all-purpose flour is a wheat flour that contains 75% of wheat grain with most of the bran and the wheat germ taken out. Maida is the type of white flour available from Indian stores.

Y

Yellow limes are available from Indian and Middle Eastern stores and are used for pickling in Indian recipes or for cooking in Middle Eastern recipes.

Z

Zathar spice is a Middle Eastern mix used in cooking and in salads.

Amin and Shenaz Shamji in China

Family having Guyanese breakfast

Mum Gulshan, her grandson Naadim and me

Aalia's 30th birthday

Fun time

Lunch in our hut

BBQ with family

Sajeda Meghji of Chachi's kitchen and me

Sherbanu Shamji and sister Amina Meghji of Chachi's kitchen

Land's End

Men family and friends

Almas Frost and mum Shireen Lakhani

Naaz Manji and me with her mum's hondwo recipe

Women family and friends

Family get together

Family photo

Cornwall

My bestie Jayshree Patel and me

Grannies and grandchildren

Cousins of Toronto

BBQ at the Younis'

Babuls at Vancouver

Family and friends

Family fun at Edmonton

Amin and Shenaz Shamji 2022

BBQ hero Amin

Amin with the Masais

Family picnic

BBQ at the Shamjis

Mojito in the sun

Family supper Toronto.

Washing up time!

Ismail Shamji brothers and wives

Host and hostess

Roshan mum and me

Venice

Taj Mahal visit

Beach time

Fehmida McCarthy and Amin making samosas

My family and me in London

ACKNOWLEDGEMENTS

This book is the final product of many years of hard work including writing, practising, editing and compiling the whole project together. It would not have been possible to accomplish this mission without the support and encouragement from the following.

My late mother-in-law **Sherbanu Shamji**. She was my mentor and guide for traditional Indian cooking for the twenty eight years that she lived with us.

I would really like to thank my lovely and sweet daughter **Aalia** for helping me with the editing and typing, and for inspiring me to bring this book to a new level. I would also like to thank my dear son **Naadim** for his constant guidance and for his research work done into the publication and formatting of this book. Both my children have been very supportive and inspirational, and I am very proud of them. In particular I would like to thank Naadim for the endless hours he has put in towards the editing of this book, especially the laborious task of standardising the terminology used throughout.

Sajeda Meghji (also known as 'Saju') my husband's first cousin and co-author of Chachi's Kitchen. Saju has been very supportive to me and has encouraged me tremendously to produce this book.

My husband and soulmate **Amin** for being my constant companion in the kitchen, for all his encouragement and feedback on my cooking. He is a great chef too, has a lot of passion for trying new foods and experimenting in the kitchen.

My children **Aalia** and **Naadim** for eating up anything their grandma, dad or I cooked. They have turned into great foodies like their mum and dad and are great budding cooks too! We share this passion as a family and bond over it, often discussing food, sharing photos of what we've cooked in our separate households that week and trying different cuisines together.

My late (adoptive) mum and dad, **Gulshan** and **Fatehali Babul** for hosting great parties with family and friends and making food the tool to bring loved ones together.

My biological mum **Roshan**, also known as **Munira Aunty**, for guiding me in creating and writing her renowned recipes. Also, to my biological dad **Bahadur** for really appreciating my traditional cooking, saying it reminded him of his mum!

I would like to thank everyone who encouraged me to produce this book including **Mohsin Meghji**; my sisters **Nina, Karima** and my late sister **Tashu**; my nephew **Aleem Jaffer**; the dear family members of my husband, **Naaz Manji** and **Salima Younis**; my friend **Almas Frost**; my cousin **Altaf Samji** and his wife – who is also my good friend - **Jyotsna** (also known as Jo); my Tanga friend **Fehmida McCarthy** and many others. Fehmida in particular has given countless hours of her invaluable time proofreading each and every recipe - this is a sign of the truest friendship. Thank you so much Fehmida!

I would like to thank **Joe Josland** of JJosland Photography for many of the beautiful photographs in this book. Joe in particular was very supportive and accommodating to my exacting needs in producing the book of my dreams.

Lastly, I would like to thank everybody who has contributed their recipes towards this book to make it a wonderful collection of treasured recipes.

Enjoy and happy cooking!

"Shenuri my sister, for as long as I can remember, you have always been so passionate about creating mouth-watering and delicious meals with so much love and care. It is truly a wonderful blessing that your hard work in writing this book with amazing family recipes will now be shared and experienced by others. Wishing you all the very best as you continue this new journey in your life. Your loving sister and greatest fan"
Karima Baboolal nee Babul

"My Shenaz aunty's (aka Sheni aunty) cooking is her way of expressing love. This is precisely why she takes so much pride in her cooking as an artist with her masterpiece whether it is mixing spices (zathar spice) or creating everyone's favourite jugu wari daal (sweet daal with peanuts) to an elaborate multi course dinner for Christmas holidays where Nana, Nani, Mom and I were fed till we could not eat anymore. The food was so tasty. This was a definite treat for us from Sheni aunty's heart. Sheni aunty expresses her love through food and creations. Sheni aunty will certainly make a foodie out of you if she hasn't already!"
Aleem Jaffer (Shenaz's nephew and her sister Tasnim's son)

"In this treasure trove of recipes, you will find something for every mood and occasion from every corner of the world. From the simplicity of Masala Mogo to the complexity of Rajasthani Biriani; from the creaminess of Kuku Paka to the crunchiness of Crispy Shredded Beef, this book is a beautiful patchwork of the author's culinary influences."
Naadim-Khan Shamji (Shenaz's son)

"A consummate chef who is passionate about eking out the best in tastes, flavours and colours. One who is not afraid to fuse various techniques she picked up as a child, growing up in East Africa to *Ismaili* parents of Indian origin. Shenaz reaches out to the recesses of her memory to remember what she learnt, gleaning over the shoulders of her grandmother and the indigenous Arab-African people in the small alleys and markets of Tanga, a coastal town of Tanzania. Be ready to cook up a storm with Shenaz!"
Altaf and Jo Samji

"It's been a pleasure for me and mum to have been Shenaz's guinea pigs. My late husband Gary loved her food especially the jugu wari daal (sweet daal with peanuts) and Gujerati Kadhi. Good job Shenaz sent lots of it, otherwise my mum who loved Shenaz's food too would not have got a look in! I am proud to book in as her first customer for this book." *Almas Frost (friend)*

'Looking back, this book was so predictable, from the array of food meticulously prepared on her weekend dining table to her love of different cuisines. Born with a discerning palate, Shenaz has taken her hobby of cooking to the next level. With a keen sense of taste and respect for authentic cuisine, from East African Ismaili Khoja to other popular international dishes, she has preserved her rich recipes in this cookbook. Her mastery is evident from a single bite. Each time, over the years, her food has transported me to many cherished moments amongst family and friends."
Nina Vellani nee Babul

"

"From a very young age I can remember mum constantly cooking up a storm in the kitchen with the music turned up and a towel draped over her shoulder. She has always loved to entertain and at the heart of her comic and vivacious character has always been food. I remember many occasions in which family and friends were invited over for big weekend meals in which mum would be preparing throughout the week to ensure the menu was befitting for the get together. Mum's food has always been delicious and as her personal taste testers, dad, Naadim and I have experienced the genius trialling variations of dishes first hand. But, as my mum never does things by half, she always ensures that along with great company and great taste, there is a feast for the eyes. Whether it is the arrangement of the food, the decorative embellishments or the beautiful serving ware, mum guarantees all the senses are awakened. I know when I entertain others for dinner that I try and emulate this spirit of cooking and entertaining although mum's larger than life character (which I sadly haven't inherited) has made the experience of eating together all that more enjoyable and memorable.

"When mum tries a new cuisine for the first time, she is quick off the mark to taste and identify the ingredients. She makes it her personal challenge to recreate that dish at home painstakingly exacting in sourcing ingredients and trialling multiple recipes of the same dish to get her own version perfectly curated for her and our family's tastebuds and preferences. All of this is to say that this cookbook has been written by a real, passionate cook who wants nothing more to share the joy she's experienced in making these dishes! My only recommendation is that you never try my mum's swiss roll (recipe not included within thankfully). My mum was never a baker, as a hilarious and traumatic childhood experience haunts and reminds me, but graciously she knows where her strengths lie (everything but baked goods)! Each recipe in this book however is sure to wow so I hope you love it as much as I do!"

Aalia-Begum Shamji (Shenaz's daughter)

INDEX

Made in the USA
Las Vegas, NV
15 July 2024

92366735R00208